The Indian: Assimilation, Integration or Separation?

RICHARD P. BOWLES
Associate Professor, College of Education, University of Toronto

JAMES L. HANLEY
Educator-Producer, History and Social Science,
Ontario Educational Communications Authority

BRUCE W. HODGINS
Professor, Department of History, Trent University

GEORGE A. RAWLYK
Professor, Department of History, Queen's University

PRENTICE-HALL OF CANADA, LTD.
Scarborough Ontario

PRENTICE-HALL, INC., ENGLEWOOD CLIFFS, NEW JERSEY
PRENTICE-HALL INTERNATIONAL, INC., LONDON
PRENTICE-HALL OF AUSTRALIA, PTY., LTD., SYDNEY
PRENTICE-HALL OF INDIA, PVT., LTD., NEW DELHI
PRENTICE-HALL OF JAPAN, INC., TOKYO

Library of Congress Catalog No. 72-4878

0-13-456954-7

2 3 4 5 76 75 74 73

PRINTED IN CANADA

Contents

Preface

The *Canada: Issues and Options* series focusses on a number of vital continuing Canadian concerns. Each volume probes the nature of a complex issue in both its contemporary and historical contexts. The issues were chosen because of their relevance to the life of the Canadian teenager as well as the general Canadian public.

Every volume in the series provides a wide variety of primary and secondary source materials. These sources are interdisciplinary as well as analytical and descriptive. They embody many divergent points of view in order to provoke critical in-depth consideration of the issue. They are arranged in a manner designed to personally involve and confront the reader with the clash of opinions and options inherent in the various issues. The historical sources have been carefully selected to provide a better understanding of the roots of the issue under consideration. It is hoped that this method will establish in the reader's mind a meaningful relationship between the past and the present.

The organization is flexible. If a chronological study of the development of the issue is desired, this can be accomplished by treating the historical sources first and later examining the contemporary manifestations of the issue. By reversing this procedure, the reader can first deal with the contemporary section. This approach will provide the reader with a brief overview of the issue, a case study designed to put it into personal and immediate terms, and a more detailed examination of the issue in its contemporary setting, prior to examining its historical roots.

Questions designed to stimulate further research are also included. These questions do not limit examination or prescribe answers, but raise more questions and suggest aspects of the issue which might be further investigated.

Throughout these volumes, a conscientious effort has been made to avoid endorsing any one viewpoint. No conclusions are drawn. Rather, the reader is presented with information which has been arranged to encourage the drawing of his own tentative conclusions about the issue. The formation of these conclusions involve the use of the skills of inquiry and the examination and clarification of personal values.

Introduction

Europeans, searching for the riches of the Indies, stumbled on present-day Canada—the land, according to a disappointed Jacques Cartier, that God gave to Cain. Nevertheless, they stayed to conquer the territory and to exploit the resources of the entire continent, forcing the two hundred thousand original inhabitants into contact with a culture sharply different from their own.

This book probes that contact and the issues which have arisen from it. It tries to arouse interest in the history of Indian-White relations by asking how and why we got where we are today. It will attempt to confront you with some of the myriad questions that make up the issues: What sort of problems do Indians face in making a living? in their relations with Whites? in getting an education? in finding justice in the courts and dignity in government dealings? Why have Indians recently become more militant? What routes are there out of the present situation? What can the Indian teach the White man? What can the White man teach the Indian?

The answers you give to these questions will make up *your* perception of the issue. How will this perception affect your choice for the future?

ACKNOWLEDGMENTS

The authors are deeply indebted to Wendy Cuthbertson for her exceptional assistance in assembling the basic material for this volume and in helping to keep it as current as possible. In the final preparation of the book, particular thanks are due Paul Hunt and Wendy Cuthbertson of Prentice-Hall of Canada Limited for their help, advice and hard work.

The authors also thank the many publishers and writers, especially the many Canadian Indians and Indian organizations, who have granted them permission to use various materials. Source references are provided with the documents.

1

The Issue: Some Opinions

The following selection of documents forms a collage of differing opinions about the situation of the Indian in Canada. What are the issues? How do you feel about them? Why do you feel the way you do?

RED POWER WHOOPS IT UP

This selection, by reporter Peter Thurling, is taken from the Toronto Telegram *of October 28, 1968.*

Red Power made it at Glendon College last night in a wild, whooping wind-up to a student conference on the Indians.

John A. MacDonald, deputy minister of the Department of Indian Affairs, was called a "liar" and "the house Nigger" by a band of heavy hecklers. . . .

Mr. MacDonald said they should listen for a change. "We've been listening for 100 years. . . ."

The Indians then started chanting: "What is the problem? What is the problem?"

"Right now, you're mine," said Mr. MacDonald.

In the rear, Tony Antoine, an advocate of Red Power, shot back: "And we're going to be yours until you give us something back."

"My office is open," said the deputy, who's only had the job since last March.

"Your office smells."

INDIAN VIOLENCE IS POSSIBLE

The comments of an Indian clergyman, James Dumont, appeared in the Toronto Star, *June 5, 1971.*

Indian violence is possible if things remain as they now are, especially as our people become aware of their real lot and the racism that does exist. I don't approve of violence—or rather, I don't advocate it. But then it's not a matter of being for or against. It is something that happens automatically if people are pushed far enough and long enough. When it does happen it will indicate something is desperately wrong. If society just looks at the violence it will be looking at the wrong end. Yet this is what constantly happens.

THE PAST IS DEAD

Indian lawyer William Wuttunee was seen on The Pierre Berton Show, *August 8, 1969.*

I follow the experience of my father. He lived for sixty years on a reservation, and he left it when he was sixty, and he took us with him. I'm very pleased he did because if I had not left the reserve I now would have been hunting rabbits perhaps, freezing to death in the one- or two-room shacks, and having one miserable time!

Whereas right now I live in a split-level home, I have running water and I have all the things that I need, and I am pleased that I live there.

The past is dead; it's as dead as a doornail. . . . We'll start from today. You know, today's a brand-new day. . . . You see, we can't weep about the past.

MY PEOPLE COMING INTO THEIR OWN

This assertion of pride and ambition by Viola Haywahe appeared in Indian News, *July 1969.*

I am an Indian. How wonderful it is to belong to this race, in this day and age, when my people are finally coming into their own. Within my veins the blood of Israel; and this land, the land of my forefathers, offers today more opportunities than ever before for my development.

BECAUSE YOU HAVE BEEN TOLD

In 1968, Peter Stewart, in an article for the Canadian Weekly, *described some incidents involving Indians and Métis.*

You are a Métis, and all your life you have known, because you have been told, that your people are dirty, lazy drunks. You received little schooling, and find jobs hard to get and harder to hold. You were fired once for roughhousing with two Whites in a company cafeteria, although the Whites were not fired. You went back to school last winter, and watched a White teacher, younger than yourself, come bursting out into the schoolyard to order grown-up natives to stop speaking Cree, their native tongue . . . and you saw them stop.

LAZY, SHIFTLESS BUMS

In a 1959 issue of Saturday Night, *a commentator gave his opinions on the Indian situation.*

The history of minority ethnic groups in this country has shown that any who were willing to work and educate themselves attained a higher standard of living than that to which they were previously accustomed.

Unlike most minority groups the Indian by and large stuck to reserves which are conducive to inbreeding and subsequent lowering of intelligence.

The Indian has been given a chance. But it seems that he can't or won't pull himself into an improved status in today's Canada. The fault is no one's but his own.

CANADIANS LIKE ALL OTHER CANADIANS

This is an excerpt from the remarks made by Prime Minister Trudeau at the Australian National University, May 1970.

We have set the Indians apart as a race. We've set them apart in our laws. We've set them apart in the ways that governments deal with them. They're not citizens of the provinces as the rest of us are. They are wards of the federal government. They get their services from the federal government rather than from the provincial or municipal governments. They have been set apart in law. They have been set apart in the relations with government, and they've been set apart socially too.

They should become Canadians as all other Canadians; and if they are prosperous and wealthy, they will be treated like the prosperous and wealthy. They will pay taxes for the other Canadians who are not so prosperous and not so wealthy, whether they be Indians or English Canadians or French or Maritimers. This is the only basis on which I see the people in our society developing as equals.

RACIAL SEGREGATION

These remarks by Kahn Tineta Horn, advocate of apartheid, appeared in the Toronto Star, *August 12, 1971.*

All Indians reject the Indian woman marrying a White man. Most of all the Indian women reject any Indian woman who marries a White man. They want no part of her, but they are too polite to say so. The law aids us by keeping these persons away once they marry White men. The Indian men reject this action too, because they know what it can mean. The Indian children do not want association with half-breeds or White children on the reserve, so they do not want it.

INTEGRATION IMPOSSIBLE

This interview between Andrew Warnock and Dr. Howard Adams, a Saskatchewan Métis, is taken from the Canadian Dimension *of April-May, 1968.*

WARNOCK: What particular problems are giving Indian and Métis people the most trouble right now?

ADAMS: There are many particular problems, but they all result from one big problem—that is, that we live in Canada, a society based on White supremacy. This is a fact that we have to acknowledge and live with. We know that as natives we will never be totally integrated into the society, so we must adjust our thinking, our action and our plans accordingly.

THE IMMENSE GUILT OF WHITE MAN'S CRIMES

John Conway, an Indian Affairs employee who was dismissed after a short period of employment, described his feelings in the Canadian Dimension, *January 1968.*

You always feel the immense guilt of all the White man's crimes about which you can do nothing, and anything you say sounds foolish. You feel, deep down, that they either hate you, feel contempt for you, are absolutely indifferent to you, or want something from you . . .

YOU HAVE TO PAY FOR YOUR OWN WAY

On the CBC radio program, The Way of the Indian, *broadcast in 1963, Leonard Crane, an Indian, said that his people must assume more responsibility for their affairs.*

I'm pretty well agreed that if an Indian needs help, give him help, you know. But we have to get out and do these things. I mean, it's too much. A White Man is just a man that's a victim of his own race and he's suffering for it now, and it's our duty as members of the human race to help him and share his problems. As the treaty reads, I think they're supposed to supply us with medical care and schools and different things like that. I'm not speaking against the treaty or with the treaty, but I figure if we get out and give the Indian department a hand in buying our medical care and trying to pay for some of our way and pay for our kids' education, it will give us more footing. Like you have to do, you have to pay for your way. I think if we start doing that now, thinking ahead, then my children will be able to take care of themselves more than I have.

What do you think?

1. *(a) Of the eleven statements you have just read, which, if any, comes closest to stating your views?*
   (b) Which statement seems to you to be the most logical and reasonable?
   (c) Was your choice the same in (a) and (b)?
2. *Summarize the views contained in any three of the above documents. Compare them. What might the speaker in each suggest for the resolution of the issue? Compare the suggestions. What do you notice?*

2

Encounter

Indian (Toronto: New Press, 1971) is George Ryga's first play. It is based on his experiences with the Cree Indians that he worked with on his father's Alberta farm. Through a series of personal encounters and reminiscences, Ryga attempts to probe the complex and contradictory nature of an Indian.

By the end of the play how have we been led from the "outside" of the Indian to the "inside"? What changes does the Indian undergo as the play proceeds? What do these changes reveal about White-Indian relations?

SETTING: Stage should be flat, grey, stark non-country. Diametric lines (telephone poles and wire on one side, with a suggestion of two or three newly driven fence-posts on the other) could project vast, empty expanse.

Set may have a few representative tufts of scraggy growth in distance—also far and faint horizon.

In front and stage left, one fence-post newly and not yet fully driven. Pile of dirt around post. Hammer, wooden box and shovel alongside.

High, fierce, white light off-stage left to denote sun. Harsh shadows and constant sound of low wind.

Back of stage is a pile of ashes, with a burnt axe handle and some pottery showing.

Curtain up on INDIAN *asleep, using slight hump of earth under his neck for pillow. He is facing sun, with hat over his face.* WATSON *approaches from stage right, dragging his feet and raising dust. Stops over* INDIAN'S *head.*

WATSON: *(loud and angry)* Hey! What the hell! Come on . . . you aimin' to die like that?

INDIAN *clutches his hat and sits up. Lifts his hat and looks up, then jerks hat down over his face.*

INDIAN: Oy! Oooh! The sun she blinded me, goddamn! . . . Boss . . . I am sick! Head, she gonna explode, sure as hell!

He tries to lie down again but WATSON *grabs his arm and yanks him to his feet.*

WATSON: There's gonna be some bigger explosions if I don't get action out of you guys. What happened now? Where's the fat boy? An' the guy with the wooden leg?

INDIAN: Jus' a minute, boss. Don't shout like that. *(looks carefully around him)* They not here . . . Guess they run away, boss—no? . . . Roy, he's not got wooden leg. He got bone leg same's you an' me. Only it dried up and look like wood. Small, too . . . *(lifts up his own right leg)* That shoe . . . that was fit Roy's bad leg. The other shoe is tight. But this one, boss—she is hunder times tighter!

WATSON: *(squatting)* Is them Limpy's boots?

INDIAN: Sure, boss. I win them at poker las' night. Boss, what a time we have—everybody go haywire!

WATSON *looks around impatiently.*

WATSON: I can see. Where's your tent?

INDIAN: *(pointing to ashes)* There she is. Sonofabitch, but I never see anything burn like that before!

WATSON: The kid wasn't lying—you guys *did* burn the tent.

INDIAN: What kid?

WATSON: Your kid.

INDIAN: *(jumping to his feet)* Alphonse? Where is Alphonse? He run away when Sam and Roy start fight . . .

WATSON: Yeh, he run away . . . run all the way to the house. Told us you guys was drunk an' wild. So the missus fixed him something to eat and put him to bed.

INDIAN: He's all right? Oh, that's good, boss!

WATSON: *(smiling grimly)* Sure, he's all right. Like I said, the missus fed the kid. Then I took him and put him in the grainery, lockin' the door so he ain't gonna get out. That's for protection.

INDIAN: Protection? You don't need protection, boss. Alphonse not gonna hurt you.

WATSON: Ha! Ha! Ha! Big joke! . . . Where are your pals as was gonna help with this job? Where are they—huh?

INDIAN: I don't know. They run away when tent catch fire.

WATSON: Great! That's just great! You know what you guys done to me?

Yesterday, ya nicked me for ten dollars . . . I'm hungry, the fat boy says to me—my stomach roar like thunder. He's gonna roar out the other end before I'm finished with you an' him! How much you figure the fence you put up is worth?

INDIAN: *(rubbing his eyes and trying to see the fence in the distance)* I dunno, boss. You say job is worth forty dollars. Five, mebbe ten dollars done . . .

WATSON: Five dollars! Look here, smart guy—ya've got twenty-nine posts in —I counted 'em. At ten cents apiece, you've done two dollars ninety cents worth of work. An' you got ten dollars off me yesterday!

INDIAN *(pondering sadly)* Looks like you in the hole, boss.

WATSON: Well maybe I am . . . an' maybe I ain't. I got your kid in the grainery, locked up so he'll keep. You try to run off after your pals, an' I'm gonna take my gun an' shoot a hole that big through the kid's head!

He makes a ring with his fingers to show exact size of injury he intends to make.

INDIAN: No!

WATSON: Oh, sure! So what ya say, Indian? . . . You gonna work real hard and be a good boy?

INDIAN: Boss—you know me. I work! Them other guys is no good—but not Johnny. I make deal—I keep deal! You see yourself I stay when they run.

WATSON: Sure, ya stayed. You were too goddamned drunk to move, that's why you stayed! What goes on in your heads . . . ah, hell! You ain't worth the bother!

INDIAN: No, no, boss . . . You all wrong.

WATSON: Then get to work! It's half past nine, and you ain't even begun to think about the fence.

INDIAN: Boss . . . a little bit later. I sick man . . . head—she hurt to burst. An' stomach—ugh! Boss, I not eat anything since piece of baloney yesterday . . .

WATSON: *(turning angrily)* You go to hell—you hear me? Go to hell! I got that story yesterday. Now g'wan—I wanna see some action!

INDIAN: All right, boss. You know me. You trust me.

WATSON: Trust ya? I wouldn't trust you with the time of day, goddamn you! *(remembers something)* Hey—there's a snoop from the Indian Affairs department toolin' around today—checkin' on all you guys workin' off the reserve. I'm telling you somethin' . . . you're working for me, so if you got any complaints, you better tell me now. I don't want no belly-achin' to no government guys.

INDIAN: Complaints? . . . Me? I happy, boss. What you take me for?

WATSON: Sure, sure . . . Now get back to work. An' remember what I told you . . . you try to beat it, an' I shoot the kid. You understand?

INDIAN *removes his hat and wipes his brow.*

INDIAN: Sure, bossman—I understand.

INDIAN *looks toward the fence in the fields.* WATSON *stands behind him, scratching his chin and smirking insolently.* INDIAN *glances back at him, then shrugging with resignation, moves unsteadily to the unfinished fence post. He pulls the box nearer to the post, picks up hammer and is about to step on the box. Changes his mind and sits for a moment on the box, hammer across his knees. Rubs his eyes and forehead.*

WATSON: Now what the hell's the matter? Run out of gas?

INDIAN: Oh, boss . . . If I be machine that need only gas, I be all right mebbe . . .

WATSON: So you going to sit an' let the day go by? . . . Indian, I've got lots of time, an' I can grind you to dirt if you're figurin' on bustin' my ass!

INDIAN: Nobody bust you, boss. I be all right right away . . . Sementos! But the head she is big today. An' stomach . . . she is slop-bucket full of turpentine. Boss . . . two dollars a quart, Sam Cardinal says to me . . . with four dollars we get enough bad whiskey to poison every Indian from here to Lac La Biche! Sam Cardinal tell the truth that time for sure . . .

WATSON: What kind of rubbish did you drink?

INDIAN: Indian whiskey, boss. You know what is Indian whiskey?

WATSON: No. You tell me, an' then you get to work!

INDIAN: Sure, boss, sure. As soon as field stop to shake. Indian whiskey . . . you buy two quart. You get one quart wood alcohol . . . maybe half quart formalin, an' the rest is water from sick horse. That's the kind whiskey they make for Indian.

WATSON: An' it makes the field shake for you . . . Christ! *You* make me sick!

INDIAN: Oh, but what party it make!

WATSON: *(irritably)* Come on . . . come on! Get on with it.

INDIAN *scrambles on box and starts to drive post into ground. He stops after a few seconds. He is winded.*

INDIAN: Sementos! Is hard work, boss! . . . I tell you, Sam Cardinal sing like sick cow . . . an' Roy McIntosh dance on his bad leg. Funny! . . . Alphonse an' I laugh until stomach ache. I win Roy's boots in poker, but he dance anyhow. Then Sam get mad an' he push Roy . . . Roy push him back . . . They fight . . . Boy, I hungry now, boss . . .

WATSON: Tough: I wanna see ten bucks work done.

INDIAN: Then you feed me? Big plate potatoes an' meat? . . . An' mebbe big hunk of pie?

WATSON: *(laughs sarcastically)* Feed ya? Soon's I get my ten bucks squared away, you can lie down and die! But not on my field . . . go on the road allowance!

INDIAN *hits the post a few more times, trying to summon up strength to get on with the work. But it is all in vain. Drops hammer heavily to the box.*

INDIAN: You hard man, boss . . . Hard like iron. Sam is bad man . . . bugger up you, bugger up me. Get ten dollar for grub from you . . . almost like steal ten dollars from honest man. Buy whiskey . . . buy baloney an' two watermelon. He already eat most of baloney and I see him give hunk to friendly dog. I kick dog. Sam get mad . . . why you do that? Dog is nothing to you? I say, he eat my grub. He can go catch cat if he hungry. I catch an' eat cat once myself, boss . . . winter 1956. Not much meat an' tough like rope. I never eat cat again, that's for sure. Sementos! But the head hurt!

WATSON: One more word, Indian . . . just one more word an' I'm gonna clean house on you! . . . You wanna try me? Come on!

For a moment the INDIAN *teeters between two worlds, then with a violent motion he sweeps up the hammer and begins pounding the post, mechanically with an incredible rhythm of defeat.* WATSON *watches for a while, his anger gone now. Scratches himself nervously, then makes a rapid exit off-stage left. Almost immediately the hammering begins to slow, ending with one stroke when the hammer head rests on the post, and* INDIAN'S *head droops on his outstretched arms.*

INDIAN: Scared talk . . . world is full of scared talk. I show scare an' I get a job from mister Watson. Scared Indian is a live Indian. My head don't get Alphonse free . . . but hands do.

Sound of motor car approaching. INDIAN *lifts his head and peers to stage right.*

INDIAN: Hullo . . . I am big man today! First mister Watson an' now car come to see me. Boy, he drive! . . . If I not get out of his way he gonna hit me, sure as hell!

Jumps down from box and watches. Car squeals to stop off-stage. Puff of dust blows in from wings. Car door slams and AGENT *enters.*

AGENT: Hi there, fella, how's it going?

INDIAN: Hello, misha. Everything is going one hunder fifty per cent! Yessiree . . . one hunder fifty per cent!

INDIAN *rises on box and lifts hammer to drive post.*

AGENT: There was talk in town your camp burned out last night . . . everything okay? Nobody hurt?

INDIAN: Sure, everything okay. You want complaints?

AGENT: Well, I . . . what do you mean, do I want complaints?

INDIAN: I just say if you want complaints, I give you lots. My tent, she is burn down last night. My partners . . . they run away. Leave me to do big job myself. I got no money . . . an' boss, he's got my Alphonse ready to shoot if I try to run. You want more complaints? *(drives down hard on hammer and groans)* Maybe you want know how my head she hurts inside?

AGENT: *(relieved)* Hey—c'mere. I'll give you a smoke to make you feel better. You're in rough shape, boy! Which would you prefer—pipe tobacco, or a cigarette? I've got both . . .

INDIAN *drops hammer and comes down from box.*

INDIAN: The way I feel, misha, I could smoke old stocking full of straw. Gimme cigarette. *(examines the cigarette* AGENT *gives him)* Oh, you make lotsa money from government boss . . . tobacco here . . . and cotton there —some cigarette! Which end you light? *(laughs)*

AGENT: Light whichever end you want. You can eat it for all I care. That's some hat you got there, sport. Where'd you get it?

INDIAN: *(accepting light* AGENT *offers him)* Win at poker, misha.

AGENT: *(examining him closely)* Aren't those boots tight? I suppose you stole them!

INDIAN: No, boss—poker.

AGENT: And that shirt—will you look at that! Have shirt, will travel.

INDIAN: I steal that from my brother, when he is sick and dying. He never catch me!

AGENT: *(laughing)* That's good . . . I must tell the boys about you—what's your name?

INDIAN: You think is funny me steal shirt from my brother when he die? You think that funny, bossman? I think you lousy bastard! . . . You think that funny, too?

AGENT: *(startled)* Now hold on—did I hear you say . . .

INDIAN: You hear good what I say.

The AGENT *takes out his notebook.*

AGENT: Just give me your name, and we'll settle with you later.

INDIAN: Turn around an' walk to road. If you want to see stealer in action, I steal wheels off your car. You try catch me . . .

AGENT: *(angrily)* Give me your name!

INDIAN: Mebbe I forget . . . mebbe I got no name at all.

AGENT: Look here, boy . . . don't give me any back-talk, or I might have to turn in a report on you, and next time Indian benefits are given out, yours might be hard to claim!

INDIAN: So—you got no name for me. How you gonna report me when you not know who I am? You want name? All right, I give you name. Write down—Joe Bush!

AGENT: I haven't got all day, fella. Are you, or are you not going to tell me your name?

INDIAN: No! I never tell you, misha! Whole world is scare. It make you scare you should know too much about me!

AGENT: *(slamming notebook shut)* That does it! You asked for it . . . an' by

God, if I have to go after you myself, I'm gonna find out who you are!

INDIAN: Don't get mad, misha. I sorry for what I say. I got such hurting head, I don't know what I say . . .

AGENT: Been drinking again, eh? . . . What was it this time—homebrew? Or shaving lotion?

INDIAN: Maybe homebrew, maybe coffee. I don't know. Why you ask?

AGENT: You're no kid. You know as well as I do. Besides, bad liquor's going to kill you sooner than anything else.

INDIAN: *(excitedly)* Misha . . . you believe that? You really mean what you say?

AGENT: What—about bad liquor? Sure I do . . .

INDIAN: Then misha, please get me a bottle of good, clean Canadian whiskey! I never drink clean whiskey in my life!

AGENT: Come on, now . . . you're as . . .

INDIAN: I give you twenty dollars for bottle! Is deal?

AGENT: Stop it! . . . Boy, you've got a lot more than a hangover wrong in your head!

INDIAN: *(points off-stage)* That car yours?

AGENT: Yes.

INDIAN: How come all that writing on door—that's not your name? Why you not tell truth?

AGENT: Well, I work for the government, and they provide us . . .

INDIAN: Thirty dollars?

AGENT: Look here . . .

INDIAN: How come you not in big city, with office job? How come you drive around an' talk to dirty, stupid Indian? You not have much school, or mebbe something else wrong with you to have such bad job.

AGENT: Shut your lousy mouth, you . . .

INDIAN: Thirty-five dollars? No more! . . . I give you no more!

AGENT: Will you shut up?

INDIAN: *(defiantly)* No! I never shut up! You not man at all—you cheap woman who love for money! Your mother was woman pig, an' your father man dog!

AGENT: *(becoming frightened)* What . . . what are you saying?

INDIAN *comes face to face with* AGENT.

INDIAN: You wanna hit me! Come on . . . hit me! You kill me easy, an' they arrest you—same people who give you car. Hit me—even little bit—come on! You coward! Just hit me like this! *(slaps his palms together)* . . . Just like that—come on! You know what I do when you hit me?

AGENT: *(looks apprehensively around himself)* What?

INDIAN: I report you for beating Indian an' you lose job. Come on—show me you are man!

He dances provocatively around AGENT. AGENT *turns in direction of his car.*

AGENT: I'm getting out of here—you're crazy!

INDIAN: *(jumps in front of* AGENT*)* No . . . you not go anywhere! Maybe nobody here to see what happen, but after accident, lots of people come from everywhere. I'm gonna jump on car bumper, and when you drive, I fall off an' you drive over me. How you gonna explain that, bossman?

AGENT: *(frightened now)* I got nothing against you, boy! What's the matter with you? . . . What do you want with me?

INDIAN: I want nothing from you—jus' to talk to me—to know who I am. Once you go into car, I am outside again. I tell you about my brother, an' how he die . . .

AGENT: Go back to your work and I'll go back to mine. I don't want to hear about your brother or anyone else. *(*INDIAN *walks off-stage to car)* Now you get off my car!

INDIAN: *(off-stage)* You gonna listen, misha. You gonna listen like I tell you. *(sounds of car being bounced)* Boy, you ride like in bed! Misha, who am I?

INDIAN *returns to stage.*

AGENT: How in the devil do I know who you are, or what you want with me. I'm just doing a job—heard your camp got burned out and . . .

INDIAN: How you know who any of us are? How many of us got birth certificates to give us name an' age on reserve? . . . Mebbe you think I get passport an' go to France. Or marry the way bossman get married. You think that, misha?

AGENT: I don't care who you are or what you think. Just get back to your job and leave me alone.

INDIAN *glances admiringly off-stage to car.*

INDIAN: Boy, is like pillow on wheels! If I ever have car like that, I never walk again!

AGENT: Get out of my way! I've got to get back into town.

INDIAN: No hurry. Mebbe you never go back at all.

AGENT: What . . . do you mean by that?

INDIAN *turns and approaches* AGENT *until they stand face to face.*

INDIAN: You know what is like to kill someone—not with hate—not with any feelings here at all? *(places hand over heart)*

AGENT: *(stepping back)* This is ridiculous! Look, boy . . . I'll give you anything I can—just get out of my hair. That whiskey you want—I'll get it for you . . . won't cost you a cent, I promise!

INDIAN: Someone that mebbe you loved? Misha—I want to tell you somethin' . . .

AGENT: No!

INDIAN *catches hold of* AGENT'S *shirt front.*

INDIAN: Listen—damn you! I kill like that once! You never know at Indian office—nobody tell you! Nobody ever tell you! . . . I got to tell you about my brother . . . he die three, four, maybe five years ago. My friend been collecting treaty payments on his name. He know how many years ago now . . .

AGENT: You coudn't . . .

INDIAN: I couldn't, misha?

AGENT: There are laws in this country—nobody escapes the law!

INDIAN: What law?

AGENT: The laws of the country!

INDIAN: *(threatening)* What law?

AGENT: No man . . . shall kill . . . another . . .

INDIAN: I tell you about my brother. I tell you everything. Then you tell me if there is law for all men.

AGENT: Leave me alone! I don't want to hear about your brother!

INDIAN: *(fiercely)* You gonna listen! Look around—what you see? Field and dust . . . an' some work I do. You an' me . . . you fat, me hungry. I got nothin' . . . and you got money, car. Maybe you are better man than I. But I am not afraid, an' I can move faster. What happens if I get mad, an' take hammer to you?

AGENT: You . . . wouldn't . . .

INDIAN: You wrong, misha. Nobody see us. Mebbe you lucky—get away But who believe you? You tell one story, I tell another. I lose nothing—but you gonna listen about my brother, that's for sure!

AGENT: *(desperately)* Look boy—let's be sensible—let's behave like two grown men: I'll drive you into town—buy you a big dinner! Then we'll go and buy that whiskey I promised. You can go then—find your friends and have another party tonight . . . Nobody will care, and you'll have a good time!

INDIAN: *(spitting)* You lousy dog!

AGENT: Now don't get excited! . . . I'm only saying what I think is best. If you don't want to come, that's fine. Just let me go and we'll forget all about today, and that we ever seen one another, okay?

INDIAN *releases the* AGENT.

INDIAN: You think I forget I see you? I got you here like picture in my head. I try to forget you . . . like I try to forget my brother, but you never leave me alone . . . Misha, I never forget you!

AGENT: *(struggling to compose himself)* I'm just a simple joe doing my job, boy—remember that. I know there's a lot bothers you. Same's a lot bothers me. We've all got problems . . . but take them where they belong.

AGENT *pulls out cigarettes and nervously lights one for himself.*

INDIAN: Gimme that!

AGENT: This is mine—I lit it for myself! Here, I'll give you another one!

INDIAN: I want that one!

AGENT: No, damn it . . . have a new one!

INDIAN *jumps behind* AGENT *and catches him with arm around throat. With other hand he reaches out and takes lit cigarette out of* AGENT'S *mouth. Throws* AGENT *to the field. The* AGENT *stumbles to his knees, rubbing his eyes.*

AGENT: What's wrong with you Why did you do that?

INDIAN: Now you know what is like to be me. Get up! Or I kick your brains in!

AGENT *rises to his feet and sways uncertainly.*

AGENT: Dear God . . .

INDIAN: My brother was hungry . . . an' he get job on farm of White bossman to dig a well. Pay she is one dollar for every five feet down. My brother dig twenty feet—two day hard work. He call up to bossman—give me planks, for the blue clay she is getting wet! To hell with what you see bossman shout down the hole—just dig! Pretty soon, the clay shift, an' my brother is trapped to the shoulders. He yell—pull me out! I can't move, an' the air, she is squeezed out of me! But bossman on top—he is scared to go down in hole. He leave to go to next farm, an' after that another farm, until he find another Indian to send down hole. An' all the time from down there, my brother yell at the sky. Jesus Christ—help me! White man leave me here to die! But Jesus Christ not hear my brother, an' the water she rise to his lips. Pretty soon, he put his head back until his hair an' ears in slimy blue clay an' water. He no more hear himself shout—but he shout all the same!

AGENT: I wasn't there! I couldn't help him!

INDIAN:. . . He see stars in the sky—lots of stars. A man see stars even in day when he look up from hole in earth . . .

AGENT: I couldn't help him—I don't want to hear about him!

INDIAN: . . . Then Sam Cardinal come. Sam is a coward. But when he see my brother there in well, an' the blue clay movin' around him like livin' thing, he go down. Sam dig with his hands until he get rope around my brother. Then he come up, an' he an' White bossman pull. My brother no longer remember, an' he not hear the angry crack of mud an' water when they pull him free . . .

AGENT: *(with relief)* Then . . . he lived? Thank God . . .

INDIAN: Sure . . . sure . . . he live. You hunt?

AGENT: Hunt? . . . You mean—shooting?

INDIAN: Yeh.

AGENT: Sure. I go out every year.

INDIAN: You ever shoot deer—not enough to kill, but enough to break one leg forever? Or maybe hit deer in eye, an' it run away, blind on one side for wolf to kill?

AGENT: I nicked a moose two years back—never did track it down. But I didn't shoot it in the eye.

INDIAN: How you know for sure?

AGENT: Well . . . I just didn't. I never shoot that way!

INDIAN: You only shoot—where bullet hit you not know. Then what you do?

AGENT: I tried to track it, but there had been only a light snow . . . an' I lost the tracks.

INDIAN: So you not follow?

AGENT: No. I walked back to camp . . . My friend an' I had supper and we drove home that night . . .

INDIAN: Forget all about moose you hurt?

AGENT: No. I did worry about what happened to him!

INDIAN: You dream about him that night? . . . Runnin', bawling with pain?

AGENT: What the hell . . . dream about a moose? There's more important things to worry about, I'm telling you.

INDIAN: Then you not worry at all. You forget as soon as you can. Moose not run away from you—you run away from moose!

AGENT: I didn't . . . hey, you're crazy! *(moves towards car off-stage, but* INDIAN *jumps forward and stops him)* Here! You leave me alone, I'm telling you . . . You got a lot of wild talk in your head, but you can't push your weight around with me . . . I'm getting out of here . . . Hey!

INDIAN *catches him by arm and rolls him to fall face down in the dust.* INDIAN *pounces on him.*

INDIAN: What you call man who has lost his soul?

AGENT: I don't know. Let go of me!

INDIAN: We have name for man like that! You know the name?

AGENT: No, I don't. *You're breaking my arm!*

INDIAN: We call man like that sementos. Remember that name . . . for *you* are *sementos!*

AGENT: Please, fella—leave me alone! I never hurt you that I know of . . .

INDIAN: Sure.

Releases AGENT, *who rises to his feet, dusty and dishevelled.*

AGENT: I want to tell you something . . . I want you to get this straight, because every man has to make up his mind about some things, and I've made mine up now! This has gone far enough. If this is a joke, then you've had your laughs. One way or another, I'm going to get away from you. And when I do, I'm turning you in to the police. You belong in jail!

INDIAN: *(laughs)* Mebbe you are man. We been in jail long time now, sementos . . .

AGENT: And stop calling me that name!

INDIAN: Okay, okay . . . I call you bossman. You know what bossman mean to me?

AGENT: I don't want to know.

INDIAN: *(laughs again)* You wise . . . you get it. I not got much to say, then you go.

AGENT: *(bewildered)* You . . . you're not going to . . . bother me anymore?

INDIAN: I finish my story, an' you go . . . go to town, go to hell . . . go anyplace. My brother—you know what kind of life he had? He was not dead, an' he was not alive.

AGENT: You said he came out of the well safely. What are you talking about?

INDIAN: No . . . He was not alive. He was too near dead to live. White bossman get rid of him quick. Here, says bossman—here is three dollars pay. I dig twenty feet—I make four dollars, my brother says. Bossman laugh. I take dollar for shovel you leave in the hole, he says. My brother come back to reserve, but he not go home. He live in my tent. At night, he wake up shouting, an' in daytime, he is like man who has no mind. He walk 'round, an' many times get lost in the bush, an' other Indian find him an' bring him back. He get very sick. For one month he lie in bed. Then he try to get up. But his legs an' arms are dried to the bone, like branches of dying tree.

AGENT: He must've had polio.

INDIAN: Is not matter . . . One night, he say to me: go to other side of lake tomorrow, an' take my wife an' my son, Alphonse. Take good care of them. I won't live the night . . . I reach out and touch him, for he talk like devil fire was on him. But his head and cheek is cold. You will live an' take care of your wife an' Alphonse yourself, I say to him. But my brother shake his head. He look at me and say—help me to die . . .

AGENT: Why . . . didn't you . . . take him to hospital?

INDIAN: *(laughs bitterly)* Hospital! A dollar he took from dying man for the shovel buried in blue clay . . . hospital? Burn in hell!

AGENT: No . . . no ! This I don't understand at all . . .

INDIAN: I . . . kill . . . my . . . brother! In my arms I hold him. He was so light, like small boy. I hold him . . . rock 'im back and forward like this . . . like mother rock us when we tiny kids. I rock 'im an' I cry . . . I get my hands tight on his neck, an' I squeeze an' I squeeze. I know he dead, and I still squeeze an' cry, for everything is gone, and I am old man now . . . only hunger an' hurt left now . . .

AGENT: My God!

INDIAN: I take off his shirt an' pants—I steal everything I can wear. Then I dig under tent, where ground is soft, and I bury my brother. After that, I go to other side of lake. When I tell my brother's wife what I done, she not say anything for long time. Then she look at me with eyes that never make tears again. Take Alphonse, she say . . . I go to live with every man who have me, to forget him. Then she leave her shack, an' I alone with Alphonse . . . I take Alphonse an' I come back. All Indians know what happen, but nobody say anything. Not to me . . . not to you. Some half-breed born outside reservation take my brother's name—and you, boss-man, not know . . .

AGENT: *(quietly, as though he were the authority again)* We *have* to know, you understand, don't you? You'll have to tell me your brother's name.

INDIAN: I know . . . I tell you. Was Tommy Stone.

AGENT *takes out his notebook again and writes.*

AGENT: Stone—Tommy Stone . . . good. You know what I have to do, you understand it's my duty, don't you? It's my job . . . it's the way I feel. We all have to live within the law and uphold it. Ours is a civilized country you understand, don't you? *(turns to car off-stage)* I'm going now. Don't try to run before the police come. The circumstances were extenuating, and it may not go hard for you . . .

INDIAN *makes no attempt to hinder* AGENT *who walks off-stage.*

INDIAN: Sure, misha . . . you're right. *(hears car door open)* Wait! Misha, wait! I tell you wrong. Name is not Tommy Stone—Tommy Stone is me! Name is *Johnny* Stone!

AGENT *returns, notebook in hand.*

AGENT: Johnny Stone? Let's get this straight now . . . your brother was Johnny Stone . . . and you're *Tommy* Stone? (INDIAN *nods vigorously)* Okay, boy. I've got that. Now remember what I said, and just stay here and wait. *(turns to leave)*

INDIAN: No, misha . . . you got whole business screwed up again! I am Johnny Stone, my brother, he is Tommy Stone.

AGENT *pockets his notebook and turns angrily to face* INDIAN.

AGENT: Look, Indian—what in hell is your name anyhow? Who are you?

INDIAN: My name? You want my name?

Suddenly catches AGENT *by arm and swings him around as in a boyish game. Places* AGENT *down on the box he used for standing on to drive posts.*

AGENT: Hey, you stop that!

INDIAN: An' yet you want my name?

AGENT: Yes, that's right . . . If it's not too much trouble to give me one straight answer, what is your name?

INDIAN: Sam Cardinal is my name!

AGENT *rises with disgust and straightens out his clothes.*

AGENT: Now it's Sam Cardinal . . . what do you take me for anyway? You waste my time . . . you rough me up like I was one of your drunken Indian friends . . . and now I can't get an answer to a simple question . . . But what the hell—the police can find out who you are and what you've done.

INDIAN: No, sementos! You never find out!

INDIAN *throws legs apart and takes the stance of a man balancing on a threshold.*

INDIAN: You go to reservation with hunder policemen—you try to find Johnny Stone . . . you try to find Tommy Stone . . . Sam Cardinal, too. Mebbe you find everybody, mebbe you find nobody. All Indians same—nobody. Listen to me, sementos—one brother is dead—who? Tommy Stone? Johnny Stone? Joe Bush! Look—*(turns out both pockets of his pants, holding them out, showing them empty and ragged)* I got nothing . . . nothing . . . no wallet, no money, no name. I got no past . . . no future . . . nothing, sementos! I nobody. I not even live in this world . . . I dead! You get it? . . . I dead! *(shrugs in one great gesture of grief)* I never been anybody. *I not just dead . . . I never live at all.* What is matter? . . . What anything matter, sementos?

AGENT *has the look of a medieval peasant meeting a leper—fear, pity, hatred.*

INDIAN: What matter if I choke you till you like rag in my hands? . . . Hit you mebbe with twenty pound hammer—break in your head like watermelon . . . Leave you dry in wind an' feed ants . . . What matter if police come an' take me? Misha! Listen, damn you—listen! One brother kill another brother—why? *(shakes* AGENT *furiously by the lapels)* Why? Why? . . . Why?

AGENT: *(clawing at* INDIAN'S *hands)* Let me go! LET . . . ME . . . GO!

AGENT *breaks free and runs off-stage for car. Sounds of motor starting and fast departure. Dust.* INDIAN *stands trembling with fury.*

INDIAN: Where you go in such goddamn speed? World too small to run 'way? You hear me, sementos! Hi . . . *sementos!* Ugh!

Spits and picks up hammer. Starts to drive post vigorously. Curtain.

What do you think?

1. *This play is based on Ryga's experiences with Cree Indians in Alberta. Do you find the play believable? Why or why not?*
2. *Which of the three characters do you find the most sympathetic? the least? Why?*

3. To what extent do you think that the actions and beliefs of Watson are typical?

4. Explain the significance of the Indian's cry: "I never been anybody. I not just dead . . . I never live at all. What is matter? . . . What anything matter, sementos?

(a) This speech is made at the end of the play, after the Indian has undergone dramatic changes in mood and behavior. Describe these changes. Why are they important to the development of Ryga's theme?

(b) In what ways does this speech explain the Indian's behavior?

5. (a) What is the play trying to say about the relationship between Indians and Whites?

(b) What does Ryga have to say about the roles that religion, the law, and the government play in Indian-White relations?

(c) Can you think of any other issues that underlie the tension between Indians and Whites?

6. Has the play explained to you why various people said the things they did in Part I? Has reading it changed the perception you had of the issues at the end of Part I?

3

The Contemporary Indian

What is it like to be an Indian in Canada today?

The following section deals with the contemporary Indian. It provides material designed to assist you in reaching a better understanding of the many factors involved in being an Indian in Canada today. We will take a look at some of the recent Indian militancy, and will examine the factors which are the focus of Indian-White tension: racial discrimination, Indian poverty, the administration of justice, the treaties, Indian Affairs, the Indian Act, the churches and schools. Finally, we will survey some of the attitudes that Whites and Indians have about one another.

What *is* it like to be an Indian in Canada today?

As you read this section, it is hoped that the materials will raise many other questions which must be considered before any useful attempt can be made to answer the first: What are the attitudes of Indians and Whites toward each other and toward each other's culture? What special problems do Indians feel they face, and what part do these problems play in determining the relationship between the two groups?

Indian Resurgence: Ends and Means

During the last decade there has been an unprecedented resurgence on the part of minority peoples. Throughout the world minority groups have asserted themselves. Sometimes the unrest erupts into violence and bloodshed; sometimes a peaceful solution is found. The way in which resolutions are found depends to a great extent on the attitudes of opposing groups.

The following selections document Indian resurgence in Canada. What are some of the demands made by Canadian Indians? What is the reaction of the White community?

1. I HAVE A PART TO PLAY

This assertion of pride and ambition by Viola Haywahe appeared in Indian News, *July 1969.*

I am an Indian. How wonderful it is to belong to this race, in this day and age, when my people are finally coming into their own. Within my veins the blood of Israel; and this land, the land of my forefathers, offers today more opportunities than ever before for my development.

My opportunities are not without challenge. Forever there will be injustices, inequalities . . . Prejudice has existed in some form throughout all time. It will always be so.

I am young and I am strong. I am proud of my heritage. Today I am preparing myself for a future full of hope and promise. I am climbing the ladder, learning all I can and taking every opportunity for my development. Education is my strongest tool against discouragement, my best weapon against ignorance, my shield against apathy.

I accept the challenge of Indian leadership. I will help myself and my people. I have a part to play in the destiny of my nation.

What do you think?

1. *Compare the mood of Miss Haywahe to the Indian in Ryga's play.*
2. *What barriers might this young girl encounter in carrying out her ambition*
   (a) from the White community?
   (b) from her own people?

2. THE FRESH ASSERTIVENESS: RED POWER

Mr. Fred Kelly, an Indian author and illustrator, was assistant to the president of the National Indian Brotherhood and vice-president of the Union of Ontario Indians. Kelly's article is taken from the Toronto Telegram *of September 27, 1969.*

There is an Indian uprising in Canada. It manifests itself in the Native Movement. It is ideological, social, legal, and political. Within the Movement is a spectrum of views. One constituent is a militancy spreading like a prairie grass fire. It is a re-enkindlement of a vision in which the destiny of the native people is in their hands. This revitalized quest for self-determination is to be pursued unswervingly and with whatever means necessary. This is Red Power. There are other terms considered more appropriate, such as, Indian Power, Native Power, Indian Assertiveness, and the like. This is mere semantic quibbling—a self-imposed division. We have already been legislatively conditioned to consider ourselves in terms of treaty or non-treaty, registered or non-registered, status or non-status, Métis or Indian. The term is sensational because it is always associated with Black Power. The connotations of racial strife as in the United States immediately arouse a defensiveness in Canadians. The fear instilled by thoughts of bloody riots, burning, and ghetto warfare affects even some of the outspoken native leaders.

Red Power neither advocates violence nor fears it. It must not be overlooked, however, that violence already exists. It is levelled against the native people. One must consider the growing frustration under governmental subjugation, second-class citizenship, poverty, and the daily provocations of discrimination to realize the seriousness of the question "How long can we restrain retaliation?"

Red Power advocacy is characterized by youth committed to the cause of native advancement. It seeks a vision through involvement in civil rights and social activism. It is also characterized by an indignant disregard for the establishment, the System, and to the colonialism which keeps native people in subjugation. It has a heated impatience for negotiation. Its ideology and terminology is derived from the third-world movement. Native youth militancy is also part of a universal resurgence of a revolutionary spirit against what has been the accepted status quo. A repudiation of traditional liberalism. A total rejection of second-class citizenship. A commitment asserting itself in a new nationalism.

What do the native people want? Any desire for change affecting the native people and its subsequent action must originate from them. The degree and direction must be decided by them. The criteria for judging their successes must be determined by them.

Equality of opportunity no longer means enough. Racism and bigotry can magically cease to exist suddenly, but the native people will still be ill-housed, ill-fed. They will still be living in substandard conditions. They will still have to contend with inadequate health services and improper education and unemployment. Until the preconditions are settled, "equality of opportunity" will remain in the lexicon of empty clichés.

While the Indians desire integration, they do not construe this to mean assimilation. They want to become equal partners in society while retaining a specific identity in the Canadian mosaic. This is not possible without mutual trust. They are not asking for love; they are demanding their rights. Many of these rights are contained in the treaties signed many years ago but now broken. Is this conducive to trust? Before they are legislated into the mainstream of society by the proposed new Indian policy, these treaties are to be honored. Integrity before integration.

There are certain facts that the native people must face in their considered action.

Indian unity must be redefined from cultural unity to mean a uniformity of cause. Indian unity until now has been used to convey a wide range of meanings, including cultural unity. Not only is this impossible, it is the advocacy of another type of assimilation—tribal. What is more urgent, possible, and workable is concerted action. This means uniting behind common grievances, supporting each other, and pressing together in a coordinated manner the remedy that is decided upon together. . . .

The struggle ahead will require a sustained effort. Therefore, new leadership must be developed, strong and dedicated. Clearly, the youth must be involved from local-level to top-level negotiations and action.

Strategies must be flexible. A foresighted constructiveness must precede any sense of destructiveness. If militant tactics are to be employed, they must be predicated on intelligent militancy not anarchistic militancy. Too often militant activism is too preoccupied by plans for destroying the prevailing system to formulate alternatives or definable programs. If moderate tactics are to be utilized, the faith and future of the native people must not be compromised.

Finally, what is required is discipline in pursuing solutions to problems that are important—patience and shrewdness in developing goals and strategies.

What is meant by?

"self-determination"
"third-world movement"
"traditional liberalism"
"integrity before integration"

What do you think?

1. *". . . violence already exists. It is levelled against the native people." Why does the author think that poverty and discrimination are acts of violence? Do you agree with him? How does this view of violence justify physical rebellion? Do you agree? Give reasons.*
2. *"Equality of opportunity is not enough." Explain.*
3. *By deriving its ideology and terminology from the third-world resurgence, is the Red Power movement endangering the very thing it wishes to preserve: Indian uniqueness? Or do these techniques improve the chances of success?*

3. KENORA: A TURNING POINT

This selection describes an attempt by a group of Indians to improve conditions in Kenora, a city which, proportionally, has the largest Indian population of any center in Ontario. The article, which appeared in Canadian Labour, *December 1966, is by civil libertarian Alex Borovy.*

In November 1965, for the first time in their history, the Indians in the area of Kenora, Ontario, exercised the art of mass political pressure. On the night of Monday, November 22, four hundred Indians marched down the streets of Kenora and engaged the Town Council in a historic confrontation.

The Indians asked the town to:

1. Petition the federal government to install radio-telephone equipment on the reserves so that they could communicate with the larger communities around them.
2. Petition the Ontario government to lengthen the trapping season in order to shorten the lay-over between the trapping season and the fishing season.
3. Petition the Ontario government to make available to the Kenora area the services of the Alcoholism Research Foundation.
4. Establish a mayor's committee to process grievances between the Indians and the town.

This demonstration created a national news sensation. Radio, television, and newspapers all over Canada headlined the story. Editorials demanded government action.

Very soon afterwards, the Kenora Town Council granted all of the requests in the Indian brief. It appointed a mayor's committee and enacted the resolutions for which the Indians had sought its support. Then the federal and provincial governments swung into action. The trapping season was immediately extended. By now, almost all the reserves have telephones. Following the dispatch of its research staff to the area, the Alcoholism Research Foundation has established a treatment center in Kenora.

This response to their demonstration infused the Indians with a sense of self-respect, pride, and hope. It has shown its effects even in other areas of Indian life. Some Indian leaders have reported, for example, that Indians in unprecedented numbers are signing up and completing government-sponsored employment retraining courses. So often government attempts to help Indians have failed because the Indians in their despair lacked the sense of hope which would motivate the exertion of effort on their own behalf. The experience of moving government and the community through the use of their own power creates that sense of hope so necessary to the success of anti-poverty activity.

Of course, this is not to exaggerate the results of the Kenora experience. The gains were modest; the problem is immense. Its importance arises from the lesson that in the field of Indian problems there is no substitute for the use of Indian power exercised on the Indians' behalf.

The good will of others is no longer sufficient. We cannot content ourselves with knitting woollies or running to the government with pious briefs demanding help for the Indians. The emphasis must be on getting the Indians into the act.

What do you think?

1. *". . . in the field of Indian problems there is no substitute for the use of Indian power exercised on the Indian's behalf." Why?*
2. *Could the gains that were made in Kenora have been achieved without resorting to the demonstration? If so, how?*

4. KENORA JUST ONE YEAR LATER

Reporter Ian Adams described the situation in Kenora a year after the agitation. Mr. Adams' report appeared in Maclean's Magazine, *February 1967.*

There are people in Kenora today who will tell you that the Indians got what they wanted: telephones for isolated reserves; a local branch of the Alcoholism and Drug Addiction Research Foundation; a one-week extension of the beaver-trapping season, and a mayor's committee to iron out difficulties between the Indians and the White townspeople. Agencies of the federal and provincial governments sent in researchers, some to find new approaches in education, some to find job prospects, and others to detail the drinking patterns of the Indians and their encounters with the law. Both governments also hired several local Indians to work as community-development officers on their own reserves. Probably the best thing to happen to the Indians was the idea to move right into the reserves with Program Five—the government's scheme to provide the unemployed with basic skills while paying them a living wage. Program Five was tried with great success at the Sioux Narrows reserve last winter. Attendance was ninety-five per cent; of 136 Indians enrolled, 124 completed their courses. This winter it is being attempted on other reserves.

But now the do-gooders and organizers have left Kenora. And over the past few months the White power structure in Kenora has re-asserted itself. The mayor's committee, which began with an equal number of Indians and Whites, has shaken down to seven Whites and one Indian. There is the same ratio on the advisory committee to the Addiction Research Foundation branch. Ontario Provincial Police say there is more drinking than ever on the reserves. At the fall assizes in Kenora there were four murder cases, more than ever before, all involving Indians. One eighteen year-old, accused of throwing his ten-month-old son into the river, was convicted of manslaughter. OPP Superintendent Larry Gartner says, "If there has been a change in the community's attitude toward Indians and law enforcement, I haven't seen it."

Perhaps one way of gauging the community's attitude is its reaction to the press. Mayor Ernest Carter fends off interviews. "There were no particular problems," he says, "until a few troublemakers stirred things up." The businessmen rail bitterly against what they call "the bad press" the town received. But if Kenora has suffered financially, it's hard to see how. Basically, it's a tourist town, and the tourist business in the Lake of the Woods area last summer was better than ever.

What do you think?

1. *What do you think caused this setback in Kenora? If you were an Indian, how would you plan in the future to avoid such a setback?*

5. THE INDIAN WHO SPOKE UP TO THE QUEEN

In the August 12, 1970, edition of the Vancouver Province *there was a report on the activities of Indian spokesman David Courchene.*

"He is," said an Ottawa official, "the man to watch. He is *the* Indian in Canada today." Said another official: "He's an advocate of moderation, tolerance, and mutual respect. He's not a militant Red Power man. But he's shrewd, really shrewd. He wants a good deal for the Indians. And he'll get it."

Dave Courchene, forty-two, was the man who told the queen, on her visit to Manitoba, that all was not well with her native subjects in Canada, that the treaties signed during her great-grandmother's reign hadn't done much for Canada's 250,000 Indians. "It is with sorrow we note," he said, "that the promises of peace and harmony, of social advancement and equality of opportunity have not been realized by the Indian people. I am sure you will note on your visits to Indian communities that Indians have not, in effect, profited well from the prosperity of this great and wealthy nation."

He went on: "We are hopeful that Your Majesty's representatives will now, though belatedly, recognize the inequities of the past, and will take steps to redress the treatment of Indian people . . .

"As the reigning monarch of the day and direct descendant of the queen with whom our treaties were originally concluded, we would ask that you see for yourself the results of a century of deprivation and ask that you advocate, on our behalf to your loyal ministers, the need for greater understanding on their part, the need to provide for greater participation of the Indian people in the decision-making process of our society. . . ."

It wasn't a spontaneous thing. Dave Courchene had been working on those words, and on just the right moment to say them, for several weeks. Nor was it an angry, aggressive, militant thing. The words came steadily, almost quietly, but with unmistakeable sincerity and feeling. They came in a way that typified Dave Courchene and his way of doing things.

Take the case of Courchene's economic development fund. In February of this year he came to Ottawa, and without the ceremony that has accompanied some other Indian presentations in the past he put his case before Indian Affairs Minister Jean Chrétien. And he walked away with a promise of $1 million. That was in addition to the $385,000 he had already extracted from the federal government for a community development program. But, it wasn't left at that. Courchene—Dr. Courchene since he received an honorary doctor of laws degree from the University of Manitoba in May—took Chrétien's $1 million promise to Manitoba's premier, Ed Schreyer. With the NDP government holding power by just one seat, with Indian votes crucial to the NDP in a number of ridings, with Indian cash going to the provincial treasury through a variety of taxes, how much, he wondered, would the province be willing to contribute. The answer—though negotiations are still going on—seems to have been, another million.

Courchene, until half a dozen years ago, was just another Manitoba Indian. A Saulteaux, he'd done some trapping, and some logging. He'd worked as a farm helper in some of Manitoba's French-speaking districts. And for something like fourteen years, he was a heavy equipment operator. But in 1964 an illness forced him to give up his job, and he turned to community affairs on his home reserve of Fort Alexander, on Lake Winnipeg, northeast of the Manitoba capital. Three years later he was elected chief. The reserve changed. The old Catholic and Anglican schools are gone, replaced by a new, bigger, non-denominational school. There's a new townsite, with water and sewers. And, there's a recreational program.

In 1968 Courchene was elected president of the Manitoba Indian Brotherhood. Founded in 1934, but long dormant, it had a staff of one and a budget of just $30,000 in that first year. Today, it has forty full-time workers, plus a list of part-time professional consultants on everything from sociology to public relations, and a budget of something over $500,000 a year. Since 1968 the Partnership Concept has been developed. That, says Courchene, was a case of getting the decision making for Indians out of the hands of Ottawa's bureaucracy and into the hands of the Indians themselves in co-operation with regional officials. "These are the people that know the needs; they should do the planning."

The Community Development Program was started in 1969. The Manitoba Indian Brotherhood got involved in Newstart, in the Mid-Canada Development Conference, in Manitoba's northern task force. The bush-clearing projects were launched through the provincial government, one for

$178,000 and employing three hundred men, the other for $83,000 and employing thirty men.

And then there was the start of the Wild Rice Co-operative. Wild rice? It's a delicacy that sells unprocessed in Manitoba for $1.45 a pound, and on the New York gourmet market for as much as $6 and $7 a pound. It's unpredictable stuff, but in a good year it can bring in about $130 an acre, ("That's a helluva lot better than wheat."), which can mean up to $500,000 for the Wild Rice Co-op and the eleven Manitoba reserves involved.

What it all adds up to—the wild rice, the economic development funds, the bush clearing—is that Dave Courchene has a talent for getting things done, both by Indians and for Indians. And that talent, taken together with the fact that he is now first president of the National Indian Brotherhood, puts him in a strong position to succeed the older, current president, Walter Dieter of Regina. It means, in short, that Dave Courchene, the man who told Queen Elizabeth that Canada's Indians weren't getting a fair shake, is, as the Ottawa man said, the man to watch, *the* Indian in Canada.

What do you think?

1. *What advantages do schemes like the Wild Rice Co-operative hold out to Indians?*
2. *Are men who operate like Courchene hurt or aided by movements like Red Power? Why?*

As Whites See Indians

How do we know what a person or a group of people is really like? If we do not know the people personally, how accurate are the impressions we receive of them from the media or from other people's opinions? To what extent does our reliance on second-hand impressions contribute to the persistence of racial discrimination?

Introducing this section is a UNESCO statement which outlines briefly the nature and origins of much racial prejudice. Following the UNESCO document are three unflattering views of the Indian taken from common sources: a magazine, a newspaper, and a textbook. Finally, there is a document dealing with specific instances of discrimination.

Do you feel that the UNESCO statement offers an explanation for the opinions held by the authors of the first three documents, and for the events described in the last document? Does it offer the possibility that racial prejudice can be eliminated in the future? What do you feel you can do as an individual to help eliminate prejudice?

What are your feelings on this question?

1. WHY PREJUDICE? THE EXPERTS' DIAGNOSIS

The UNESCO conference held in Paris issued a statement on race and racial prejudice, September 26, 1967.

1. The conference of experts meeting in Paris in September 1967, agreed that racist doctrines lack any scientific basis whatsoever. It reaffirmed the propositions adopted by the international meeting held in Moscow in 1964 which was called to re-examine the biological aspects of the statements on race and racial differences issued in 1950 and 1951. In particular, it draws attention to the following points:
   (a) All men living today belong to the same species and descend from the same stock.
   (b) The division of the human species into "races" is partly conventional and partly arbitrary and does not imply any hierarchy whatsoever. Many anthropologists stress the importance of human variation but believe that "racial" divisions have limited scientific interest and may carry the risk of inviting abusive generalization.
   (c) Current biological knowledge does not permit us to impute cultural achievement to differences in genetic potential. Differences in the achievements of different peoples should be attributed solely to their cultural history. The peoples of the world today appear to possess equal biological potentialities for attaining any level of civilization. Racism grossly falsifies the knowledge of human biology.
2. The human problems arising from so-called "race" relations are social in origin rather than biological. A basic problem is racism, namely, anti-social beliefs and acts which are based on the fallacy that discriminatory intergroup relations are justifiable on biological grounds.
3. Groups commonly evaluate their characteristics in comparison with others. Racism falsely claims that there is a scientific basis for arranging groups hierarchically in terms of psychological and cultural characteristics that are immutable and innate.
4. Racism has historical roots. It has not been a universal phenomenon. Many contemporary societies and cultures show little trace of it. It was not evident for long periods in world history. Many forms of racism have arisen out of the conditions of conquest—as exemplified in the case of Indians in the New World—out of the justification of Negro slavery and its aftermath of racial inequality in the West, and out of the colonial relationship. Among other examples is that of anti-Semitism, which has played a particular role in history, with Jews being the chosen scapegoat to take the blame for problems and crises met by many societies.
5. The committee of experts agreed on the following conclusions about the social causes of race prejudice:
   (a) Social and economic causes of racial prejudice are particularly ob-

served in settler societies wherein are found conditions of great disparity of power and property, in certain urban areas where there have emerged ghettos in which individuals are deprived of equal access to employment, housing, political participation, education, and the administration of justice, and in many societies where social and economic tasks which are deemed to be contrary to the ethics or beneath the dignity of its members are assigned to a group of different origins who are derided, blamed, and punished for taking on these tasks.

(b) Individuals with certain personality troubles may be particularly inclined to adopt and manifest racial prejudices. Small groups, associations, and social movements of a certain kind sometimes preserve and transmit racial prejudices. The foundations of the prejudices lie, however, in the economic and social system of a society.

(c) Racism tends to be cumulative. Discrimination deprives a group of equal treatment and presents that group as a problem. The group then tends to be blamed for its own condition, leading to further elaboration of racist theory.

6. The major techniques for coping with racism involve changing those social situations which give rise to prejudice, preventing the prejudiced from acting in accordance with their beliefs, and combating the false beliefs themselves.
7. Ethnic groups which represent the object of some form of discrimination are sometimes accepted and tolerated by dominating groups at the cost of their having to abandon completely their cultural identity. It should be stressed that the effort of these ethnic groups to preserve their cultural values should be encouraged. They will thus be better able to contribute to the enrichment of the total culture of humanity.

What is meant by?

"hierarchy"
"genetic potential"
"anti-social"
"immutable and innate"
"cultural identity"

What do you think?

1. *The conference of experts meeting in Paris in September 1967, agreed that racist doctrines lack any scientific basis whatsoever. How did the experts support this assertion?*
2. *Outline the social causes of racism. How does the racist's belief in biological differences between peoples permit anti-social attitudes?*
3. *In what ways are anti-scientific beliefs and anti-social attitudes directed against Indians?*

4. *"Racism tends to be cumulative." Explain. To what extent can this account for White prejudice against Indians?*
5. *In Clause 6, the UNESCO statement broadly outlines ways to eliminate racial prejudice. Suggest some techniques that would put these proposals into practice.*
6. *In Clause 7, the UNESCO statement asserts that ethnic groups should be encouraged in the preservation of their cultural values, their uniqueness. Would such an effort increase or decrease the likelihood of racial prejudice? Explain.*

2. LO! THE POOR INDIAN

In this thirteen-year-old article originally published in Saturday Night, *November 1959, a commentator made several assertions about the Indian. Are his opinions widely held today?*

A few weeks ago the goose boss of a Hutterite colony in southern Alberta was showing me around the farm. I saw I was not the only visitor. A carload of Blood Indians was departing with a large package of freshly baked buns from the communal bakery.

"Our Indian friends have paid us a visit again," commented the wife of the goose boss. "They come around here to beg every time we bake. I can't understand them at all. They won't work—those big lazy fellows."

This remark of pity and scorn, coming as it did from a member of one of Canada's most oppressed minority groups, is a succinct comment on the status of the Canadian Indian in the West.

It is a departure from comments made by his many champions who regard him as a downtrodden aristocrat—champions who disregard the fact that he is a dull, slow, untidy person and a careless workman.

Many who espouse his cause are merely sentimentalists whose knowledge of Indian affairs stems from having paid an occasional visit to a reserve or who have seen him dressed to the hilt in native costume—buckskin, beads, lipstick, feathers and dyed underwear—holding forth at Ohsweken Indian Fair, the Calgary Stampede or Banff's Indian Days. They do not realize that nine times out of ten to be present at these affairs, the Indians will have gone off and left crops and livestock unattended.

At a recent meeting of the Calgary Friends of Indians Society, a district agriculturist cited instance after instance of local bands' poor records as farmers. When the urge comes upon them they up and leave their homes to spend a week or two with relatives. Dozens of times he has seen bright Indian 4H Club members raise top calves only to be dragged off by their parents to leave the calves shift for themselves.

The Blackfoot reserve at Gleichen, Alberta, is 174,595 acres. Years ago the band used to lease 140,000 acres to the White man as grazing land for $300,000 annually.

A few years ago they decided to cancel the grazing leases and put their own young people on the land to farm it. And what's happened to that farming venture? It's $330,000 in the red! They even had to hire outside help!

Because the Indian has a built-in sense of irresponsibility many employers who demand good, steady, sober personnel are averse to Indian labor. I know one large farm employer who hires twice as many Indians as he needs on the assumption that half will have taken off by mid-season.

The Indian never worries. What tomorrow will bring is of no concern today. He won't put in a sustained effort at anything. He can do it, really, but just hasn't the inclination.

The history of minority ethnic groups in this country has shown that any who were willing to work and educate themselves attained a higher standard of living than that to which they were previously accustomed.

Unlike most minority groups the Indian by and large stuck to reserves which are conducive to inbreeding and subsequent lowering of intelligence.

The sooner the Indian forgets about the reserves and treaties written in the time of Queen Victoria the better. Both served their purpose in an agricultural economy; both are now obsolete in an industrial economy. Both offer an easy security and the temptation to remain living in untidy shacks surrounded by hulks of wrecked cars.

William Wuttunee, a young Cree Indian lawyer in the employ of the Saskatchewan government, said at a recent Western Citizenship Seminar in Banff: "The treaties should be done away with. At the time they were signed they brought peace but they mean nothing now.

"What is needed now is a radical approach with a real desire to attack the problem. I once thought that in 35 years there would be no more Indian problem. At the rate we are going now, we are going to have it with us now 150 years."

It would not be thoughtless or unkind to say the average Indian has not the slightest understanding of the colossal sums set aside by the Ottawa government for him and his family. I suspect the government set up the joint Commons-Senate committee not so much to assist the Indian in raising his status, as to devise ways of halting treasury giveaways which are predicated on the fact the Indian firmly believes the government owes him a living. This belief has been inculcated into the young by parents and by the Indian residential schools where education, clothing and food are provided "for free."

Although the standard of intelligence varies from band to band, I was amazed to learn from a man who has been connected with Indian residential schools for thirty years that on Prairie reserves and even in some areas of British Columbia and Ontario children are admitted to school without knowing a word of English.

It is a losing battle because Indian parents don't yet seem to realize that turning a child loose from school merely able to read and write just isn't enough today. Many leave school at sixteen and thereafter make little or no attempt to improve their knowledge of English. They shy away from speaking English on the reserve for fear of ridicule from their own people and off the reserve for fear of the silent scorn of the White man.

They have no incentive to seek further training—academic or vocational. Some, such as the ones I saw in the Yukon, proved to be smart enough to hold a job and do enough work to become eligible for unemployment insurance.

The Indian has been given a chance. But it seems that he can't or won't pull himself into an improved status in today's Canada. The fault is no one's but his own.

What do you think?

1. *"The author is judging the Indian by the standards of the White culture." Do you agree or disagree? Explain.*
2. *This article was published in 1959. Has the upheaval of the '60s changed the attitude of Canadians?*
3. *How does the UNESCO statement explain the attitudes expressed in this article? What are the possible effects of this type of journalism?*

3. THE DRUNKEN INDIAN

In the Edmonton Journal *of March 4, 1967, a reporter related experiences he had in a beer parlor not too far from the Blackfoot reserve south of Calgary.*

"Hey Art! You wanna be my brother-in-law?"

An Indian friend took another pull at his beer and watched my reaction. His sister offered a dirty hand. "Have a corn cheese. They good for you."

We were sitting in this town's controversial beer parlor, the one that the Alberta Liquor Control Board has promised to investigate. The room was full of native people with the exception of five or six Whites. My friend jabbed a finger into my ribs—"Hey brother-in-law! Gimme a dime for beer."

Drunken Indians continue to plague this community bordering the Blackfoot Indian reserve, forty-five miles southeast of Calgary. I drifted into

Gleichen, dirty and in need of a shave, to investigate the situation. No one knew who I was. Everyone was friendly at first. But some of their attitudes grew ugly the next day when I pretended to be broke.

The hotel bar was doing a smashing business. One Indian was so drunk he could hardly sit on his chair. "Art! How much money do you want to spend on beer?"

"Not much. I'm just about broke and have to look for a job tomorrow."

My thoughts turned to an Indian who was sleeping off a seven-day bender in my car. He had mumbled something about lemon extract before falling asleep. Five natives, seated at the next table, cast envious eyes in our direction. It was obvious they wanted money for beer. Small children played on the streets and ran around in the pool hall and a dirty cafe on Main Street while their parents drank. News came in that two juvenile girls, one from Gleichen and another from Cluny, were suspects in a Calgary murder. Someone offered me two dollars to take him and his wife to the Cluny bar, nine miles away. "Don't go. It's too rough over there."

The warning came from the Indian who had been sleeping in my car. He had the shakes. "Gimme a dollar for beer. You can stay at my place."

Three other natives asked me to stay with them. I accepted an offer from a six-foot-plus, 235 pounder. His size discouraged argument. Before sales closed, my friend put in another pitch for me to be his brother-in-law for the night. He was refused.

I spent the night driving people around the reserve and then ended up in a two-room home, with one door, about eight miles from Gleichen. The host was drunk but friendly. Two young children slept on the floor and I was told to sleep on a couch. It wasn't the time for refusals.

The attitude of many natives began to sour about noon Saturday when I told them my wallet was empty. "Hey! C'mon, you got some money. You drive big car. Buy us some beer."

The bar had been open for one hour and at least ten natives had already got off to a good start. Others were drunk from the night before. And then I ran into the fellow who had slept in my car. He had walked ten miles into town. "Why didn't you sleep at my place? Aren't we good enough for you?"

Someone else asked me to buy him a beer. "You think you're too good for us? Give me some money for beer and we'll go out to my place now."

Another Indian stood outside the beer parlor. His nose was bandaged and he carried a bag full of beer. "Some of the boys jumped me last night. Broke my nose and kicked me in the stomach."

I walked away but he grabbed my arm. He wanted a ride home. There wasn't a friendly face in sight.

What do you think?

1. *This document formed part of a series of newspaper articles designed to expose, and thereby arouse public opinion to the situation in Gleichen.*
   (a) *Do you feel this article would help or hinder Indian-White relations with regard to Gleichen? Explain.*
   (b) *In your opinion, does the author present a complete picture? If not, what might be added?*

4. FROM OUR HISTORY

This selection is taken from a popular Canadian history textbook published in 1951.

It is probable that all the American Indian tribes, in the course of their wanderings, lived for some generations in the frozen wastes of Alaska. This experience developed in them a stolidity and endurance that gave them exceptional physical vigor and courage. But it deadened their minds; it killed their imagination and initiative, just as even today years in the frozen north play havoc with the mind of almost any White man. Further, except in a few favored spots, agriculture was for the Indian impossible, and agriculture has been the basis of all progressive cultures. It would be interesting to speculate on the civilization that the Iroquois might have developed. They had made a beginning in agriculture but they clashed with a vastly superior White civilization before they had a chance to make any important advances. By reason of his historical background, the Indian was wholly unfit to cope with the more civilized, more intelligent White man. He was forced by changing circumstances to imitate the White man in order to make a living, a task for which he was very poorly equipped. He tended to lose his proud and independent spirit, to become an outcast in the land of his fathers.

What do you think?

1. *If you were an Indian student, how would you feel about this extract? What effect might this passage have on non-Indian children*
2. *"It is the author's opinion of White civilization that determines his opinion of the Indian." Discuss.*
3. *Have you ever before encountered the climatic theory of race? What is it, and how valid do you think it is?*
4. *What arguments advanced in the UNESCO statement might help to explain the opinions of this author?*

5. LIVING WITH DISCRIMINATION

These cases are taken from an article by journalist Peter Stewart called "Red Power," which appeared in the Star Weekly Magazine *in the spring of 1969.*

Almost every Indian I talked to carries the memory of some racial incident burning in his gut. Larry Seymour remembers sitting in the Indian gallery in the theatre in Duncan, British Columbia, so he wouldn't contaminate the Whites. Terry Lavallee, twenty, a Cree from Broadview, Saskatchewan, remembers being called "chief" and watching faces go dead when he said no, he was not an Italian, with his dark skin—as a matter of fact, he was an Indian. Duke Redbird remembers being told in the nine foster homes he drifted through that he would come to no good, because everyone knows Indians are depraved. He remembers, too, being turned out of a hotel when a group of Indians came to visit his room while he was working for the Company of Young Canadians, because, once they knew what he was, the hotel was sure he wouldn't pay his bill. Stan Daniels, forty-two, president of the Alberta Métis League, remembers the favorite sport in Edmonton area where he grew up—"kicking the asses of the half-breeds all the way to school." He carries a scar on his buttock from a White man's knife.

Project yourself into the tawny skin of Rod Bishop, thirty, at Green Lake, in north-central Saskatchewan. You are a Métis, and all your life you have known, because you have been told, that your people are dirty, lazy drunks. You received little schooling, and find jobs hard to get and harder to hold. You were fired once for roughhousing with two Whites in a company cafeteria, although the Whites were not fired. You went back to school last winter, and watched a White teacher, younger than yourself, come bursting into the schoolyard to order grown-up natives to stop speaking Cree, their native tongue . . . and you saw them stop. You are an adult, with a wife and four children, but have no say in running your community. Although there are six elected native councillors, their role is advisory; the decisions are made by White civil servants. Not long ago, the Whites condemned some Métis homes, and moved the natives into government houses. The Métis were not asked, of course, what kind of houses they would like, or where they should be placed, or how they should be painted—even though they will be buying them. Some Métis wondered if their old homes couldn't be fixed up for less than the $7,500 cost of the new ones, but the Whites said that was impractical, the old houses were beyond repair. Now they have been sold, to a White man, who is fixing them up. There may be an explanation for this, but you have not heard it; and when the council protests, the protest is not even recorded in the council minutes, which are kept by the Whites. What would you do?

For a few minutes, become Geraldine Larkin, a pretty little girl who went to school at Alert Bay, near Vancouver. You learned to be called "squaw" and to be followed by the White boys and teased about what an easy make the squaws are—all in fun, of course. You met a nice White boy and he used to take you out; then one day he came to explain he couldn't see you anymore; he wanted to become an accountant, see, and personally, he has nothing against Indians, but it just wouldn't look right. You understand? You do, of course, and later you marry a nice White boy and have a lovely baby, but do you ever forget your humiliation?

Stand for a time in the shoes of Matthew Bellegard, twenty, at Little Black Bear Reserve in southern Saskatchewan. You have a White friend, too; an okay guy who doesn't mind coming to the reserve, doesn't mind the poor houses and strange smells. You drive around town a lot, and people stare at the White kid riding with an Indian, in a town where Whites and Indians have lived since 1908, but nobody says much until your friend starts to date an Indian girl, and then the remarks begin. One day, on the street, a White boy comes up to you both and says, "Hey, Matt, who's the Indian-lover?" So you bust him one, and a fight breaks out, and it gets pretty nasty. You know it was a stupid thing to do, busting him, but didn't it feel good?

What do you think?

1. *"You are a Métis, and all your life you have known, because you have been told, that your people are dirty, lazy drunks." How would this sort of thing influence a young Métis?*
2. *Why would a White school teacher discourage Indians from using their native tongue? Why does this author find it shocking?*
3. *Do you feel the UNESCO statement helps to clarify the causes of these incidents? If so, how?*

As Indians See Whites

Are you part of a majority culture? If so, you are probably aware of certain attitudes that exist towards the Indian. But in assessing the Indian-White relationship it is just as important to know how the Indian views the White man.

What images does the Indian have of White society? What view does he have of his role in relation to that society?

1. HELLO RED

Eli Jacko, a young Indian from Manitoulin Island, expresses his feelings in his poem "Hello Red," which appeared in Indian News, *July 1969.*

I walk along in a long empty
corridor. I feel happy today.
"Lord," I say to myself, "thanks
for being so loving to me and
giving me all I need, especially
your love."

But like the striking of a sword into
the flesh, my world of happiness
was shattered to pieces.

"Hello Red." It keeps coming
    to me.
Like a child I cry in anguish, "O
    Lord,
drive this hatefulness away from me.
You taught me how to love and
    to love my enemy.
Stand by me and lead me to the
road of forgiveness."

But how can I forgive now, when
    it is almost too late?
Please give me strength to
    forgive and not to hate.

I am not a Red man and there is
no one on this earth that is Red.
People call me a Red man, which
    I am not.

But Lord, why do my people have
    to suffer so much.
We want to be friends, but no one
will accept us. I cannot bear it any
    longer,
and Lord, please help me to forgive.

What do you think?

1. *Why is the speaker happy in the first stanza? Who shatters his happiness? What is his reaction and why?*
2. *What does the poet mean when he says, "I am not a Red man and there is / no one on this earth that is Red"? Would Kahn Tineta Horn agree (page 4)? Do you? Why or why not?*

2 BEWARE OF ANTHROPOLOGISTS

In this excerpt, taken from his book, Custer Died for Your Sins *(New York: Macmillan, 1971), Vine Deloria Jr., an American Indian author, comments on those anthropologists who make him and his fellows statistics.*

Into each life, it is said, some rain must fall. Some people have bad horoscopes; others take tips on the stock market. McNamara created the TFX and the Edsel. American politics has George Wallace. But Indians have been cursed above all other people in history. Indians have anthropologists.

* * * * *

Abstract theories create abstract action. Lumping together the the variety of tribal problems and seeking the demonic principle at work that is destroying Indian people may be intellectually satisfying, but it does not change the situation. By concentrating on great abstractions, anthropologists have unintentionally removed many young Indians from the world of real problems to the lands of make-believe.

* * * * *

One example: The Oglala Sioux are perhaps the most well known of the Sioux bands. Among their past leaders were Red Cloud, the only Indian who ever defeated the United States in a war, and Crazy Horse, most revered of the Sioux war chiefs. The Oglala were, and perhaps still are, the meanest group of Indians ever assembled. They would take after a cavalry troop just to see if their bowstrings were taut enough. When they had settled on the reservation, the Oglala made a fairly smooth transition to the new life. They had good herds of cattle, they settled along the numerous creeks that cross the reservation and they created a very strong community spirit. The Episcopalians and the Roman Catholics had the missionary franchise on the reservation and the tribe was pretty evenly split between the two. In the Episcopal Church, at least, the congregations were fairly self-governing and stable.

But over the years, the Oglala Sioux have had a number of problems. Their population has grown faster than their means of support. The government allowed White farmers to come into the eastern part of the reservation and create a country, with the best farmlands owned or operated by the Whites. The reservation was allotted—taken out of the collective hands of the tribe and parceled out to individuals—and when ownership became too complicated, control of the land passed out of Indian hands. The government displaced a number of families during World War Two by taking a part of the reservation for use as a bombing range to train crews for combat. Only last year was this land returned to tribal and individual use.

The tribe became a favorite subject for anthropological study quite early, because of its romantic past. Theories arose attempting to explain the apparent lack of progress of the Oglala Sioux. The true issue—White control of the reservation—was overlooked completely. Instead, every conceivable intangible cultural distinction was used to explain the lack of economic, social and educational progress of a people who were, to all intents and purposes, absentee landlords because of the government policy of leasing their lands to Whites.

* * * * *

Then one day a famous anthropologist advanced the theory, probably valid at the time and in the manner in which he advanced it, that the Oglala were "warriors without weapons."

The chase was on . . . Outfitting anthropological expeditions became the number-one industry of the small off-reservation Nebraska towns south of Pine Ridge. Surely, supplying the Third Crusade to the Holy Land was a minor feat compared with the task of keeping the anthropologists at Pine Ridge.

Every conceivable difference between the Oglala Sioux and the folks at Bar Harbor was attributed to the quaint warrior tradition of the Oglala Sioux. From lack of roads to unshined shoes, Sioux problems were generated, so the anthro's discovered, by the refusal of the White man to recognize the great desire of the Oglala to go to war. Why expect an Oglala to become a small businessman, when he was only waiting for that wagon train to come around the bend? The very real and human problems of the reservation were considered to be merely by-products of the failure of a warrior people to become domesticated. The fairly respectable thesis of past exploits in war, perhaps romanticized for morale purposes, became a spiritual force all its own. Some Indians, in a tongue-in-cheek manner for which Indians are justly famous, suggested that a subsidized wagon train be run through the reservation each morning at nine o'clock and the reservation people paid a minimum wage for attacking it.

* * * * *

Real problems and real people become invisible before the great romantic and nonsensical notion that the Sioux yearn for the days of Crazy Horse and Red Cloud and will do nothing until those days return.

* * * * *

The rest of America had better beware of having quaint mores that attract anthropologists, or it will soon become a victim of the conceptual prison into which Blacks and Indians, among others, have been thrown. One day you may find yourself cataloged—perhaps as a credit-card-carrying, turnpike-commuting, condominium-dwelling, fraternity-joining, church-going, sports-watching, time-purchase-buying, television-watching, magazine-subscribing, politically inert transmigrated urbanite who, through the phenomenon of the second car and the shopping center, has become a golf-playing, wife-swapping, etc., etc., etc., suburbanite. Or have you already been characterized—and caricatured—in ways that struck you as absurd? If so, you will understand what has been happening to Indians for a long, long time.

What do you think?

1. *What were the real problems of the Oglala Sioux? According to Deloria, why and how were these real problems obscured?*
2. *"The rest of America had better beware of having quaint mores that attract anthropologists. . . ." Why?*

3. IF THE TABLES WERE TURNED

In a Letter to the Editor which appeared in the Globe and Mail, *July 8, 1969, Mr. J. S. Powless of the Six Nations Reserve near Brantford, Ontario, draws an analogy which illuminates some Indian attitudes towards the White man.*

Let us create a hypothetical situation and suppose that Japan invades or infiltrates Canada, and proceeds to take over all reins of authority and also proceeds to enforce its language, customs, and institutions on the Canadian people. The Canadian people would naturally rebel against the Japanese. The Japanese would have two alternatives: annihilate the natives, as the English did in Newfoundland; or divide and conquer, as the Europeans did on the North American mainland. If the divide-and-conquer theory were used by the Japanese, a terrific resentment against them would be built up by the Canadian people. This is exactly what happened between the White Europeans and the North American native people.

Down through the years many schemes were used by the Europeans to divide, conquer, and subdue the North American native people. They cajoled them, cheated them, stole from them, made unrealistic promises, and at the same time, by using their armed forces and police, bossed them with an iron fist.

Can you honestly wonder why the North American native people are in many instances a bitter, hostile people, and why, in many areas, there is enmity toward the people who forced their will upon them?

Let us now go back to the hypothetical Japanese invasion or infiltration of Canada. They are now, after three or four hundred years, firmly in the driver's seat. During these several hundreds of years, the Japanese have continually attempted to brainwash the Canadian people and induce them to accept their customs, traditions, institutions, and language. While attempting this brainwashing technique, they have tolerated the Canadian people and have watched those Canadians who refused to accept their customs and traditions slide lower and lower into the valley of despair, poverty, and deprivation.

The Japanese have offered the Canadian people the right to live among them—on condition that the Canadian people adopt their customs, language, traditions, and institutions. They have offered to educate the Canadian people—on condition that the Canadian people accept the Japanese form of education and learn the things that the Japanese want them to learn. The Japanese have also offered the Canadian people religion—on condition that it is the Japanese religion and is taught by Japanese clergy.

The years have rolled by since this hypothetical Japanese invasion; generations of people have come and gone. The Canadian people have almost completely lost their culture, customs, traditions, and language. Most of the Canadian people who have adopted the Japanese way of life have intermarried with the Japanese, and although many still call themselves Canadians, they are often almost completely Japanese.

The Canadians have become so much like their Japanese conquerors that they no longer present an obstacle in the path of Japanese development of their resources. The Canadian people are attending Japanese institutions of higher learning and are gradually leaving their reserves and entering into the mainstream of Japanese life. Thousands of Canadians are now working for and with the Japanese.

Down through the years, the Japanese in Canada have also lost and/or discarded many of their Japanese homeland customs and traditions, and have come to think of themselves as Canadians rather than Japanese. They have adopted a distinct Canadian flag with no trace of the homeland Japanese flag. They have appointed a Canadian to the Senate. A Canadian has even been elected by the Japanese to represent them in the federal Parliament.

End of hypothesis.

I do not believe that we will ever solve the "Indian problem" because we will never be able to pinpoint what the "problem" really is.

What do you think?

1. *What do you think is Powless's attitude towards White society? Why does he feel the way he does?*
2. *Powless says, "I do not believe that we will ever solve the 'Indian problem' because we will never really be able to pinpoint what the 'problem' really is." How does he arrive at this conclusion? Do you agree with his arguments? Why or why not?*

4. THE ADVENTURES OF CHARLIE SQUASH

Duke Redbird, a many-talented Canadian Indian, illustrates a dilemma which is faced by many Indians.

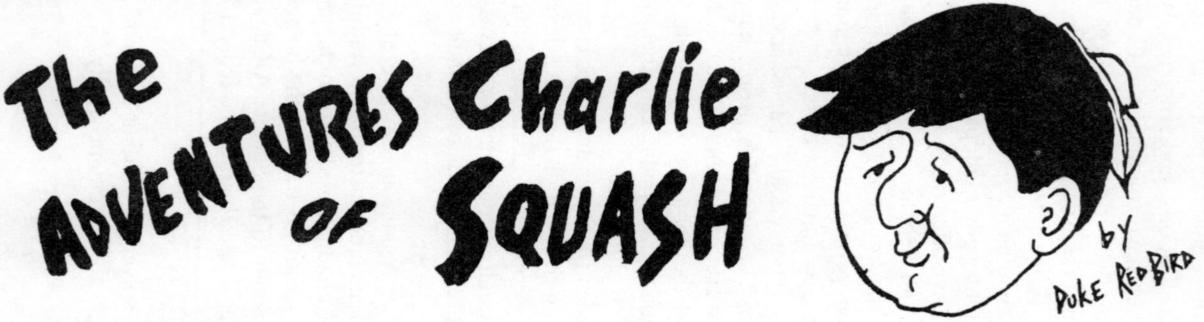

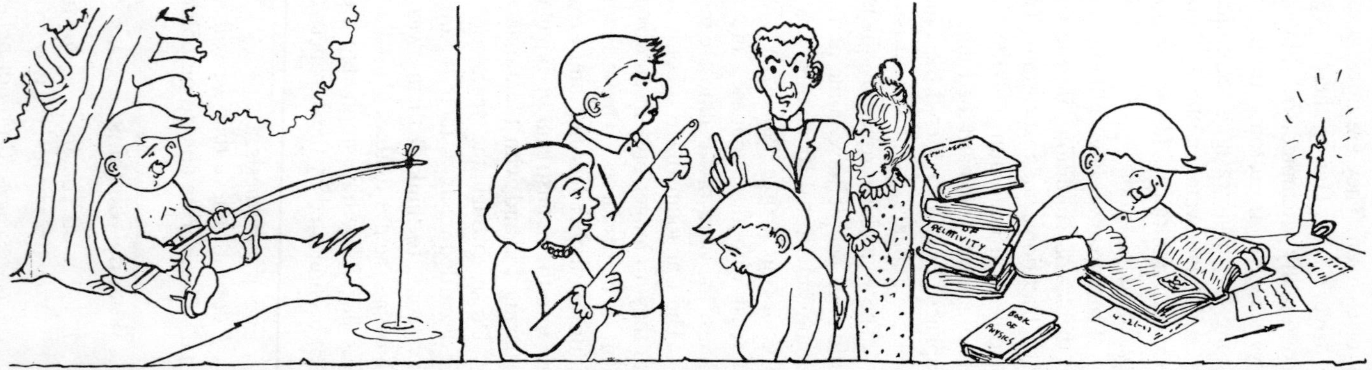

When I was a youngster on the reserve, I was a happy little savage. I was the kind of Indian boy everybody reads about in books. I fished, hunted, played, and danced.

But my parents told me I had to grow up. My minister told me I had to face my responsibility. My teachers said I must prepare to face the modern world.

So I stored away the breechcloth, my bows and arrows, and my dancing costumes. I bought all kinds of books and studied like a mad Indian to be a success in the big outside world.

Then I graduated from high school and I left the reserve to find my place in the world. People didn't believe I was an Indian, because I acted just like they did. I didn't even wear feathers.

When I visited the reserve my parents were mad because I sounded like a White man. My minister was mad because I didn't praise the traditions of my people, and the teachers were mad because I didn't get a job with the National Indian Council.

So I studied Indian lore like mad. I learned all I could about the North American Indians and I got a membership with the National Indian Council.

Now my friends at work complain because I am always pushing the Indian cause. They say that I should try to adjust and blend with the White society, and quit lobbying to make Indians different and independent of the rest of society. So I quit work.

But I couldn't get a job. I took what little money I had and made some Indian war bonnets. They sold like mad. So I paid another Indian to make them for me and run the shop, and now I spend my time fishing, hunting, and dancing on the reserve.

Everybody should have let well enough alone.

What do you think?

1. *What is the problem portrayed in this cartoon?*
2. *How do Whites perpetuate it? How do Indians?*
3. *Can you see a resolution? Explain.*

Making a Living

Many rural Indians, especially those in the North, live in conditions of appalling poverty. Yet those who seek relief by moving to the city often find only more poverty, except that in the city it is too often accompanied by loneliness and anxiety.

What effects does poverty have on people's lives? How does it influence their attitude towards the rest of society, particularly if they are part of a racial minority group?

This section offers material to assist you in your examination of these questions.

1. SOME STATISTICS ON INDIAN POVERTY

The following table graphs the family incomes of Indians. The information provided here was taken from the Canada Yearbook *of 1969, and arranged by the Indian-Eskimo Association of Canada.*

What do you think?

1. *Which income group showed the most significant change between 1958 and 1969? Why?*
2. *Draw up a budget for an Indian family of four with an income of $2,000. Use as a guide the prices found in your own area. What adjustment would have to be made for northern Indians?*

INDIAN FAMILY UNIT INCOME

Percentage of numbers earning:

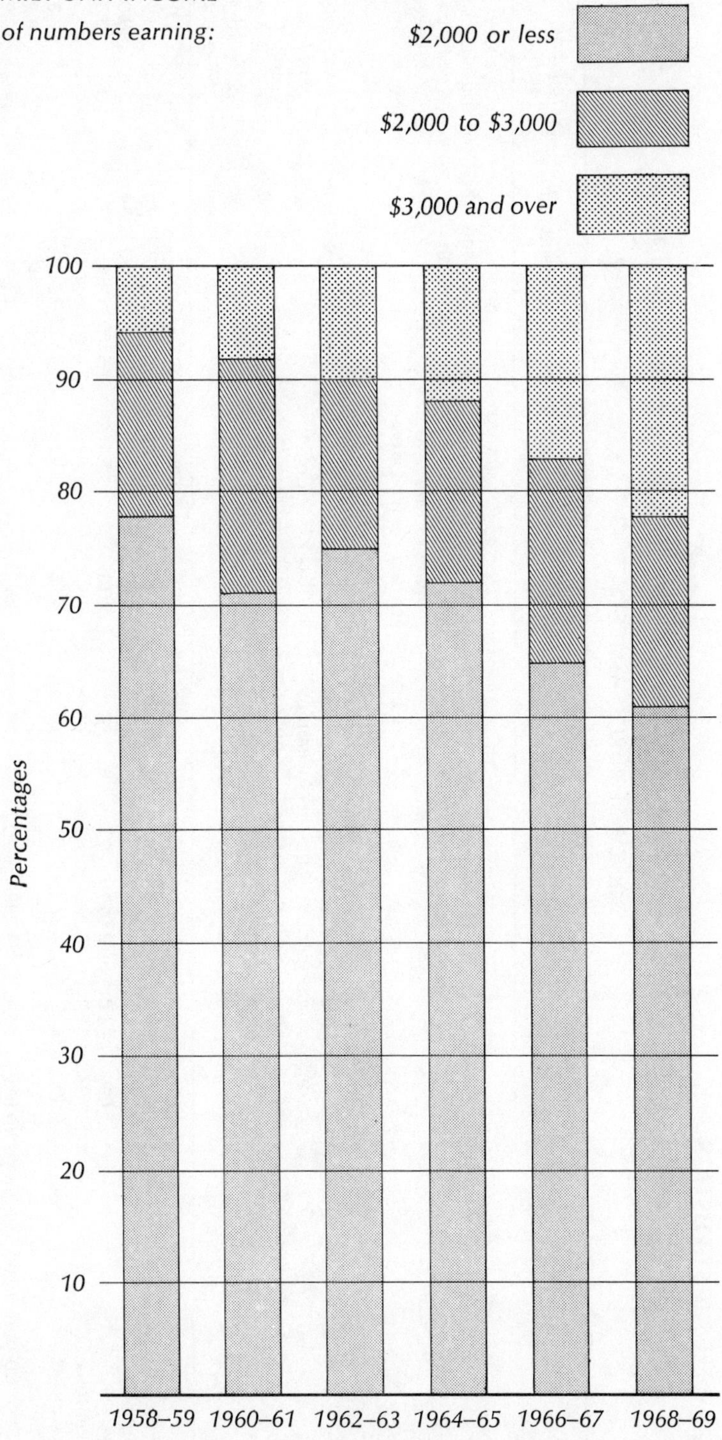

By comparison: in 1966 less than 1% of Canadian taxpayers had a taxable income below $1,000. Less than 16% had a taxable income below $3,000.

2. WELFARE STATISTICS

The following table, taken from Indian Facts and Figures *(Information Canada, 1969), shows the number of Indian welfare recipients.*

SURVEY OF PUBLIC ASSISTANCE 1966

	Total No. of Relief Recipients		*Adults*		*Employable Adults*			*Heads of Households*			*Frequency of Assistance*	
								Adult recipients who were heads of households			*Employable Heads of households who received help each month in previous 11 months or more*	
									Employable			
Agency or Region / *NATIONAL TOTAL*	*No.*	*Percentage of resident population**	*Total No. of Adults assisted*	*Percentage of resident adult population assisted***	*No. of adult recipients who were employable*	*Percentage of adults assisted who were employable (Col. 6 over 4)*	*Percentage of adults resident on reserves who were employable and rec'd assistance (Col. 6 over **)*	*Total No.*	*No.*	*% (Col. 10 over 9)*	*No.*	*Percentage of heads of households assisted (Col. 12 over 9)*
(1)	(2)	(3)	(4)	(5)	(6)	(7)	(8)	(9)	(10)	(11)	(12)	(13)
Maritime	3,832	56.7	1,402	44.4	624	44.5	19.8	698	535	76.6	281	40.3
Quebec	6,949	36.2	3,104	32.6	1,371	44.2	14.4	1,582	1,339	84.6	475	30.0
Ontario	7,096	33.0	2,911	27.9	1,189	40.1	11.4	1,558	1,130	72.8	300	19.3
Manitoba	13,734	51.3	5,289	45.2	2,046	38.7	17.5	2,621	1,804	68.8	459	17.5
Saskatchewan	16,592	60.3	6,362	54.9	2,702	42.5	23.3	3,433	2,526	73.6	956	27.8
Alberta	8,280	38.0	3,212	35.6	1,211	37.7	13.4	1,628	1,084	66.6	297	18.2
British Columbia and Yukon	9,889	24.4	3,730	20.2	1,355	36.3	7.3	2,128	1,263	59.4	359	16.9
District of Mackenzie	1,355	25.5	557	20.9	207	37.2	7.8	345	202	58.6	87	25.2
Canada	67,727	40.0	26,567	34.7	10,705	40.3	14.0	13,993	9,883	70.6	3,214	23.0

N.B. * Resident Population: 169,35 (Including 1,649 "Off Reserve" in the Yukon Agency)
** Resident adult population (Reserves and Crown Land): 76,565 (Including 750 "Off Reserve" in the Yukon Agency)

What do you think?

1. *Which part of Canada has the lowest percentage of Indians on welfare? The highest? Account for these differences.*
2. *How many Indian adults were on assistance? How many families? How many children? What effect would the receipt of welfare have on the family as a whole, and the children in particular?*
3. *What percentage of welfare recipients were employable? What, if any, are the special problems created by this situation?*
4. *What is column 13 trying to show? Account for the variations between the Maritimes and Ontario.*

3. INDIANS DON'T WANT TO BE POOR

Glen Allen, a staff reporter for the Toronto Star, *described the Indian poverty which he saw in northern Ontario. His account appeared in the* Star, *June 22, 1969.*

Last November, J. Herbert Dawson of the Children's Aid Society in northern Ontario, visited Gull Bay, a community of treaty Indians, and wrote a report about them. It said in part that on entering an Indian person's house, "I found three small children huddled under an old wet blanket in a bedroom and a baby in a crib. They had been alone since the previous evening and were in bad condition as there was no heat or food. At first we thought the baby was dead. Never have I felt a colder body."

Of another Indian home Dawson reported, "A mother has eight children born out of wedlock. There are two bedrooms in the house. One is used for wood storage, and in the other is one bed without springs. . . . There were no blankets, dishes, or towels, and very little food."

Some Indian people of Ontario live with a kind of poverty unknown to the darkest, most abjectly poor corner of inner Toronto. They are poor partly because of what history has left them—in the case of Gull Bay, an almost inaccessible spot of land on a cliff overlooking a lake somewhere west of Lake Nipigon. They are poor because people—White people—have gotten so used to thinking about Indians as being poor that they think of their poverty as a condition as fixed as the stars. "This is a poverty with a difference," says Victor Valentine of Carleton University, a sociologist. "It is a poverty with a national frame of mind built around it. People say 'Oh yes, the poor Indians' and then forget about it."

But if anything can be learned from visiting Indian communities in northern Ontario it is that Indian people don't want to be poor. They don't want the values of middle-class Ontario, but they do want shelter that is warm. They want enough food to eat and some—Heaven forbid—want indoor plumbing. "There is nothing in our culture that says we must use an outhouse in 30-degree-below-zero weather," an Indian said.

What do you think?

1. *"White people think of Indian poverty 'as a condition as fixed as the stars.'"*
   (a) Why?
   (b) Is this an example of cumulative racism (page 33)? Why or why not?
   (c) What effect would this attitude have on government spending, local taxpayers, and Indian workers?
2. *(a) Debate the proposition: "One cannot reject middle-class White values and expect to enjoy things like indoor plumbing."*
   (b) How does this dilemma compare with the Charlie Squash cartoon by Duke Redbird on page 46?
3. *In the excerpt taken from his book* Custer Died for Your Sins, *Vine Deloria wrote very negatively about social scientists. How does the article above suggest, indirectly, that there is a role for the social scientist in Canada?*

4. RESERVATION LIFE: PRO AND CON

Indian reserves are often located in the most remote and infertile parts of the country. As a result they often become pockets of terrible poverty. Comments from Indians on the reserve life appeared on the CBC radio program The Way of the Indian, *broadcast in 1963.*

CHIEF JOHN ALBANY: There's 2,200 reserves across Canada, and very few of them are near towns. So if you've got a house and some land on the reserve, how do you get a job? You do what you can—farm maybe. And there's a lot to be said for living on the reserve. It gives us our own land, our own way of life.

MRS. DAVE CROWCHILD: There's no harm living on the reserve. Here on the Sarcee Reserve, near Calgary, Alberta, I've found that out. As long as we can live by ourselves, and make our own living, I think it's all right.

DR. GILBERT MONTURE: The reserves today, even in the far North, are becoming depleted of game and fish. And this will grow progressively worse as the industrialization of the marshland takes place, so that the opportunities for hunting and fishing and enjoying the primitive life will grow less and less. Consequently, what is the Indian to do? He is beyond the agricultural belt in most cases. He cannot supplement his living by raising a few vegetables or things of that sort. And so, for those types of food he must pay money to buy them, either as canned goods or goods that come up from the agricultural area. Now, if he has no job opportunity, where is he going to find the money to maintain himself at even a very low standard of living? I would say that the opportunity for them to pursue their former natural way of life is rapidly disappearing and this presents the big problem that's facing the Indian.

BURTON KEWAYOSH: When I was a boy we had a reserve here which was all wood, all marsh. No White men. Which made it a very nice reserve. And these were some of the happiest times of my life when I was a boy, just wandering all over the reserve. Everything was just ideal—just trees and marsh and grass and wild plums and cherries and apple trees. There was no such thing as hurry, no idea of time—we didn't even have a clock. Now we have a reserve here, possibly fifty thousand acres. We have a reserve here that's just as good as it ever was, but now it has to be farmed like the White man's community. Even our muskrats and ducks have to be farmed, whereas a long time ago we had broad expanses of duck marsh, and the White man never hunted there. Now we have to commercialize on everything we have in order to stay in the picture—like renting out the hunting to the White man. But then, you see, you get to realize that these things have to be. You have to live with them. It's progress you know.

What do you think?

1. *What problems does reserve life pose for the Indian? What promise?*
2. *To the native people reserves are one way of insuring the survival of their culture. What problems might the economic development of the reserves create for this function? What are some solutions?*

5. THE URBAN MIGRATION

Glen Allen reports some of the experiences that Indians often have after moving to the city. Allen's article appeared in the Toronto Star *on June 26, 1969.*

One day last fall, an eighteen-year-old Indian girl we'll call Mary Lee X arrived in Toronto from British Columbia. Not long after, on October 28, she was arrested for being in possession of a stolen painting valued at more than fifty dollars. Bail was set at one thousand dollars. Mary Lee couldn't raise it, and she spent a month in the Don Jail, appearing in court five times without a case being brought against her by the Crown. The charge was finally withdrawn November 28 for lack of evidence.

Mary Lee's lawyer, P. T. Matlow of Toronto, wrote a letter to a Toronto newspaper saying that "she left without a word of apology or explanation from anyone for the injustice to which she had been subjected and without any compensation for the loss of earnings and the suffering she endured." Mary Lee disappeared almost as soon as she left the court. There was an address of a Bay Street hotel, and a house on Winchester Street. Someone thought she might have moved on to Montreal. Two social workers more than a little piously said she was "a bad girl" anyway. Mary Lee, wherever she is now, is a sad example of the Canadian Indian who leaves home for the city only to find that urban Canada can be a huge and terrifying underground.

Ontario's Indians leave their communities and reserves for the city in increasing numbers. There are an estimated ten thousand Indian people in the city of Toronto. Many survive, some splendidly. Recently, five hundred members of the North American Indian Club of Toronto, a largely middle-class gathering of teachers, factory workers, engineers, and social workers—people who live in their own homes in places like Rexdale and Scarborough—met for their annual meeting in an Etobicoke assembly hall.

But, says Victor Pelletier, an Indian from northern Ontario who is program director for the Indian Centre of Toronto, "too many come down here and end up in the slums." Life on the reserve is a world away, says Pelletier. "A man comes to my door, just off the bus from the North. He's got seven kids and five dollars in his pocket and he says he was told I could get him a job. I ask him if he has any trade and he says no. I ask him if he has any schooling, and he says grade two. I ask him if he has a place to stay, and he says he was told that I would help him get one. I ask him if he wants to rent a house and he asks 'What's rent?'

"On the reserve people have never had a boss; nobody has ever told them how many furs to trap, how much wood to cut. So it's more than simple adjustment when a man gets a job on an assembly line. It's a new, upside-down way of life. A man gets very discouraged, very depressed.

"And there are the girls. Every day you see them getting off the bus. And the sharpies are down there to meet them. They make a career of it. 'You new here?' they say. 'Could I take you out for breakfast?' Well these kids don't know what's going on. Inside of six weeks they've become prostitutes. Short of having someone meet every bus that comes to town I don't know what to do about it."

Walter Currie, an Indian who is president of the Indian-Eskimo Association, says that while Indians in Toronto don't live in the readily identifiable ghettos they occupy in Winnipeg and Vancouver, they have enormous difficulties equipping themselves for urban life. The Indian has to learn about budgets and thrift, getting to places on time, and steady work habits. He has to adjust to the noise of the city, to the number and varieties of functionaries in the bureaucracies that control his life, and to a language he may not speak. He has to learn about everything from transportation to trade unions, when to take the garbage out, and when to pay a gas bill.

"Agencies both public and private are not aware of the Indian in the city," says Currie. "They don't know what to do with him when he walks in the door. He goes to the Indian Affairs Branch and they say, 'You've already been here six months—so your problems are up to the city. Go and see them.' He goes to the city and they say, 'You're an Indian—go to the Indian Affairs.' And this whole business of sitting in an office waiting for people, Indians or any kind of people, is so wrong. What good is a Manpower (employment) counsellor to a man just off the reserve when he tells him to sit down, fill out a form and 'We'll call you if we need you.' They're not speaking the client's language. Boy that makes me mad."

The one agency that exists solely to help Indian people in the city, the Indian Friendship Centre, serving fifteen hundred people in a big old Beverley Street house, says it has been hard to get official recognition of the need for their kind of work.

Indian people come to the city for most of the same reasons people go anywhere new: for adventure, for employment, and sometimes because a contemporary has already tried the city. Indian people themselves sometimes decide that moving to the city was the best move they ever made, or that, at least, it is better than what they left behind.

Mrs. Valerie McHugh who lives in an aging apartment off Beverley Street with four children, says she will never go back to the reserve where she grew up, at Cutler, eighty-five miles north of Sault Ste. Marie. "There was never anything to do. And I don't see how any government couldn't spend its budget. Up there on the reserves everything is so much worse than what people everywhere else have."

But Norbert Cameron, a former chief of White Dog Reserve north of Kenora, came to Toronto to take a carpentry course at George Brown College and says he was "never so glad to leave anywhere. All that noise, everyone's so busy."

Helen Domenchuk, an Indian woman from the Cape Croker Reserve who now lives in Toronto, says, "I have a home here and my husband, but the reserve is still the place you call home—a place where you can be free with your people."

There is a wide gulf between Helen Domenchuk's "home" and the cities where the Indian so often finds himself unwelcome.

What do you think?

1. *Why do you think Indians move to the city?*
2. *What problems would city life pose for any newcomer from the country? What particular difficulties would Indians in this situation encounter?*
3. *What can be done to ease these problems?*

6. TWO KINDS OF POVERTY

In this article published in the Indian-Eskimo Association Bulletin *of November-December 1965, Canon E. W. Scott tells how efforts to lessen Indian poverty can actually increase it.*

First, we need to remind ourselves of two basic factors: (1) The cultures of Indians and Eskimos have not been, historically, centered on possessions, nor have they been exploitive or individualistic. (2) When the cultures of these groups first came in contact with White "civilization," the ability of the European settlers to establish themselves depended on the skills of the native. But as the dependence decreased, these groups became more and more separated from the newcomers, and for the last century or more, the pattern of relationships can be generally described as "out of sight, out of mind." During this period, the relatively similar economic condition which existed in both groups in the period of initial contacts has altered. The effects of industrialization brought greater material benefits to the urban dweller than to the rural person; and much improved health services and altered patterns of living led to a rapid increase in population. The combination of these factors has led to growing contrasts between the economic situation of the White community and that of their Indian neighbors.

At the present time, new developments are breaking down the separation between the two groups and the contrasts are becoming obvious. In areas such as Kenora and Minaki, the development of tourism, summer homes, and fishing and hunting lodges shows up the differences in their most extreme form. Such contrasts can be stimulating and challenging. They can also be frustrating to a degree which leads to destructiveness and violence.

When these contrasts are seen to be owing to conditions over which Indians and Eskimos have no control, this situation negates the system of values which is traditional in their cultures. Success, for them, had been measured, not in terms of possessions, but in terms of ability to cope with the environment, to grapple with the elements, to exercise skills in hunting and fishing, etc. When they feel they can no longer cope with their environment, it becomes more and more difficult to maintain any sense of self-worth. At the same time, alternative cultural values are pressing in upon them, especially upon the young people. So we see a coincidence of cultural and economic poverty. Steps taken to alleviate the economic poverty often tend to deepen the cultural poverty. This is the real dilemma we face.

Our country is wealthy enough and has enough technical skill to enable us to grapple with the economic poverty of Canada, certainly with that of our Indian and Eskimo people who are not a large part of our population. The real danger is that under pressure we may deal with poverty only in economic terms, and in so doing create a more insidious and pervasive kind of poverty that cuts right into the core of people's beings.

We must approach the problem, therefore, not only on "welfare" terms but in human terms, on the basis of personal capacities and creativity. On the North American continent our governments spend a great deal of money on "welfare," in providing a bare minimum level of economic existence. A comparatively small amount is spent on maintaining employment.

In the Scandinavian countries, on the other hand, a great deal of money is spent on maintaining full employment, making large welfare expenditures unnecessary. The North American approach tends to divide society between those who believe they are self-sufficient and those who have to be assisted. Between these two groups exist strong undertones of bitterness and judgment.

Which group we belong to does not any longer depend primarily upon individual factors, but in the vast majority of cases is determined by the family into which we were born. This pertains particularly to Indian and Eskimo people. They are poor not because they are afraid to work, but because they were born into the wrong racial group.

We must, therefore, go farther than maintaining that poverty must be dealt with in economic terms. We must call for action in human terms that will enable native people to maintain (or if need be, regain) a true sense of dignity and worth. Their existence must have meaning for them as persons. They must be able to feel that they are making a real contribution to our well-being as a nation and to the well-being of the whole human family, of which they are valuable members.

What do you think?

1. *(a) How does the author explain how efforts to ease the poverty of Indians can actually worsen their situation?*
   (b) How can this dilemma be solved, if at all?
2. *Does welfare deepen Indian "poverty"? If so, how and why? What alternatives are there to welfare?*

Finding Justice

Nowhere is the potential for misunderstanding between Indians and Whites more prominent than in the area of the law. What are the problems that Indians face in following the White man's law, and in obtaining just treatment in court?

1. STATISTICS ON INDIAN DELINQUENCY

This table is taken from Indians and the Law, *a pamphlet prepared for the Department of Indian Affairs and Northern Development by the Canadian Corrections Association in 1967.*

What do you think?

1. *What questions or statements do these statistics raise?*
2. *From what you know, what answers would you suggest?*

NUMBER OF INDIAN, METIS AND ESKIMO ADULTS IN SELECTED PROVINCIAL CORRECTIONAL INSTITUTIONS IN CANADA FOR CERTAIN PERIODS IN 1965 OR 1966

Prov.	*Institution*	*Period*	*Total Admitted*[1]	*Total in Detention*[2]	*Indian, Métis and Eskimo*	*Indian, Métis or Eskimo per cent*
N.B.	N.B. Central Reformatory	Jan-Aug 66	70		3	4
	Interprovincial Home for Young Women	Since 1963	20		0	0
Que.	New Carlisle Jail	Jan-June 66	242		29	12
	Roberval	1965	834		245	29
Ont.	Mercer Reformatory (F)	Aug 66		68	7	10
	Brampton	Aug 66		130	4	3
	Burtch	Aug 66		135	22	16
	Algoma	Jan-June 66	370		91	24
	Kenora District (M)	Jan-June 66	587		418	71
	Kenora District (F)	Jan-June 66	281		266	95
	Sudbury District	Jan-Jun-66	1120		195	17
Man.	Headingly	Aug 66		454	99	22
	Brandon	Aug 66		79	47	59
	Dauphin	Aug 66		66	52	78
	The Pas (M)	Aug 66		38	32	84
	The Pas (F)	Aug 66		17	17	100
	Portage La Prairie	Aug 66		63	44	69
Sask.	Regina P.C.I.	Aug 66	222		106	48
	P.A. P.C.I. (M)	Aug 66	153		101	66
	P.A. P.C.I. (F)	Aug. 66	30		24	80
Alta.	Fort Saskatchewan (M)	Aug 66	648		181	28
	Lethbridge	Aug 66	318		208	66
	Calgary	Aug 66	563		88	16
	Fort Saskatchewan (F)	Aug 66	109		81	74
B.C.	Oakalla Prison Farm	Apr 66	741		100	13
	Vancouver Island Unit	Apr 66	100		10	10
	Kamloops	Apr 66	170		69	41
	Prince George	Apr 66	89		21	24
	Oakalla Prison Farm (F)	Apr 66	76		35	46
	Kamloops (F)	Apr 66	11		11	100
Y.T.	(RCMP Whitehorse Guardroom)	Aug 66	176		95	54
N.W.T.	Fort Smith	Aug 66	131		108	82
	RCMP Inuvik (Guardroom)	Aug 66	85		81	95
	Frobisher Bay	Aug 66	25		22	88

[1]Total number admitted during period of time indicated.
[2]Detained in jail at the time of the collection of data.

2. INDIANS AND THE LAW: A CASE STUDY

The jailing of two Indian women in August of 1969 created alarm among concerned people. This report is from the Toronto Telegram *of October 26, 1970.*

Two young Indian mothers, angry at their world and its future, went on a drinking spree last August, and ended up throwing rocks through nearly three thousand dollars worth of windows. Judge J. V. Fregeau sentenced one of them to twelve months definite and six months indefinite on one charge and another twelve months concurrent on another. The other mother got nine months definite and six months indefinite. Judge Fregeau said later he believed the stiff sentences were needed as a warning to others. This severe punishment, although causing little stir here [Kenora], has brought an outcry from southern civil libertarians and Indian leaders. Short cuts were made in the two cases. The fact that both were staggering drunk at the time the windows were broken, maybe too drunk to be legally responsible, was not argued. Nor was the full involvement of some juveniles probed in any effort to reveal that the women didn't do all the damage.

"You tell me the answer," says Judge Fregeau. "I've tried everything I know. What was I going to do with these women? They broke over three thousand dollars worth of windows for apparently no reason."

Judge Fregeau, a former Kenora mayor appointed to the bench about twelve years ago, explained that with the high native population here, he is constantly facing "unusual circumstances" that other judges don't face. "The Indian here is a different breed of cat. It seems like this has been the dumping ground for the worst. I know jail doesn't seem to do any good, but it takes them out of circulation," he said.

"At least by sending them to jail, I told a doctor one night, I probably extend their lives fifteen years. They are warm, clothed, and well fed in jail. Some never had it better."

Civil rights lawyer Jack Doner, a close friend of Indians here, said of Judge Fregeau's remarks: "You have to try to understand what the judge is saying and what is behind his words, because he is a fair and just person. His remarks are the result of a decade of frustration where he has tried everything ever suggested about dealing with native people. Certainly Indian people are different here from the Indian of another culture somwhere else, just like you and I are different from Americans. I agree jail isn't the answer. But what is the alternative when we must act within the law which applies to all Canadians?"

He was, however, critical of the sentences given Mrs. Henry and Mrs. Land, calling them "not punishment but retaliation." Mr. Doner learned about it too late to lodge an appeal. "Everyone in Kenora is looking elsewhere for the answers and blaming others for the racial tensions here. It is time the White people started blaming themselves and tried themselves to find the answers."

A social worker dealing with the Ojibway mothers at Vanier Institute for Women at Brantford, where they are serving their sentences (about twelve hundred miles from their families and culture), described their cases as "shocking." "How can we rehabilitate someone like this if 'rehabilitated' is the word? We know nothing about their life and they know nothing about our ways. The cultural shock for them must be terrible. It is cruel to send such people here," said the social worker.

P. J. Hare, area supervisor of Indian Affairs, was aware of the women's cases. But he says he did not intervene even though the damage was to property under his control. Mr. Hare drew attention to Treaty No. 3 between Kenora area Indians and the Queen, pointing out that they promised ". . . in all respect to obey and abide by the law."

White Dog Reserve Chief, Roy Mcdonald laughed out loud when told Mr. Hare had referred to Treaty No. 3.

"Maybe he would like to explain why sections of the treaty beneficial to the Indian people have not been upheld. That treaty also promises schools for our people, but today forty children are not in school because there is no room for them," said Mr. Mcdonald.

* * * * *

He agreed with Mr. Doner that the two mothers should have been punished, but felt a small jail sentence or probation would have been enough.

Asked if it was significant that the women damaged only property of an agency which has controlled their lives for as long as they can remember Mr. Mcdonald just smiled and shrugged.

Lawyer Bruce Finlay, who sometimes acts as Crown prosecutor, was more forceful when asked to comment on the cases: "The southern press and radio and TV like to come up here and make an instant analysis. If there is any discrimination it is against the White offenders. The client who is really suffering now is the White paying client and the White from the poverty background who has little education."

What do you think?

1. *Why do you think this incident of vandalism might have been brought about by frustration?*
2. *What are the issues raised by the Kenora jailings?*
3. *Compare the attitudes of Judge Fregeau, Mr. Doner, the social worker and Chief Mcdonald. How do they each see the issues? What might they each suggest for a resolution to the problem?*

3. CAUGHT BETWEEN TWO CULTURES

The pamphlet Indians and the Law *explains part of the difficulty that Indians have with the law.*

A fuller understanding of what it means to be caught between two cultures would result in a more sympathetic application of our laws and legal system to Indians and Eskimos. Our law is a foreign law to the Indians and Eskimos, not based on their culture or their history and not reflecting their values. They, therefore, do not understand it and often resent it.

A simple example has to do with personal possessions. In the traditional Indian community, if one member of the group is fortunate he is expected to share his good fortune with the others. In the primitive conditions of the past this principle had obvious advantages. However, it does not apply as smoothly under modern conditions, and sometimes the individual Indian will say it is not worth being the only working member of his immediate group since on payday his relatives simply move in and share his wages until they are gone. Also, doors are not locked in an Indian community and any member of the group feels free to make use of the house of another without asking permission. When this attitude is carried into a non-Indian community, the result is apt to be a charge of breaking and entering or trespassing.

* * * * *

It appears that Indians have little understanding of their legal rights, of court procedures or of resources such as legal aid. The vast majority in conflict with the law appear in the magistrate's court where offences such as liquor infractions, petty theft and assaults are heard in general, the magistrates seem to have great compassion for the Indian people and to be lenient in their treatment of them in comparison to non-Indians appearing before them on similar offences. There are exceptions to this rule, places where magisterial attitudes are reflected in sterner treatment of the Indian people. But these are rare, and were encountered primarily in those areas where the court docket was almost exclusively composed of Indian or Métis people and where general conditions among the Indian people were at their worst.

Occasionally, leniency shown by the magistrate towards Indians tended to irritate local authorities, particularly the police, and may well contribute to the attitude on the part of some Indian people that the law itself is not only a joke but that the magistrate or justice of the peace bases his decisions on whim and caprice.

It appears that most Indian people enter guilty pleas either because they do not really understand the concept of legal guilt and innocence, or because they are fearful of exercising their rights. Access to legal counsel is seldom possible for them. In remote areas, the Indian people appear confused about the functions of the court, particularly where the Royal Canadian Mounted Police officers also act as Crown prosecutors, or where the magistrates travel about in police aircraft.

In the southern part of Canada, there appears to be no real language barrier because most Indian people have had relatively close contact with either the French- or English-speaking dominant group and have an understanding of either the English or the French language. The field workers observed, however, that communication, with full understanding and good rapport, is practically non-existent. The use of interpreters does not alleviate this fully because, for the most part, the interpreters themselves were not able to grasp the significance of court language. In addition, there is no well-organized system of locating good interpreters or paying them adequately for their services. An example was quoted—and this apparently happens quite often—in which an accused Indian, who had already been sentenced for an offence and had been removed to jail, was subsequently returned to court and pressed into service by the magistrate as a court interpreter for other Indians undergoing trial.

What is meant by?

"legal aid"
"court docket"

What do you think?

1. *What problems with understanding the White man's law does the Indian have in everyday life? Why? What problems does he encounter in court?*
2. *Suggest ways in which cross-cultural misunderstanding could be dispelled. How detrimental to the survival of the Indian culture could this process be?*
3. *How could a confusion between the courts and the police affect Indians' attitude toward the law?*

4. INDIANS AND ALCOHOL

Alcohol is more often than not at the root of Indian crime. It is also a source of much White resentment towards Indians. The pamphlet Indians and the Law *tries to explain Indian drinking.*

A recent paper by R. C. Dailey shows how early concern about the misuse of alcohol among Indians is recorded in scores of references in the Jesuit relations of the seventeenth and eighteenth centuries. It was realized even during that early period that the Indians had no strong controls of a social and psychological kind to structure and contain their drinking behavior. Once the belief was established that, somehow, the Indian could not control himself when drinking, it became part of the folk-belief system, and generations of Indians grew up, indeed still grow up, learning that, for some biological reason, they are incapable of drinking in a "normal" manner. In more recent times, the Eskimos have been encouraged to have the same beliefs about themselves. Social scientists have shown that, once such beliefs get established about an ethnic group and the people in that group get to accept those beliefs, a kind of self-validating process gets under way in which the people act in the ways expected of them, even though there is no biological basis for their presumed inherited behavior. It requires a massive educational campaign to break up this circular process of belief-begetting behavior reinforcing belief-begetting behavior and so on and on. What makes the task particularly onerous is that psychological "gains" in acting as though this belief were true give people a vested interest in retaining them and in retaining the behavior associated with these beliefs. The matters referred to here are the functions served by alcohol. Several investigators argue that many Indian and Eskimo people unconsciously use drinking as a release from an ugly world, as a means of making legitimate certain illegitimate things that they might want to do (e.g. assault, rob or insult police).

* * * * *

There is a related pattern of offences such as breaking and entering, theft and assaults, committed while intoxicated or in an attempt to obtain funds for liquor. In urban and semi-urban areas the problem is most noticeable and the incidence of this type of law breaking decreases in remoter northern areas. In fact, the rate of involvement in any type of crime is relatively low wherever access to liquor is either impossible or difficult.

There is evidence that crimes of violence are on the increase and that juvenile delinquency is also rising, with liquor playing a significant role.

There appears to be less social control to inhibit excessive drinking among Indians and Eskimo people with proportionately less social ostracism from the group as a result of arrest, conviction and detention for liquor infractions. While the use of alcohol serves, at least in part, to provide an escape mechanism from present circumstances and problems, there is also evidence that in terms of social acceptance it enhances the status of the offender in the eyes of his colleagues. Only fear of unpredictable and violent behavior seems to arouse expressions of condemnation from other Indians. Hence, the real limiting factor on the purchase and consumption of intoxicants appears to be availability of funds.

What do you think?

1. *What are the apparent reasons for Indian drinking? What do you think the real reasons are?*

2. *Why is Indian drinking often uncontrollable, resulting in delinquent behaviour?*
3. *How does the argument of this document bear out the UNESCO contention that "racism is cumulative"?*
4. *What recommendations would you make in an effort to correct this problem?*

5. INDIANS ON SKID ROW

Hugh Brody, in Indians on Skid Row *(Information Canada, 1971), explains why Indians do not quit drinking.*

The explanation of Indian skid row drinking . . . is begun with an answer to the question, Why not drink?

Not drinking for the skid row Indian involves the renunciation of pleasure. The justification which mainstream Canadian society would provide for such a renunciation is threefold. First, drinking consumes a great deal of money; that money could be used for self-advancement. Equally, drinking prevents the earning of money, and that also inhibits one's social possibilities. Second, large-scale consumption of alcohol is bad for the health. Third, drinking is morally bad: a good and decent person does not spend his time drinking. To the first of these we can reply: self-advancement is no part of the Indian's social consciousness or practice—at least as the mainstream Canadian understands it: it would be irrational to sacrifice a rewarding life-style for the remote chance of some social success. Indeed, the social success and advancement entails integration into non-Indian society. For many Indians that is neither a realistic hope nor a pleasing prospect. The second point is true, but it must be said that mainstream life is not noted for its healthiness: there is a strong likelihood that reference to physical sickness has a great deal to do with a sense of moral and social impropriety. . . . Third . . . the Indian is remote in his own most real terms, from the morality that sees drinking as sinful.

The truth is that skid row Indians have more to gain in social terms than they have to lose by drinking. . . The skid row Indian is unlikely to find in the standard . . . argument against drinking any real strength until his socio-economic position is radically altered. Until that time he will probably go on drinking, just because drinking is or seems to be more pleasant than not drinking.

What do you think?

1. *In your own words explain why Indians find no incentive to stop drinking. How does this explain why they drink?*

2. *What is a socio-economic position? Why does the author feel that only if the socio-economic position of a person is changed will he cease to drink? Does this mean that the Indian must assimilate into White society in order to stop drinking? Explain.*
3. *Is the problem solely one of economics? What other factors might there be? What solutions would you suggest for them?*
4. *Could the author of the Gleichen article (page 36) have used the material presented in the last two documents? How?*

As a Citizen

Has the traditional policy of dealing with Indians as a distinct group been wise? For example, should a separate government bureaucracy have been set up, or special legislation enacted? Should the treaties, which represent Indian distinctiveness, be preserved or terminated?

Opinion is varied on these questions. Some feel that these provisions are discriminatory and prejudicial to Indian welfare. Others regard them as essential for the protection of Indian rights and for the survival of Indian culture

This section deals with three areas that are at the center of this debate on the nature of Indian citizenship:

1. Treaties,
2. The Indian Affairs Branch,
3. The Indian Act

Where do you stand in the debate over "special" status?

Treaties

British colonial policy in the United States and later in Canada included the practice of making treaties with various Indian tribes. Indian leaders were forced by circumstance to see Indian land title extinguished in return for such benefits as educational and medical facilities, cash payments, and economic assistance. In addition certain rights and privileges were guaranteed by the Crown for "as long as the grass will grow."

For Indians today the treaties are no less crucial than they were for the chiefs who signed them. The settlement of treaty claims and grievances has become a focal point for many Indians, radicals and moderates alike.

1. TREATIES BEAR UPON ALL ISSUES

In the pamphlet Indians and the Law, *the crucial importance of the treaties is explained.*

Many of the people of Indian and Eskimo descent are alienated from the economic, social, and political structures [of mainstream Canadian society]. This alienation is bound to be reflected in their attitudes towards the law. In their Kamsack study, Shimpo and Williamson noted that the attitudes of Indians towards the law could not be understood without, at the same time, considering their attitudes towards the treaties and the Indian Act. As they say:

> Their (the Indians) observations of the local scene . . . where White men broke their own laws in dealing with the Indians and with each other, did not help to clarify for the band members their understanding of the law.

This study, and others, indicates that the abrogation of treaties and laws by the non-Indian majority encourages the questioning, in Indian eyes, of much of the White people in general.

It was the conclusion of the field workers that the question of treaty rights pervades the field of Indian/non-Indian relationships to such an extent that resolution of these differences is a pre-condition to acceptance by the Indian people of most programs for their benefit and advancement. In specific terms, what the Indian people regard as the failure of successive governments to live up to the terms and the spirit of the original treaties is, in the eyes of most Indian people interviewed, a stumbling block to their acceptance of the White man's law in its widest terms. Many of them do not know the exact terms of the treaties that were signed; others are not so much disturbed by the specific treaty commitments—in the legal sense—as they are by the failure of governments to meet their moral obligations to preserve Indian rights.

The evidence from this survey, from that of the Hawthorn group [a government-sponsored inquiry into Indian affairs, published in 1967], and others, suggests that treaty rights are increasing in importance as more Indian people become better organized and develop a more vocal approach to government.

What do you think?

1. *Why is the settling of the treaties so important for the future of Indian-White relations?*
2. *What might the government's "moral obligations" be?*

2. BROKEN TREATY PROMISES

This selection is from Native Rights in Canada. *(Indian-Eskimo Association of Canada, 1970.)*

A number of treaty promises have been matters of contention and deserve specific consideration.

1. HUNTING AND FISHING RIGHTS

The curtailing of treaty-protected hunting rights by the Migratory Birds Convention Act is an issue everywhere in the country. However vague other issues may be, this one is clear. The Supreme Court of Canada has stated that the government broke the treaties [as the Court agreed that the treaties did contain these rights]. The issue is both recent enough and clear enough that it has become symbolic–a focal point for dissatisfaction. In the same way treaty-protected fishing rights have been cut away by federal fishing legislation.

Treaty-guaranteed hunting rights are protected against provincial legislation. The federal government was so scrupulous about this early in our history that in 1890 it disallowed the Northwest Territories Game Ordinance because it violated Indian hunting rights guaranteed by treaty.

The protection of hunting and fishing rights was, without question, of paramount concern to the Indians called upon to enter treaty. The comment of the commissioners for Treaty Number Eight would be typical:

> Our chief difficulty was the apprehension that hunting and fishing privileges were to be curtailed.

2. OUTSTANDING RESERVE ALLOTMENTS WITHIN PROVINCES

When the treaties were made there were areas where extensive settlement could not be anticipated in the near future. Indians often expressed concern about being forced to live on reserves and were assured that they would not be pressed. To refer again to the report of the commissioners for Treaty Number Eight:

> As the extent of the country treated for made it impossible to define reserves or holdings, and as the Indians were not prepared to make selections we confined ourselves to an undertaking to have reserves and holdings set apart in the future, and the Indians were satisfied with the promise that this would be done when required. There is no immediate necessity for the general laying out of reserves or the allotting of land. It will be quite time enough to do this as advancing settlement makes necessary the surveying of land. Indeed the Indians were generally adversed to being placed on reserves. It would have been impossible to have made a treaty if we had not

> assured them that there was no intention of confining them to reserves. We had to very clearly explain to them that the provision for reserves and allotments of land made for their protection, and is secured to them in perpetuity a fair portion of the lands ceded in the event of settlement advancing.

The matter of settling the outstanding allotments has been overly slow. By the British North America Act of 1930, the Prairie provinces are to transfer to the Dominion out of ungranted Crown lands sufficient area to meet treaty obligations. The reluctance of at least one province is fairly well known. Apparently there have been disputes about what acreage is required. Since the allotments are tied to population, is the population figure at the date of the treaty or the present population figure to be used? Certain Indian bands have come to feel apprehensive. They have repeatedly asked for their allotment and do not understand why the delay is continuing. The slowness of the governments sustains the Indians' sense of grievance and the feeling that Indian Affairs is distant and unresponsive. Their isolation and what is for them the inscrutable character of Indian Affairs create a frustrating realization of powerlessness.

3. THE MEDICINE CHESTS

In 1935 the case of *Dreaver v. The King* [*sic*] was heard by the Exchequer Court. The Court interpreted the Medicine Chest promise in the following way:

> As I have previously pointed out, the treaty stipulates that a medicine chest shall be kept at the house of each Indian agent. This, in my opinion, means that the Indians were to be provided with all the medicine, drugs or medical supplies which they might need entirely free of charge. . . .

The judge admits that the above conclusion was based in large part upon the evidence of Chief Dreaver himself who was present when the treaty was signed in 1876 and was then approximately twenty years old. Dreaver testified that he remembered the conversation between the commissioners, the chiefs and headmen acting for the Indians about medicines, and said that it was understood that all medicines were to be supplied gratuitously to the Indians from that date until 1919. There was no mention of the case of any objection being raised using this oral evidence for the purposes of interpreting the terms of a written treaty. In 1966 there was a second case on the medicine chest provisions. An Indian had been charged with failure to pay hospital tax under the Saskatchewan Hospitalization Act. The magistrate at the trial level stated:

> Referring to the medicine chest clause of Treaty Number Six it is common knowledge that the provisions for caring for the sick

and injured in the areas inhabited by the Indians in 1876 were somewhat primitive compared to the present-day standards. It can be safely assumed that the Indians had limited knowledge of what provisions were available and it is obvious that they were concerned that their people be adequately cared for. . . . I can only conclude that the medicine chest clause and the pestilence clause in Treaty Number Six should properly be interpreted to mean that the Indians are entitled to receive all medical services, including medicines, drugs, medical supplies and hospital care free of charge. . . .

The Indian Association of Alberta in their paper *The Native People*, June 1969, urged treaty Indians in that province to boycott the Alberta medical plan until the question of premium payment is resolved. They claim that the policy of Indian Affairs to provide free medical services only to the indigent is a breach of treaty promises. Apparently the federal government has agreed to pay the premiums, at least for the first year.

Indian medical services were traditionally under the Department of Indian Affairs. By an Order-in-Council dated November 1, 1945, the service was transferred with the personnel to the Department of National Health and Welfare. After this transfer there was a cutback of services and free medical services became based solely on indigency.

What do you think?

1. *What effects could the abrogation of hunting and fishing rights have on the Indians of the Mackenzie River Basin (page 50)? Why?*
2. *Why would the delay in reserve allotment be a crucial issue in treaty discussions? In what areas of Canada would this question be particularly important?*
3. *What is your position on the medical insurance issue? Why?*

3. NATIVE RIGHTS IN THE NORTHWEST TERRITORIES

Datelined Inuvik, September 11, 1970, this article is taken from the Toronto Star.

The fireball behind the burgeoning Northwest Territories Native Rights Movement is a plump middle-aged Indian woman who plots assaults on federal policies from the incongruous confines of a government-operated handicrafts shop. . . . Mrs. Semmler is also president of the Committee of Original Peoples' Entitlement, a five hundred-member coalition of Eskimos, Indians and Métis formed this spring to force changes in Ottawa's northern development policies. . . .

About 22,000 of the 33,000 people living in the 1,300,000 square miles of the Northwest Territories are of pure native extraction or mixed blood, with the 11,000 Eskimos forming the largest single ethnic unit. . . .

Mrs. Semmler spelled out a few of the realities of being a Stone Age Eskimo in twentieth-century Canada. "The natives who have moved to Inuvik and the other towns have forgotten how to live off the land," she said. "Now they're all more or less on welfare; they've lost their boats, their hunting equipment and their traps."

The Eskimos have traded living off the land for welfare cheques, the freedom of roaming the tundra for better education and improved health standards. Unemployment is the rule rather than the exception. The problem is that the overwhelming majority of adults have little or no education at all and adult education efforts are at best sporadic. Mrs. Semmler says that because of the educational gap, the Eskimos by and large are getting little or nothing out of the current oil exploration boom in the Arctic. The companies, many of them operating out of Inuvik, are spending $50 million this year. She said she is deeply concerned that by the time educated Eskimo children come out of the schools, the oil boom will be over and there won't be anything to take its place.

The key to the problem, as Mrs. Semmler and the committee see it, is for the federal government to recognize aboriginal rights to the land and the resources it contains. The Eskimos, unlike the Indians to the south, signed no treaties with the Crown and never formally surrendered title to anything. Technically, they have no rights to anything under Ottawa's current definition. The seven thousand treaty Indians of the territories signed agreements with Ottawa in the 1920s, but do not live on reserves. Ottawa is technically holding lands in trust for them, but exactly what lands and where they are has yet to be spelled out. Both the committee and the Northwest Territories Indian Brotherhood cite the United States government's pending billion-dollar settlement with the fifty-five thousand natives of Alaska as a precedent for similar action by the Canadian government. Mrs. Semmler said such a settlement with northern natives would give them a cushion of land and cash to fall back on should the oil boom go bust. She wants a percentage of oil and mineral revenues allotted directly to the natives, under native control.

Ottawa has, so far, flatly refused to negotiate on aboriginal rights. Revenues accruing from mining and oil go directly to federal coffers in Ottawa.

What is meant by?

"aboriginal rights"

What do you think?

1. *Why is the recognition of aboriginal rights in the Northwest Territories so important to the native people who live there?*

2. *Why do you think the government is refusing to negotiate on aboriginal rights? Would you favor negotiations on aboriginal rights? Why or why not?*

4. NO RECOGNITION FOR ABORIGINAL TITLE

This is part of a speech given by Prime Minister Trudeau on August 8, 1968, in Vancouver.

I think Canadians are not too proud about the past way in which they treated the Indian population of Canada, and I don't think we have very great cause to be proud.

We have set the Indians apart as a race. We've set them apart in our laws. We've set them apart in the ways governments deal with them. They're not citizens of the province as the rest of us are. They are wards of the federal government. They get their services from the federal government rather than from the provincial or municipal governments. They have been set apart in law. They have been set apart in the relations with government and they've been set apart socially too.

So this year we came up with a proposal. It's a policy paper on the Indian problem. It proposes a set of solutions. It doesn't impose them on anybody. It proposes them—not only to the Indians but to all Canadians—not only to their federal representatives but to the provincial representatives too and it says we're at the crossroads. We can go on treating the Indians as having a special status. We can go adding bricks of discrimination around the ghetto in which they live and at the same time perhaps helping them preserve certain cultural traits and certain ancestral rights. Or we can say, "You're at a crossroads—the time is now to decide whether the Indians will be a race apart in Canada or whether they will be Canadians of full status." And this is a difficult choice. It must be a very agonizing choice to the Indian peoples themselves because, on the one hand, they realize that if they come into the society as total citizens they will be equal under the law but they risk losing certain of their traditions, certain aspects of a culture, and perhaps even certain of their basic rights. This is a very difficult choice for them to make, and I don't think we want to try and force the pace on them any more than we can force it on the rest of Canadians. But here again is a choice which is in our minds: whether Canadians as a whole want to continue treating the Indian populations as something outside, a group of Canadians with which we have treaties, a group of Canadians who have, as many Indians claim, aboriginal rights, or whether we will say forget the past and begin today. This is a tremendously difficult choice. For example, one of the things the Indian bands often refer to are their aboriginal rights; and in our policy, the way we propose it, we say we won't recognize aboriginal rights. We will recognize treaty rights. We will recognize forms of contract which have been made with the Indian people by the Crown and we will try to bring justice in that area and this will mean that perhaps the treaties shouldn't go on forever. It's inconceivable, I think, that in a given society one section of the society have a treaty with the other section of the society. We must be all equal under the laws, and we must not sign treaties amongst ourselves. Many of these treaties, indeed, will have less and less significance in the future anyhow. But things that in the past were covered by the treaties—things like so much twine or so much gun powder—and which haven't been paid, must be paid. But I don't think that we should encourage the Indians to feel that their treaties should last forever within Canada so that they be able to receive their twine or their gun powder. They should become Canadians and if they are prosperous and wealthy they will be treated like the prosperous and wealthy. They will pay taxes for the other Canadians who are not so prosperous and not so wealthy whether they be Indians or English Canadians or French or Maritimers. This is the only basis on which I see the people in our society developing as equals. But aboriginal rights? this really means saying, "We were here before you. You came and you took the land from us. Perhaps you cheated us by giving us some worthless things in return for vast expanses of land. We want to re-open this question. We want you to preserve our aboriginal rights and to restore them to us." And our answer—it may not be the right one and may not be one which is accepted; but it will be up to all of you people to make your minds up, and to choose for or against it, and to discuss it with the Indians—our answer is "no."

If we think of restoring aboriginal rights to the Indians, what about the French who were defeated at the Plains of Abraham? Shouldn't we restore rights to them? And what about the Acadians who were deported—shouldn't we compensate for this? And what about the other Canadians, the immigrants? What about the Japanese Canadians who were so badly treated at the end or during the last war? What can we do to redeem the past? I can only say as President Kennedy said when he was asked about what he would do to compensate for the injustices that the Negroes had received in American society. We will be just in our time. This is all we can do. We must be just today.

What do you think?

1. *Describe the Prime Minister's position on aboriginal rights. Do you agree with him? Why or why not?*
2. *"We will be just in our time. This is all we can do. We must be just today."*
   (a) How do you feel about this statement? Why?
   (b) Is the analogy to the American Negro a fair one? Explain your answer.

5. THE TREATY MENTALITY OF DEPENDENCE

William I. C. Wuttunee, a Calgary lawyer, is a well-known Indian spokesman. Wuttunee was born on the Red Pheasant Reserve near Battleford, Saskatchewan, and has been a prominent member of numerous Indian organizations. His views on the treaties appeared in his book, Ruffled Feathers *(Calgary: Bell Books, 1971).*

A great injustice to Indian people is being done if we tell them that the White man did not keep his promises under the treaties. . . .

We must therefore make every effort to re-educate all Canadians to the facts of history. The federal government has kept its promises under the treaties. Since the turn of the century the government has paid out on behalf of the Indians the sum of two billion dollars. This does not take into account the amounts which may have been spent on programs for Indians by other federal agencies such as the Secretary of State, Regional Economic Expansion, or Manpower. Concerning the medicine chest which the Queen's commissioners may have promised to be maintained on behalf of the Indians, the federal government, under its Indian Health Services budget, spent the sum of $35,978,000 for the 1970–71 period. In the same period the federal government will be spending a total of $100,000,000 for the education of Indian people. The amount to be spent on housing alone for the Indian people in 1970–71 is in the sum of $17 million. This is no mean cash settlement for the purchase of any possessory rights which the aboriginals may have had in this country.

One would have to spend $2.00 every minute since the birth of Christ in order to spend $2 billion, and even at that rate there would still be some money left over. The enormity of such a purchase price would blow the mind of even the greatest capitalist. Considering the minimal holdings of the Indian people at the time of the initial occupation of Canada and with their low population figures, they have been well paid for their undeveloped lands.

The treaty mentality of dependence is being prolonged by some Indian leaders today who are encouraging it among their people. It is unlikely that the government is going to renegotiate these treaties or to read more into them than was actually provided for. It is time that the Indian leaders recognized this principle. Nothing has been taken away from the Indian that was rightfully his. . . .

The Indians have built up the treaties to such an extent that nearly everything in their lives hinges upon them. They have developed a mentality which, like the treaties, is dependent. The treaties were negotiated at a time when the Indians were no longer strong and powerful; they were peaceful and wanted good relations with the White man. They wanted the assistance which the White man was prepared to give to them and which they eventually received. It is this continuing form of dependence which the Indians cannot overcome. The Queen Victoria Treaty Protective Association was formed to put emphasis on the treaties. This organization eventually lost most of its adherents and there was some indication that this form of mentality was dying out. However, it has been regenerated with the new thrust that Harold Cardinal has put into the Indian Association of Alberta, and its emphasis on the treaties.

Those people who have a treaty mentality, who want to be fed, clothed, cared for, spoon-fed from the cradle to the grave, are out of date. They cannot now look for assistance in the form which was provided to their ancestors.

If the old ways have died, then new ways have been opened up to the Indian people with new challenges. If the treaties can be buried once and for all and if they can be relegated as tombstones to an ancient culture, Indians can build a new future. . . .

If Canada can remove the bitterness from the Indian, this change will remove a great deal of his cause of pain and suffering which he has brought about on himself. The cause of the problem is not so much what the White man has done to him, but what the Indian does to himself through his interpretation of what transpired in the past.

One cannot overstress the significance of ending these treaties and of ending the treaty mentality which has spread throughout the country. It has embedded itself so firmly in the Indian mind that it clouds all his thinking and he cannot seem to see his way clearly, for his feelings work more strongly than his mind on this subject. The Indian people cannot keep living in the past. They can never rewrite what actually transpired at the signing of the treaties because the cold facts of history have indelibly written themselves in the hearts and minds of the people. We cannot re-interpret them; we cannot give more significance to either the one side or the other, we cannot improve the bargaining position of either side, and neither can we take away. We can realistically look at the past, the present and the future, and learn from the hard lessons of history those truths which will assist us in facing the problems of the day.

The people who negotiated the treaties have died and we should leave them in peace. They did the very best they could in the circumstances and they left to us a commission to fight new battles for a new era. It is our responsibility to settle this land peacefully and to look to the new boundaries. Let us then gather the old treaties, the Queen Victoria medals, the flags and the chiefs' uniforms and put them in the museums of our land, so that they can forever remind our children that this land was built and created out of the hopes and frustrations of ancestors who earnestly desired the peaceful development of Canada. Let us consider them hereafter without frustration, and regard the treaty period as a necessary development in the process of fusing together the Red and the White.

What do you think?

1. *Debate the following assertions of Wuttunee's:*
   (a) *"Considering the minimal holdings of the Indian people . . and . . . their low population figures, they have been well paid for their undeveloped lands."*
   (b) *"If the treaties can be buried once and for all, and if they can be relegated as tombstones to an ancient culture, Indians can build a new future."*
   (c) *"The cause of the problem is not so much what the White man has done to him, but what the Indian does to himself through his interpretation of what has transpired in the past."*

Why do you feel Wuttunee feels the way he does? What is your reaction to Wuttunee's views and why? How would other Indian leaders you have encountered react? Why? How do you think they might rebut him, if they wished to do so?

The Indian Affairs Branch

Another facet of the Indian's role as a citizen is his relationship with the Indian Affairs Branch, the federal bureaucracy evolved over the last century which deals with Indian matters.

You have already seen how the deputy minister of Indian Affairs was heckled by Indians and students at the 1968 Glendon conference. Why do many Indians resent Indian Affairs?

1. NOTES FROM CARRY-THE-KETTLE

John Conway, in the Canadian Dimension *of January 1968, described his experiences as an Indian Affairs employee on a Saskatchewan reserve.*

According to the local people, the agent for this reserve is one of the most corrupt, clever and dangerous men around here. He lets it be known ever so subtly that the road to regular relief depends on the women being "nice" to him. He has a $20,000 house, a brand-new car, paid for, sends one kid to university, is sending his family on a trip to Expo with new matching sets of luggage and is considering buying a motel—all on less than $6,000 a year! It is rumored that for the last couple of years he has had on the payroll of one of his reserves a carpenter who does not exist.

*　*　*　*　*

Today in the agent's office (where I bed down, and to which the agent has not come since he was appointed a number of weeks ago) I found scotch-taped to the wall a sick racist joke dealing with Indians. There was an Indian "squaw" sitting in front of a teepee surrounded by children; talking to her was a White insurance agent who was saying "And when you retire you get fifty bucks a month." She replies to this, in the miserable mind of the cartoonist, "I get plenty bucks now." Sexuality asserts itself again and again as being central to the White man's racism. The man who taped this to his office wall is responsible, under the Indian Act, for the health and welfare of around two hundred families, if you count all the reserves for which he is responsible.

*　*　*　*　*

I get paid as much a day as a single adult Indian gets to live on in one month. What a situation! A perfect colonial administrative situation—millions are spent to maintain a huge and complex bureaucracy ostensibly established to "look after" a small, impoverished group, and so pathetically little is allowed to filter down to them. This year Indian Affairs Branch will get $180 million of Canada's tax dollars to look after 225,000 (about) Indians. That's $800 a year for each man, woman and child. Where does it go? It certainly doesn't get to the people. I feel like a blood-sucker.

*　*　*　*　*

Only one person showed up for school today. I was disappointed. So far I have seven registered for evening classes and five for day classes.

Today I got hold of something that I wasn't supposed to. A copy of the Saskatchewan Assistance regulations which the Indian Affairs people use to base their welfare cheques on. Following is an accurate facsimile:

Amendments to Saskatchewan Assistance Regulations
Ordinary Food Allowance

		Week	Month
Adults		$6.05	$26.50
Children	0-4 years	3.60	14.50
	5-9	4.05	21.00
	10-14	6.05	26.00
	15-19	6.60	28.00
Necessities for personal care (per month)			
Adults		$3.25	
	0-4	.45	
	5-9	.60	
	10-14	.85	
	15-19	1.75	

$4.00 more per month for old age (over 65 years)

I couldn't believe my eyes! For a family of man and wife and three children (one five, one ten, and one fifteen) this would give $122.90 per month to live on—that is for everything! And, in application, if you have more than three children you do not get any more welfare, even if you have fifteen children. Apparently Indian Affairs differs from the Saskatchewan welfare only in that three-child limit on their handouts. This may not be quite genocide, but it is barely enough to keep the physical hunger pangs to a minimum. It cannot provide even reasonable sustenance.

* * * * *

I visited another reserve today. It is unbelievable, but on the road I met two men within half an hour of each other who were badly in need of medical attention. But the Indian Affairs doctor didn't think so, since he had discharged them. One man had had hot doughnut grease thrown into his face and then a broken water glass shoved into his face by his wife during a quarrel. His face was a mess and needed, in my lay opinion, more than a superficial dressing; it needed surgery. The second man had just come from having his jaw lanced; the dressing was just casually put on, and the wound was still bleeding. Both had seen doctors, Indian Affairs doctors, that day. I was appalled.

* * * * *

Today is Treaty Day. Two Indian Agents came out with a clerk and a secretary. They set up shop in the school-room. There is much ritual and formality surrounding this day. There is an R.C.M.P. constable in full dress who hands out the cheques as the queen's representative. "The group" (representing White society, the queen, and our institutions) sat at a table. They were insufferable and arrogant; they exchanged smart remarks and racist jokes and humiliated most of the Indians. I took pictures as unobtrusively as possible.

* * * * *

This is also T.B. X-ray day. In fact, no one gets paid until they are X-rayed; as they are X-rayed they are handed orange slips of paper which allow them to receive their treaty money. I never realized until now that this "treaty money" about which we hear so much amounts to five dollars per person per year. The chief and councillors receive fifteen or twenty dollars and a new suit of clothes every two years.

There was a carnival atmosphere among the people away from the agents and the constable. Downstairs the cooking class sold food and such so that they could bring films to the recreation hall. I felt very relaxed with the people for the first time. But you always feel the immense guilt of all the White man's crimes about which you can do nothing, and anything you say sounds foolish. You feel, deep down, that they either hate you, feel contempt for you, are absolutely indifferent to you, or want something from you since you work for Indian Affairs.

I saw the agent approached by three Indians with pressing problems (seed and housing). He hasn't been out here since he was appointed. He put them all off with miserable lies which amounted to "write me a letter."

What do you think?

1. *To what extent does Mr. Conway's article explain the relationship between the Indian and the Indian agent in George Ryga's play?*
2. *How believable did you find George Ryga's play when you read it? Does this article change your opinion? Why?*

2. DICTATORS AND TYRANTS

Harold Cardinal, author of The Unjust Society, *a highly critical account of the White man's dealings with Indians, is one of the major spokesmen for the native movement. At the Glendon conference in 1968, Cardinal attacked the Indian Affairs Branch.*

The Indian Affairs Branch was originally created to administer the annuities and to implement promises contained in treaties negotiated on behalf of Her Majesty the Queen and the Indian peoples of this country. They were to further protect our rights given to us as payment when our forefathers surrendered title to this land. Over the years, this role has been redefined–naturally without consultation with our people–to the extent whereby those who were hired by the government to protect our rights became *oppressors* instead of protectors. Instead of honoring our rights, these civil servants developed many schools of thought. Some thought that our treaties were to be honored; others thought that they should be interpreted out of existence, etc. In this changing world of the bureaucrats hired to serve our people, they gradually brainwashed themselves into believing that they were sacrificing their lives to the cause of Indian peoples. In the process, the servants became the dictators, the tyrants, the empire builders; the people to be served became the oppressed, the victims of colonial White supremacist mentality. The situation to date has changed little. The same structure that has bred this colonial mentality remains. The bureaucrats that make decisions for us still continue to do so.

However, in view of the developing, articulate leadership arising in every province of this country, and the cry for participation by these leaders in the decision-making process affecting their lives and the lives of the people they represent, the Department of Indian Affairs has developed a new rhetoric proclaiming its commitment to helping Indians help themselves, and the need to work themselves out of a job; but strangely enough, their staff is increasing rather than decreasing. In fact . . . they proudly point to the increasing millions the federal government allots for Indians Affairs. However, they always neglect to point out to the public how this money is spent, and who really benefits from it. In fact, intentionally or otherwise, the bureaucrats, and some politicians, leave the false impression that the major portion of these millions reach the Indian peoples of this country.

No honest man can suggest that the accomplishments have been remotely commensurate with the effort. In this situation the late Sir Winston Churchill would have said, "Never have so many done so little for so few." With this in mind, one sometimes has the feeling that the Department of Indian Affairs and Northern Development almost welcomes failure, for failure, if repeated frequently enough, only demonstrates the need to expand their services still more. They have concentrated far too much on symptoms, and not enough on causes. Their goal has been to force Indians to assimilate, to teach them how to adapt themselves to society as it is, rather than to change those aspects of society that make the individuals what they are. It is our contention that the problems stem far less from individual maladjustment than from an objective lack of opportunity, from a social system that denies the individual dignity and equality. Hence the present policy of Indian Affairs toward assimilating Indians or making them nice "little brown White men" is doomed to failure. Unless they are willing to accept our culture and our identity, they, the bureaucrats, the faceless, anonymous decision-makers for the federal government, will continue to multiply the social problems they have created, instead of solving them. Unfortunately, we are the ones left holding the bag, the negative image and the taunts of our fellow citizens.

The Department of Indian Affairs and Northern Development has used welfare programs, etc., the way the Romans used bread and circuses–to keep the poor happy and unthreatening.

In the final analysis, however, the failure of the Indian Affairs Branch effort stems from the same factor that has produced the political strain between Negroes and Whites in the U.S.A.–their preoccupation with doing for people instead of doing *with* them–a preoccupation that destroys the dignity and arouses the hostility of the people who are supposed to be helped. The bureaucrats have proved beyond a shadow of doubt that they are completely incapable of changing. They have over and over proved that their progressive sounding clichés mean little more than an attempt to further solidify their acquired positions of power.

What do you think?

1. *What is Cardinal's chief objection to the Indian Affairs Branch?*
2. *Why does he say that the policy of the branch is doomed to failure? What does this tell us about the Indian culture?*

3. *Compare Cardinal's views to those of:*
   (a) Prime Minister Trudeau (page 71),
   (b) George Ryga (page 7),
   (c) John Conway (page 75).

3. INDIAN AFFAIRS: A COMMENT

Burton Kewayosh, an Indian, describes his feelings about the Indian Affairs Branch in The Way of the Indian, *a CBC-produced radio program broadcast in 1963.*

The Indian Affairs Branch have too many people sitting around on their fannies up in the office doing nothing. They're do-gooders, sitting there in a nice warm office, but a lot of them know nothing of the conditions on these reserves. And they have too much to say about what goes on in a reserve. We had a few resolutions passed through our council when I was just a young councillor. Well, they came back again. The government said, "Nothing doing," you know. We think they're all right here but they go to "head office" and come back "No." And its our own affairs we want to run. I think this affects a lot of Indian reserves. What I would like to see, if there were to be a "head office," is an organization of Indians right across Canada sitting there, who know the conditions on the reserves.

What do you think?

1. *What is the issue here? How peculiar is it to the Indian?*
2. *How does Mr. Kewayosh propose to resolve it?*

4. INDIAN AFFAIRS BRANCH BUDGET

Taken from figures in the Canada Yearbook of 1969, this graph charts the increase in government spending on Indians and shows where some of that money is spent.

What do you think?

1. *What was the Indian Affairs Branch budget in 1961–62? What was it in 1969–70? What is the percentage increase? Can you account for this?*
2. *What percentage of the budget was spent on education? On the development and maintenance of Indian communities? How effective do you think this spending has been? Give reasons.*

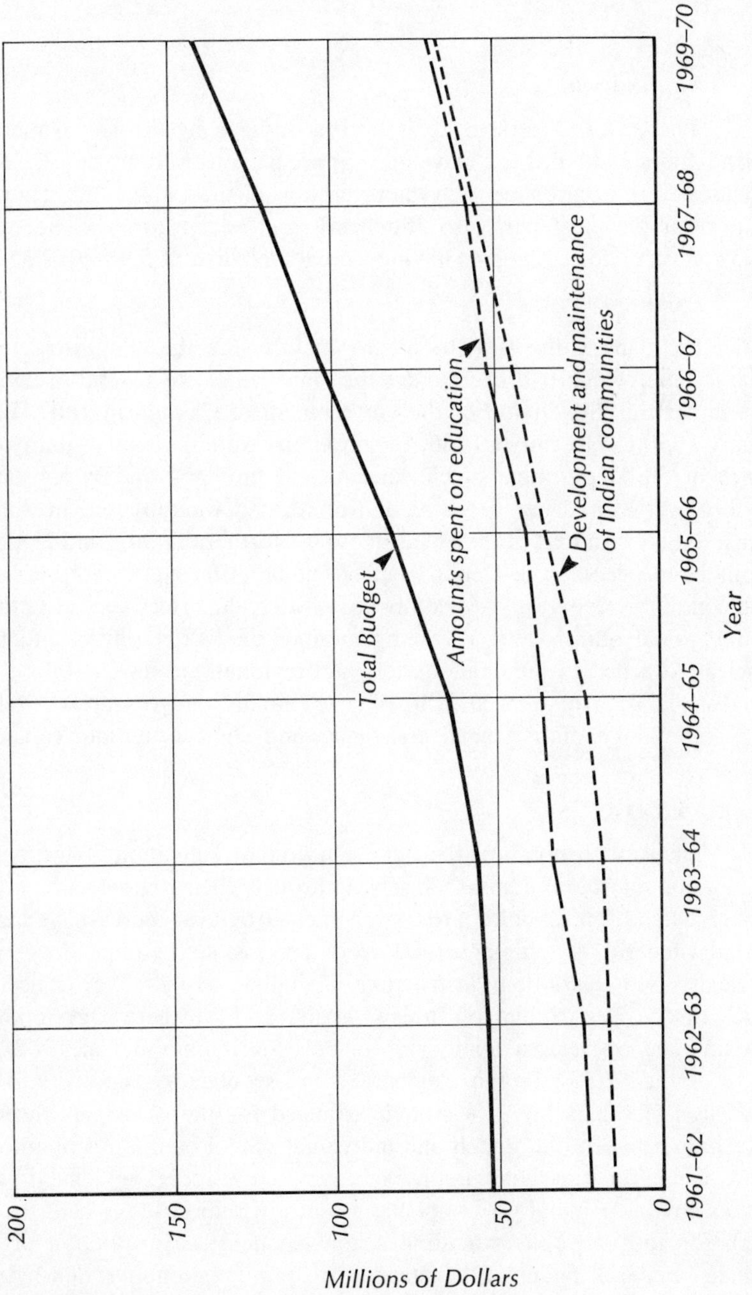
Total Budget
Amounts spent on education
Development and maintenance
of Indian communities
0
50
100
150
200
Millions of Dollars
1961–62
1962–63
1963–64
1964–65
1965–66
1966–67
1967–68
1969–70
Year

5. ACTIVITIES OF THE INDIAN AFFAIRS BRANCH

This summary of the Indian Affairs program appeared in the 1970–71 Canada Yearbook.

THE INDIANS

The 237,490 persons registered as Indians by the Department of Indian Affairs and Northern Development are persons who are entitled to be so registered in accordance with the provisions of the Indian Act. They are grouped for the most part into 556 bands and occupy or have access to 2,263 reserves and settlements having a combined area of 5,983,072 acres.

ADMINISTRATION

Pursuant to the British North America Act, the administration of Indian affairs, which had been under the management of several provinces, came under the jurisdiction of the Government of Canada in 1867. From January 1950 to December 1965, Indian affairs were the responsibility of a Branch of the Department of Citizenship and Immigration. By legislation (SC 1966, c. 25) a new department was formed whereby Indian Affairs Branch joined with part of the Department of Northern Affairs and National Resources to become the Department of Indian Affairs and Northern Development. This department is composed of a headquarters staff at Ottawa, seven regional offices, and a varying number of district offices and field agencies. Attached to the headquarters and regional and district offices are specialists in such matters as education, economic and resource development, community affairs, social assistance, and engineering and construction.

EDUCATION

The key to continued progress in Indian education is the active participation of the Indians themselves through their school committees and membership on school boards, strengthened by ever-increasing support from non-federal governments and from professional groups concerned specifically with classroom instruction of Indian pupils. The Education Branch of the Department of Indian Affairs and Northern Development maintains and operates a number of schools for Indians but in 1968–69, 33,351 of the 62,834 Indian elementary and secondary school pupils attended non-federal schools, a system arranged for the most part through agreements between the branch and individual school boards. In Manitoba, British Coumbia and New Brunswick, however, under agreement with the respective provincial governments, a uniform tuition fee is paid by the branch for Indian pupils attending schools under the jurisdiction of the province. Federal financial assistance for pupils attending non-federal schools varies from payment of tuition fees to full maintenance. Promising senior students are awarded scholarships to attend university or vocational school and scholarships are given to those who show promise in the arts.

Federal schools for Indian children are in operation in all provinces except Newfoundland and school residences care for children who, because of isolation or for other reasons, are unable to attend local schools. Standard classroom supplies and authorized textbooks are used in federal schools, which follow generally the curriculum of the province in which they are located.

A two-year kindergarten program has been instituted to give a head start to children who will receive their classroom instruction in a language other than their mother tongue. It has developed very rapidly and it is anticipated that all five-year-olds will be enrolled in school by 1971 and all four-year-olds by 1973. The 1968-69 kindergarten enrolment was about 6,000.

COMMUNITY DEVELOPMENT AND IMPROVEMENT

The community development program, in operation since 1965, has led to much closer involvement of the Indian people in the management of their own affairs. In their efforts to accept such responsibility, many Indian bands across the country are developing their own municipal-type administration. In 1969–70, this program was assisted by six regional superintendents of community affairs and 46 community development workers (18 of Indian status), together with four workers on contract with the department and 36 hired by provincial governments. A grants-to-bands program makes it possible for participating bands to operate and administer their own programs through financial and advisory assistance. Expenditure under this program increased from $71,065 in 1965 to $2,023,059 in 1969–70, and in the latter year community affairs turned over a sum of $9,966,808 in program funds to Indian bands for administration.

Federal-provincial community development agreements extending provincial services to the Indian people exist with Ontario, Alberta, Manitoba and Saskatchewan. Costs are shared on a population basis where both Indians and non-Indians are involved. An additional step forward was taken on October 1, 1969, when the federal government, the Manitoba government and the Manitoba Indian Brotherhood agreed that the Brotherhood should take over the responsibility for community development in that province. Community development services for seven reserves in the Cape Breton area of Nova Scotia are provided under an agreement with the extension department of St. Francis Xavier University at Antigonish.

Over the past few years, encouragement has been given to the Indian people in the development and perpetuation of their own culture. Grants, subsidies and scholarships have been given to individuals, groups and organizations for the development of their creative and performing talents—Indian fine arts and crafts, literature, dancing, folk songs and related activities. Such grants amounted to over $300,000 since the inception of the program in 1965.

In 1969–70, training courses were carried on continually in all seven regions across the country in such fields as leadership, human resource development, band government, homemaking and folk activities and in many related areas. These courses involved 2,000 Indian people and 500 departmental staff, for an estimated 13,000 man-days. The human resources development program alone had an attendance of 43 Indians and non-departmental staff and 27 departmental staff, for a total of 1,091 man-days.

The Technical Services Branch of the Department assists with the physical development of Indian communities—community planning on reserves, housing accommodation, water and sanitation, electrification, construction and maintenance of roads and bridges, etc. Such service is given either directly through the efforts of the community concerned, indirectly through consultant planners, or through provincial or regional planning offices.

There were 1,794 houses constructed on Indian reserves in the year ended March 31, 1969. Financing and operation of three housing programs on reserves and one off-reserve program, under way in 1970, may be described as follows:

1. Subsidy housing program	Direct subsidy by the federal government.
2. Band-administered housing program	Band councils may, by resolution, request authority to administer federal appropriation, either as the sole source of financing or in conjunction with band funds and housing loans from the Central Mortgage and Housing Corporation.
3. Indian on-reserve housing program	Individual housing loans from the Central Mortgage and Housing Corporation as a sole source of financing or in conjunction with federal subsidy.
4. Off-reserve housing program	Indians living away from reserves may secure mortgage funds from the Central Mortgage and Housing Corporation or approved lenders in conjunction with forgivable ten-year second mortgage funds from the federal government.

In recent years, emphasis has been placed on overcoming the isolation of many reserves by the building of roads to facilitate movement between Indian and non-Indian communities, the upgrading of roads on reserves adjacent to urban communities, the participation of Indian children in off-reserve school programs, the commuting of Indian people to and from centres of employment, and the development of marketing of reserve resources. Where economically feasible, electric power is being installed at Indian reserves, and a potable water supply and adequate sanitation facilities are requirements at all reserves.

In the 1968 tourist season, 114 Indians owned and operated tourist-outfitting establishments, providing employment on a seasonal basis for 520 people. In addition, in the field of tourism and recreation, Indians owned and operated 31 tent and trailer parks, 36 picnic grounds, 36 businesses providing overnight accommodation, eight marinas, six museums and villages, two sightseeing tour businesses and six other operations that combined such facilities. There are approximately 6,700 Indians engaged in producing Indian arts and crafts, 70 of whom operate their own retail outlets. Gross sales for 1968–69 were estimated at $1,500,000. Participation is encouraged by the department through the provision of raw materials and the operation of a central marketing service and, recently, Indian business leaders in the arts and crafts industry formed an advisory group to work with the department in devising improved production and marketing facilities. Indian people are actively involved in 123 co-operatives, which had a total membership in 1968–69 of 7,800, fixed and current assets of $3,300,000 members' equity of about $1,200,000 and revenue from business conducted of over $5,000,000.

The Indian Loan Fund continues to provide financing for Indian enterprises. In 1968–69, 139 loans totalling over $1,000,000 were made to farmers, fishermen, lumbermen, craftsmen, bus operators, merchants, tourist-facility operators and others. Advisory services in business planning and operation are available to prospective Indian businessmen in conjunction with the operations of the Fund.

An industrial, commercial, and real estate development program was started in January 1969 to encourage the development of secondary industry on or in proximity to Indian reserves. During the year two textile plants were established on reserves and negotiations were under way with a number of manufacturers for the establishment of branch plants on reserves.

RESOURCE AND INDUSTRIAL DEVELOPMENT

The department, through its Indian-Eskimo Economic Development Branch, assists individuals and bands in their efforts to create business and employment opportunities in service and secondary industries and in the areas of resource utilization and land development, including mineral resources on Indian reserves. Assistance is in the form of loans, grants, technical and management advice and specialized training. Many programs are conducted in co-operation with other federal departments, provincial governments and private organizations.

Statutory responsibilities covering reserve and surrendered lands and the administration of Indian estates are administered by the branch. At the end of March 1969, some 11,097 leases of or permits to use Indian reserve lands by non-Indians, excluding oil and gas resource leases, were in effect, providing over $5,000,000 annually in income to individuals and bands. Oil and gas resources, which are developed through leasing to non-Indians, continue to provide major revenues for Indian bands in Alberta, and bands in other western provinces and in Ontario also receive revenues from these resources. In 1968–69, revenues from royalties, bonuses and rentals totalled $4,278,795; 2,000,000 acres of Indian oil and gas rights were under contract, 598 under lease and 65 under permit.

The mining resources of the Indian reserves, for many years left under developed, are receiving increased attention, largely because of a change in policy for disposing of mineral rights and of an increasing interest of band councils in the development of minerals. Since late 1968, Indian band councils may negotiate mining leases and permits direct with the mining companies as an alternative to disposal by public tender.

During 1968–69, some 1,300 Indians were engaged in farming, either full-time or part-time, on 200,000 acres of reserve lands, and another 1,012 operated ranches extending over 530,000 acres. Under the Rotating Herd Program, 9,346 head of cattle in 335 herds were out on loan. The total value of agricultural production on reserve lands exceeded $4,800,000.

Many Indians still depend on fishing and trapping for all or part of their earned income. In 1968–69, 2,300 fishermen produced about 20,000,000 lb. of fish having a gross value of $8,400,000, and over 11,000 trappers brought in furs with an approximate value of $4,000,000 accounting for 30 per cent of the total wild fur production in Canada. Timber produced from reserve lands amounted to 323,862 cunits (a unit of stacked wood containing 100 cubic feet of solid volume within its outside dimensions) with a value of over $6,000,000, which represented 69 per cent of the volume of timber cut from all federal lands.

WELFARE

Indians, like other Canadians, are eligible for benefits from a number of welfare programs which are administered by different levels of government, Indian bands, and private agencies. Like other Canadians, not all Indians have the same programs available to them, for some programs vary between and within provinces and on and off reserves.

Some Indian bands administer social assistance and child care for persons living on the reserve of the band. The criteria of eligibility and rates of payment for social assistance are generally based on those of the province in which the band is located. Family allowances, youth allowances, old age security and the guaranteed income supplement are paid to Indians by the Department of National Health and Welfare on the same basis as they are paid to other Canadians.

Indians are eligible for benefits from some, but not all, provincial welfare programs except in the Northwest Territories. Generally speaking, the provincial programs from which Indians are eligible for benefits are programs for specific categories of persons, such as the blind. Benefits from less specific programs, such as social assistance, are not generally available to Indians living on reserves, although they are in some parts of some provinces.

The federal Department of Indian Affairs and Northern Development provides social assistance, care for children and care for physically handicapped adults for Indians where these are not available from other sources. The criteria of eligibility and the rates used in calculating the amount to which an application for social assistance is entitled are based on those of the provinces in which the person applies for assistance.

[*Another federal agency involved in Indian affairs is the Department of National Health and Welfare.*]

Medical and public health services are made available to registered Indians and Eskimos who are not included under provincial arrangements and who are unable to provide for themselves. Much of the service in treatment and health education is rendered to the patients through 46 departmental out-patient clinics and 91 health centers staffed by medical and other public health personnel. In remote areas, the key facility is frequently the departmental nursing station, a combined emergency treatment and public health unit usually having two to four beds under the direction of one or two nurses; 57 of these are operated throughout Canada.

Where practicable, there has been considerable integration of Indians in provincial and municipal health agencies, so that the number of hospitals and other facilities provided specifically for them have been reduced accordingly. In 1970, the department maintained 13 hospitals at strategic points and co-operated elsewhere with community, mission or company hospitals. Indians are included under all provincial prepaid insurance plans for hospital care and other forms of medical care. Indian and Eskimo health workers are trained to give instruction in health care and sanitation.

What do you think?

1. *How much is being done by the Indian Affairs Branch for the Canadian Indian? Too much? Too little? Explain.*
2. *(a) Describe the extent and type of participation in Indian affairs of the provincial governments.*
   (b) Explain why the federal government encourages provincial involvement in Indian affairs.

3. (a) *From your reading of this report judge to what extent the Indian people are involved in the management of their own affairs.*
   (b) *What seems to be the branch's position on this question? Justify your answer.*
   (c) *What are your feelings on this issue?*

6. AN INDIAN DEFENDS INDIAN AFFAIRS

Mrs. Sheila McGrath, an Indian from the Golden Lake Band in Ontario, tells of her experience with the Indian Affairs Branch.

Indian Affairs Branch. This was just a name holding no meaning until one day I realized that I faced a grim future without the aid of this organization. My education began in an Indian day school on the Golden Lake Reservation, Ontario. As a critic I cast judgment on teaching methods then. The one major point is that everything was provided for the pupil free of charge. This tended occasionally to lead to carelessness for teachers as well as pupils. However, this was very rare and I am happy to recall my school days on the reservation as being happy and unforgettable.

The Convent of Mary Immaculate in Pembroke, Ontario, prepared me for my grade twelve diploma. The years spent in boarding school were difficult, happy, but most of all, satisfying. It was extremely difficult to become accustomed to routine. Home-sickness was a constant companion until graduation day arrived and banished all feelings but pride and happiness. Between school years, I held summer employment which I obtained through the Indian Affairs Branch. This began my acquaintance with this organization.

My major disappointment and decision came when I realized that the nursing profession was not for me. After four months of training, I approached the Indian Affairs Branch for assistance to attend business college for the remainder of the school year, and when June arrived, I had completed a stenographic course. That summer my services were used by the Indian Affairs Branch. They weren't much to offer but becoming acquainted with the work and staff was a bigger lesson to me than all else.

My experience in the Indian Affairs office revealed my potential to be a teacher, so, come September, I commenced training in Teachers' College. This lasted two years. This course, too, had its trials and happinesses. I seemed to turn to the Indian Affairs Branch each time I was confronted with any problem I thought was major. I experienced disappointment and unhappiness, but co-operation and perseverance brought joy and, most of all, satisfaction in achievement. On completion of my course, I was accepted on the staff of the Toronto Separate School Board.

Now, as a happy housewife and mother, my summation is that Indian Affairs personnel are understanding, helpful and review each problem presented to them with wholeheartedness. They work for the benefit of those with whom they are concerned—the Indian people. My sincere gratitude goes to the Indian Affairs Branch and all concerned in making my life a successful and happy one.

What do you think?

1. *Why do Mrs. McGrath's views differ from the others you have read?*
2. *What criticism of Mrs. McGrath's point of view might Harold Cardinal make? What might Mrs. McGrath say to him?*

7. WHOSE RESPONSIBILITY IS IT?

The following article from the Toronto Star *of June 2, 1967, underlines Indian impatience with jurisdictional problems.*

Ontario Indians are a little tired of hearing about which government has constitutional responsibility for their well-being. It is true there is no iron-clad rule outlining responsibilities. In fact either the federal or provincial governments can do almost anything they want for Indians depending on their generosity. Under Section 91 of the British North America Act, exclusive legislative authority is given to the Parliament of Canada over "Indians and lands reserved for Indians." This does not mean that the federal government has any real legal obligation to provide services to them, although as a matter of policy it has provided a broad range of services to Indians living on reserve lands.

But the province has legislative authority to include all residents of the province within the ambit of its social programs and that includes Indians. It has in practice served Indians who do not have treaty and reserve status and Indians who have such status but who have left the reserve. Provincial services are in some cases provided only to people living on "organized territories," that is, in municipalities or townships, and, for purposes of provincial welfare and one or two other services, Indian reserves. But in a pinch, the province has given services to unorganized territories such as Armstrong, (near Lake Nipigon), where there are urgent problems to solve.

There are about 52,000 treaty Indians in the province and an estimated 50,000 non-treaty Indians. A treaty Indian is one who lives under the terms of the Indian Act, has the right to live on a reserve where he is on a band list and gets certain benefits, such as subsidized housing from the federal Indian Affairs Branch. He or his forebears have in most cases signed a treaty with the federal government and he gets "treaty money" of about four dollars a year (it varies per tribe). A non-treaty Indian is one who by reason of his parentage or a curious practice called enfranchisement (by which the government bought out his treaty rights for his share of the band funds) has lost his reserve and treaty status. He is then solely in the care of the province, which despite his generally lamentable conditions of life, is painfully slowly lumbering to his rescue.

What do you think?

1. *What issues are identified here?*
2. *What would you do to resolve them?*

The Indian Act

In the controversy surrounding the separate treatment of Indians by government the Indian Act has provoked perhaps the clearest statements of opinion in the debate. Passed in 1951 the revised Indian Act has never been very popular with Indians or with many Whites for a variety of reasons. What are some of these reasons? Why do those who oppose the Act disagree among themselves?

1. LEGISLATED DISCRIMINATION

Walter Currie, an Ojibway Indian, is director of the Indian studies program at Trent University in Peterborough, Ontario. Mr. Currie's remarks on the Indian Act are taken from an article which appeared in Human Relations, *May 1968.*

. . . The picture I have painted shows reservation communities at the bottom of the economic totem pole, lowest on the scale of social and economic progress. The people on these reservations have a culture, but these people live under a culture of poverty. Join this poverty to isolation, add a substandard quality of education, substract economic growth, bracket with one hundred years of paternalism, and you have a modern math problem too tough for the Indian alone to answer. The people of Canada, through their governments, must find a solution.

I could speak with you of many factors which have, and are, contributing to this situation, but for today, let us examine "legislated discrimination," which I hold as the major cause of this shameful mess.

Am I an Indian? My mother came from Walpole Island Reserve, my father from Muncey Indian Reserve, but I am not an Indian because I do not fit the legal definition of what an Indian is! It says here [in the Indian Act that] "Indian" means a person who, "pursuant to this Act is registered as an Indian or is entitled to be registered as an Indian" (Section 2.1.g.).

What is this? It is the Indian Act, unilaterally passed by the House of Commons in 1951. Here is "legislated discrimination." Name me another piece of legislation which defines a people. (By the way, I am not sure what I am.) If you fit this definition your name is entered on the roll in Ottawa and you get a number.

Let me tell you of Indians and marriage. If an Indian girl, with treaty status, marries a non-Indian, she ceases to be an Indian. Or, if a non-Indian girl marries a treaty Indian, she, the non-Indian, becomes an Indian–complete with number.

A few sentences back I mentioned that this Indian Act was unilaterally passed by the House in 1951. For your further information, you might be interested in knowing that the Indian people were not asked if they approved of or disapproved of the Act. They were not asked what they thought of this piece of legislation at all. As a matter of fact, in 1951, when this Act was passed, the treaty Indian of Canada could not vote in federal elections. This right of a Canadian citizen was not given to the treaty people of Canada until 1960. If my history memory is functioning, I recall a country losing a package of colonies over legislation without representation.

May I point out just how backward our country has been in recognizing the rights of its native people. In 1958, Prime Minister Diefenbaker appointed to the Upper House a gentleman by the name of Gladstone. Mr. Gladstone was and is a Blood Indian from the Blood Reserve of southern Alberta. Ironically, when he was apointed to the Upper House in 1958, he could not vote in a federal election but he sat in our Parliament as a senator. As a matter of fact, Senator Gladstone and all the treaty Indian people of Alberta were not given the, right to vote in their provincial elections until 1965.

RESERVES

Most people believe that under the Indian Act reserves belong to the Indian bands who reside therein. But Section 2.1.0 says, "reserve means a tract of land, the legal title to which is vested in Her Majesty, that has been set apart by Her Majesty for the use and benefit of a band"; or Section 18.1 ". . . reserves shall be held by Her Majesty for the use and benefit of the respective bands . . . and subject to this Act and to the terms of any treaty or surrender, the Governor in Council may determine whether any purpose for which lands in a reserve are used or are to be used for the use and benefit of the band"; or Section 18.2: "The Minister may authorize the use of lands in a reserve for the purpose of Indian schools, the administration of Indian Affairs, Indian burial grounds, Indian health projects . . ."; or Section 19; "The Minister may . . . divide the whole or any portion of a reserve into lots or other subdivisions, and . . . determine the location and direct the construction of roads in a reserve"; or Section 20.1: "No Indian is lawfully in possession of land in a reserve unless, with the approval of the Minister, possession of the land has been allotted to him by the council of the band"; or Section 20.4: "Where possession of land in a reserve has been allotted to an Indian by the council of the bands the Minister may, in his discretion, withhold his approval."

Some of you may have heard those words "as long as the sun shall rise, the grass shall grow, and the rivers shall flow." That is what Indian people think is meant by "This is our reserve"; "This is Indian land"; "The treaty makes this our land." But read Section 35, parts 1–4, and learn, as the Indian has bitterly learned that reservation land can be expropriated (and has been expropriated). You may say, "But so it is for any one in Canada." I must agree except for two vital facts,

1. When this legislation was passed Indians were unable to vote. That's like taking candy from a kid who is bound and gagged.
2. For the ordinary people of Canada, the land they own was purchased. The Indian's land–his reservation–was and is his small retention of what was once all his. This reserve of a few acres he kept, and in turn gave away the forests, plains, mountains, rivers, and streams upon which depended his way of life.

There's the difference and the unfairness. Those two facts put the Indian in a different position to a citizen of Canada. To the Indian is owed a legal and moral debt.

Have I answered the question "Do Indians own their reservations?"

FREE ENTERPRISE

Are Indians citizens with equal rights? equal opportunities? Listen to Section 32.1: "A transaction of any kind whereby a band or a member thereof purports to sell, barter, exchange, give or otherwise dispose of cattle or other animals, grain or hay, whether wild or cultivated, or root crops or plants or their products from a reserve in Manitoba, Saskatchewan, Alberta, to a person other than a member of the band, is void unless the superintendent approves the transaction in writing."

DEATH AND WILLS

Sections 42 to 50 inclusive make for weird reading. Briefly they say that "all jurisdiction and authority in relation to matters and causes testamentary, with respect to deceased Indians, is vested exclusively in the Minister. . . ." In essence, complete authority is in the Minister's hands. For example, Section 46 says that the Minister may declare a will void in whole, or in part. Even into the grave, the Department of Indian Affairs runs the affairs of Indians.

* * * * *

ENFRANCHISEMENT

Section 108.1 deals with treaty Indians wishing to give up their treaty rights:

> On the report of the Minister than an Indian has applied for enfranchisement and that in his opinion the Indian
> (a) is of the full age of 21 years,
> (b) is capable of assuming the duties and responsibilities of citizenship, and
> (c) when enfranchised, will be capable of supporting himself and his dependents,
>
> the Governor in council may by order declare that the Indian and his wife and minor unmarried children are enfranchised."

From 1955 to 1965, 7,725 Indians were enfranchised. I wonder what tests were used to assess their capabilities of citizenship and self-support? My mother when enfranchised could neither read nor write!

EDUCATION

According to the B.N.A. Act, education of the people of Canada rests in the hands of the provinces—except for Indians. The authority for the education of Indian children rests wholly in the hands of the Minister. Nowhere in the Act, nor in reality, do Indian parents have any say in the education of their children. School boards or boards of education do not exist on reservations; and where Indian children are integrated into schools of neighboring White communities, the parents are neither elected to seats on these boards nor invited to even sit on them.

There lies one of the major reasons why a 90 per cent dropout rate occurs among Indian children. Only as a man is involved will he concern himself. Until Indian parents are given greater opportunity to be responsible for and to participate in the decisions relating to their children's education, . . . only minor positive improvements will occur.

Section 119. Did you realize that an Indian child who is expelled or suspended from school, or who is not a regular school attender is labeled as a "juvenile delinquent". Is this true for all other school children across Canada?

You have often heard how we Indians cannot "hold our liquor"–in either hand. The Act covers this, and in turn' forces reservation Indians to break the law.

Most provinces now permit the Indian to buy a drink in a hotel or retail store. But the Indian Act (Section 96) says the Indian may not bring his legal purchase home onto the reserve to drink it! So he has to drink it in some alley or in a parked car. He is then picked up for being drunk; or he becomes a hazard driving his car.

The band members of a reserve may vote for a local option, it is true. But, in non-Indian communities which are dry, a member of that community may still buy and bring onto his property a case of beer without arrest. Is this equality before the law or is it special laws for special people?

All too briefly in the preceding comments I have covered some of the injustices incorporated in the Indian Act–an Act passed by our country's top legislators. Maybe some are asking why have I not touched on color discrimination, job discrimination. Do they not exist? They do. But remember that I said I believe that this "legislated" discrimination is the major cause of the mess in which the Indian people of Canada find themselves.

You must understand that the Indian people have existed under an Act which has treated them paternalistically, which has excluded them from the Canadian way of life, which has isolated them from a world of progress and growth. You must understand the effect this Act and its execution has had, and does have, upon the mental set of my people. The Indian people have believed and still believe in too many cases, that whatever the Indian agent says is Law. They do not realize their own human rights, their right to take their problems to succeeding levels, including the prime minister. You cannot live as my people have lived for generations without acquiring the inertia against acting for oneself. As Josh White says in one of his songs, "I been down so long, I ain't never thought of standing up."

What then is to be done? The federal government, which is the people of Canada, must examine its policies and role toward its native people. The provincial governments must get off their tailbones and . . . accept the fact that these people are citizens as much as anyone else in the provinces and therefore deserve equal opportunities and equal services. It is high time that the provinces stopped hiding behind the idea that "Indians are a federal responsibility." One sometimes gets the idea that the only time provinces fight for provincial rights is when a source of revenue is involved.

The Indian people want to accept, and must be given, the responsibility for their destinies.

In closing, two thoughts. When I had finished speaking to a group recently, one gentleman came to me and said, "Mr. Currie, I am ashamed for what my forefathers have done to your people." My reply: "Do not be ashamed for what they did, but be ashamed if you do nothing." His Excellency, the late Governor General Georges Vanier, said in his Brotherhood Week message:

> The first prerequisite of unity is mutual understanding and a willingness to serve. To live for oneself alone is not to live at all. Only as we develop an awareness of the needs and feelings of others can we hope to rise to real stature and spiritual manhood. Our country as a whole will be great in proportion to the compassion its citizens show for each other. Let us remember that just as

none of us can be perfectly free until all our people are free, so none of us can be perfectly happy until the well-being of every Canadian is assured.

What do you think?

1. *"If my history memory is functioning, I recall a country losing a a package of colonies over legislation without representation." Why does Currie make this reference to the American Revolution?*
2. *Do Currie's arguments convince you that the Act is "legislated discrimination"? Why or why not?*
3. *Would Currie support the repeal of the Indian Act? Give reasons for your answer.*

2. KAHN TINETA HORN DEFENDS ACT

Kahn Tineta Horn is a Mohawk Indian from the Caughnawaga Reserve near Montreal. She has become noted for such attention-getting tactics as releasing live rats in an Indian Affairs meeting. Miss Horn's views on the Indian Act are found in her Letter to the Editor which appeared in the Toronto Star, *August 12, 1971.*

As the executive director of the Indian Legal Defence Committee, allow me to inform you that of the 250,000 registered Indians in Canada, at least 249,000 would reject the spirit, principle and arguments in your editorial charging "bias" in the Indian Act concerning the fact that when an Indian woman marries a White man she loses her rights. [According to the Indian Act, when an Indian woman marries a White man, she loses all her rights as a member of a band. If an Indian man marries a White woman, his wife acquires all the rights of a band member. The editorial asked that the government equalize the status of men and women under the Indian Act].

As a Mohawk, a member of the Six Nations Iroquois Confederacy, and one of the most widely travelled North American Indians, who is entirely self-supporting and not controlled or aided by an charity, tax, government or other source, I can speak freely for the Indians.

All Indians reject the Indian woman marrying a White man. Most of all, the Indian women reject any Indian woman who marries a White man. They want no part of her, but they are too polite to say so. The law aids us by keeping these persons away once they marry White men. The Indian men reject this action too, because they know what it can mean. The Indian children do not want association with half-breeds or White children on the reserve, so they do not want it.

The White man did rob the Indian of nearly everything. When White men come along and marry an Indian woman, some wonder if somehow they can grab some of the land they think that the parents of the Indian woman might have. For example, suppose such a couple were married about fifteen or twenty years ago, and the parents of the Indian woman are now dead. Suppose the White husband would like to figure out how he could somehow get the land he thinks rightfully belongs to his wife. It is very obvious and clear that all land is held in the name of the Crown. There is a "location certificate" issued allowing an Indian to use the land, never to own or sell it, so that the White husband with dreams of a rich Indian real-estate bonanza is thoroughly misguided. This is the main reason that some Indian women—ten to twenty years away from the reserve—are suddenly being pushed to scream for their "rights."

You say that "the Royal Commission on the Status of Women has recommended that the discriminatory sections of the Indian Act be repealed immediately." The findings of the royal commission concerning Indians were unanimously rejected by all Indians. The conclusions, which I studied with Indian women on many reserves, simply showed us the impossible gap in understanding between the "Women's Lib," and "White bleeding hearts"–even normal White society, and the Indians. There is nothing in that report except damage to Indians. However, if Indian Affairs Minister Jean Chrétien does not agree with the Indian Act, he should not stay in office.

If you would bother to study the Assessment Act of the province of Ontario, as it applies for example on the Cornwall-St. Regis Reserve, you would see just how vicious the law can be against Indians when it suits the White people. Under that law the property in which a non-Indian stays for a week or so can be declared part of the Cornwall municipality forever and taxed forever, until it is wiped out of the reserve, and sold over the head of the Indian owner. That law alone would not permit an ex-Indian to return to the reserve.

If your editorial writer knew more about the subject, he would not harp on the same things which were in the Chrétien White Paper and which were unanimously rejected by Indians all over Canada. "The tempest in a teapot" is designed to bring White children to live on the reserve, and to get Indian lands for ambitious White husbands of Indians. It is a shame that men so wise, important and highly placed as the editors of the *Star* could be so innocently cruel to the interests of Indians in Canada. With respect to the girl who had abandoned her people and then after being separated from her husband wished simply to live with her own people again: this girl knew all that before she deserted her people and married a White man. Now she must respect us for what we stand for, and she cannot return to the reserve again unless she marries an Indian man.

What do you think?

1. *Compare Miss Horn's views with those of Walter Currie (page 90).*
2. *Many Indians are coming to feel that certain forms of "legislated discrimination" are a good thing, if they serve to protect the inter-*

ests of a small, vulnerable group. Does Miss Horn agree with this contention? Do you? Why or why not?

In the Church and School

How important are a man's faith and values to him? How vital to their survival is the language in which these things are expressed?

If you were a member of a minority, would the threat of losing these cultural traits influence the way you looked at the majority society? How do you feel Indians are influenced by this threat? Do you feel that Indians can or should maintain their beliefs and language in the midst of groups which have different languages and different values?

1. INDIAN CLERGYMAN: A CRISIS OF FAITH

James Dumont, a young Indian minister is the central figure in this article by journalist Tom Harpur from the Toronto Star, *June 5, 1971.*

Indians in Canada are caught in the agony of rediscovering their true identity. As they struggle, it is becoming clearer that their traditional religion, a faith almost as old as the waters, woods, and mountains it celebrates, will play an ever-increasing role. The question, however, for them and for the churches, is whether or not this must inevitably mean a rejection of the Christian faith and the whole missionary past.

James Dumont, twenty-six, an Ojibway from Shawanaga, near Parry Sound, is a man caught in the middle of this "crisis of faith." In 1970, with a B.A. degree from Laurentian University and a bachelor of divinity degree from Emmanuel College, Toronto, he turned down initiation as a minister in the United Church to take instead a post at the Indian Friendship Centre here. He is currently director of youth as well as being editor of the *Toronto Native Times*, a monthly paper devoted almost entirely to Indian culture. He is a shy man by nature and deliberate in speech; but as he recalls his inner battle about the ministry his eyes flash and the words begin to flow freely: "I came at last to see that the churches have been guilty of what amounts to cultural genocide. By considering everything Indian as heathen and pagan, and by demanding that native peoples renounce all that their fathers and forefathers cherished, they were in fact asking them to deny their past. But once you deny your past you have no link with your history and, therefore, no identity. This was the last devastating blow of all. The Indian did not know who he was."

As he sees it, the situation has changed from the early missionary days, but not that much. Some in the larger churches are alert to the problem and are working on reforms; but the old approach is still going on, he charges. "They're careful about overseas missions, but almost anyone can be sent to minister on an Indian reserve. For some it's a last resort; they don't make it anywhere else. Because they get isolation pay. They don't know our culture and don't care to learn."

"On many northern reserves evangelical sects are now coming in by plane and trying to convert my people from being Anglican or Roman Catholic to something else. Consequently, Indians see only a divided church in competition for souls, bringing dissension and confusion in its wake."

Dumont decided to be a minister at the end of his high-school career in Parry Sound, seven years ago. "Christians teach that the thing of ultimate value is service to others," he says. "That's what I really grasped on to. I did not have a mature concept of Christianity, but I did want to serve–not just my own people, but humanity in general."

This was enough to carry him for the next five years. Helped by church funds and summer earnings, first with his father at the sawmill on the Shawanaga Reserve, then on various summer missions, he completed arts and the first two years of theology. Then he was assigned as a student to the Toronto Indian Centre. "From grade eleven on I had not had much contact with my own people," he relates. "Once placed with them I suddenly realized I was so much more comfortable there than at any time in my educational career. It was not just a matter of race; their lifestyle, their values, even though not always put into words, spoke to me as formal theology had not. Gradually, as I reflected, I became aware of all that was wrong in the church's relationship with Indians and I found it hard to finish my final term."

Dumont, however, is too perceptive to accept any easy black-and-white analysis. He is keenly aware that what many European missionaries meant by Christianity, in the early days, was not the good news of the gospel, pure and simple, but a whole "package" of Western ideas along with it. They did it in good faith, but they did it all the same. "They thought they were preaching Christ, but often what they were really doing was trying to impose their own culture, their own aggressively individualistic way of life," he says. "The results, however, were devastating."

The quarrel then, he admits, is not so much with Christianity as with the values and traditions which overlaid it. In fact, the core of ancient Indian spiritual beliefs, as outlined by Dumont, is strikingly in harmony with the heart of the Christian faith. "We believe in a Great Spirit who created all things. Each Indian has to experience in his own way a personal link with Him. This personal relationship is the ground of one's inner strength and central to everything else. Each must be left free to develop his spiritual life without interference from others. We believe also in a deep reverence for mother earth, in the need for a shared, communal life and strong family ties. The circle where the common pipe is smoked is for us a form of communion service."

Dumont himself believes in the historic Jesus as Son of God, in His death for mankind and in His resurrection. He prefers, however, to use the terms of his Indian past to describe his spiritual life. "I find it hard to use the Christian language without getting hung up on all the old associations—its identification with an alien lifestyle and outlook," he says.

This touches a point of similar concern for most thinking Christians in the West today: How do you disentangle what it means to be a Christian from "the great American way of life"? There is increasing awareness that Christian values and North American culture cannot be simply identified: that, in fact, they are in tension.

Dumont sees his main task with Indian young people as educational. "We hold seminars, travel from reserve to reserve, trying to communicate what's happening in other communities and exposing our youth to the kind of issues they should be concerned with," he points out.

Asked just what these issues are, he replied; "Basically, what it means to be an Indian today. This is hardest of all in the cities. If you try to uphold the ancient values of sharing, communal life, non-interference and respect for nature, everything around you denies them. North American society has a compulsion to make everyone believe and do the same things. It's a conversion-obsession and I just don't mean in religion. If an Indian does not conform to the competitive, aggressive, individualistic ethic, then Manpower or some other agency will feel they must make him conform. Yet this is the very life-style that is destroying society itself.

"Indians are convinced that Western society is rushing headlong to destruction and that Indian people and their values could provide an answer. From pollution to the obvious lack of spiritual depth in people's lives we see problems for which Indian ways of looking at things offer insight."

Dumont had these comments on Red Power and violence: "For me Red Power—or being a Pink Panther—means simply being proud of your heritage and color. It means living and rejoicing in this fact. In this sense of being, and not in politics, lies true strength.

"Indian violence is possible if things remain as they now are, especially as our people become aware of their real lot and the racism that does exist. I don't approve of violence—or rather, I don't advocate it. But then it's not a matter of being for or against. It is something that happens automatically if people are pushed far enough and long enough. When it does happen it will indicate something is desperately wrong. If society just looks at the violence it will be looking at the wrong end. Yet this is what constantly happens."

He prophesies a resurgence of Indian religion among his people as they become aware of their identity, and argues that its value system will provide a "mirror" in which the rest of us will be able to see where we are going wrong. Some Indians will undoubtedly reject the outward trappings of Christianity in this process. Others, perhaps the majority, led by people such as Jim Dumont, will work slowly and painfully toward a synthesis of the old with the new—discarding what is irrelevant or false in either.

Insofar as they are successful, they will benefit us all.

What do you think?

1. *Dumont admits that "the quarrel is not so much with Christianity as with the values and traditions which overlaid it." What are those values and traditions? Why might Indians object to them, and not to Christianity?*
2. *"Indians are convinced that Western society is rushing headlong to destruction and that Indian people and their values could provide an answer." Why would Indians feel this way?*

2. CHRISTIANITY DISPELLED SUPERSTITION AND FEAR

These comments from the Right Reverend James A. Watton, Anglican bishop of Moosonee, were reported in the Toronto Star, *June 5, 1971.*

Right Reverend James A. Watton, Anglican bishop of Moosonee—a diocese of 350,000 square miles, including most of northern Ontario and central Quebec north of the Canadian National Railways—told the *Star* in a phone interview that the accusation of cultural genocide is the "oldest chestnut of all." The bishop makes no claim to be an expert on Indian affairs, yet most of his ministry since ordination in 1938 has been spent in close association with Cree, Ojibway and Chipewyan people. He has many hundreds of Indians under his care, including five Indian priests.

"There is precious little written about Indian culture," he stated. "What there is was written mainly by churchmen. After all, it is easy to forget that before the coming of the missionaries the Indian here had no written language." The syllabic alphabet which made literacy possible was the invention of Anglican clergymen, James Evans and Bishop Horden, first bishop of Moosonee. Without this as a tool, reading, even about their own culture, would have been impossible.

"It is Western society as a whole and not Christianity that has demanded of the Indian that he deny his values and whole routine of life. In fact, these Indian values and religious beliefs coincide with basic Christianity much more than Western civilization does at the present time. What the missionaries did do was offer freedom from superstition and fear. No one realizes just how much fear lay behind the power of the conjurer or medicine man in the primitive community."

Bishop Watton says that it is understood by all parties concerned in his diocese that the church will continue to work with the Indians only as long as it is wanted. "We are there by their invitation," he insisted. "We could not stay on without it. It's as simple as that."

Asked for comment on the new flood of other sects into areas traditionally cared for by either the Anglican or Roman Catholic Church, he replied tersely: "It is a supreme tragedy. What could be more confusing?"

In spite of this, and in spite of all the criticism, he remains convinced that the Indians, at least in the far north, will continue to be Christian while increasingly affirming their distinctive "Indianness."

What do you think?

1. *In what ways do Bishop Watton and James Dumont agree? Disagree?*
2. *Can Indians "continue to be Christian while increasingly affirming their distinctive 'Indianness' "? Why or why not?*

3. A COLONIAL PLOT?

Howard Adams was born in St. Louis, Saskatchewan, a Métis community, and has completed a Ph.D. in the history of education at the University of California. Adams has become recognized by the Indian and Métis people of Canada as one of their most articulate spokesmen. This interview with Andrew Warnock is taken from the Canadian Dimension *of April-May 1968.*

WARNOCK: The mass media has given some publicity to Indian and Métis protests against the school system and the role of the churches. Would you like to comment on that?

ADAMS: It is a typical colonial pattern, one that has existed in all other imperialist systems of the world, for churches to be given control of education of the native people. A study of the history of African countries in the colonial period shows how completely the churches dominated native education. In their liberation struggle these countries have had to fight the church and other authorities in order to overcome this situation. This is true with us. On our reserves the schools are administered by the Catholic or the Anglican church, and are staffed by priests, nuns, or lay people chosen by the churches. This is definitely a feudal arrangement, as well as being colonial, and it seems that the situation is never going to be rectified by the government working through its own policies. The change must come through the struggle of the native people.

The residential schools, of course, are already in serious trouble. The native people no longer want these residential schools because they disorganize and break up the home by taking the child away for ten months of the year. They bring him to the residential school where he is taught by White people and where he learns to look down on his own culture. The residential schools will be going quickly because the native people are already moving militantly against them.

We have already started to move against church control of our education on the reserves and in the Métis communities. This will develop a little more slowly because of the religious factor involved. It means that the native people, in order to criticize their educational system, have to criticize their God, and for many of them this is a very difficult thing to do. With the Métis people, in most cases the Catholic church controls our educational system. It is disastrous for our own culture not to have any of our own teachers in our schools. The teachers there now are all White and of course represent the urban, middle-class value system. This denies us the possibility of developing, reinforcing and strengthening our culture. What we say, as native people, is that we are being brain-washed into believing that we are shy and retiring and withdrawn, and this denies us the possibility of developing aggressive and confident leadership qualities. We simply cannot have a feudal system of education in the twentieth century, in a highly technical world. It doesn't allow us to develop the social and psychological skills that are necessary today. Too many of the students drop out, and why? Because the schools are foreign institutions right in our own communities. We have to make them meaningful and relevant to ourselves, and this cannot be done unless we as native people begin to insist on control. As it is, we have no control over our school system. We have no rights which allow us to be trustees on school boards, we have no right to determine the curriculum, no right to determine the hiring and firing of teachers, no say in what textbooks are used. We are completely powerless in this situation. How can we preserve our own culture when the whole program and policy of the Department of Indian Affairs and the Department of Education is directed at making middle-class White men out of us?

What do you think?

1. *Would you support an Indian take-over of Indian schools? Why or why not? How could this be done?*
2. *What sort of education might a segregated school system offer? How would it help or hinder Indians?*
3. *What effects did the religious control of education have on Indian education? How would this influence the opinions of James Dumont (page 97)?*

4. ACHIEVEMENT LEVELS OF INDIANS IN SCHOOL

The Canada Yearbook of 1969 provides figures which allow a comparison between the education achievements of Indians and non-Indians.

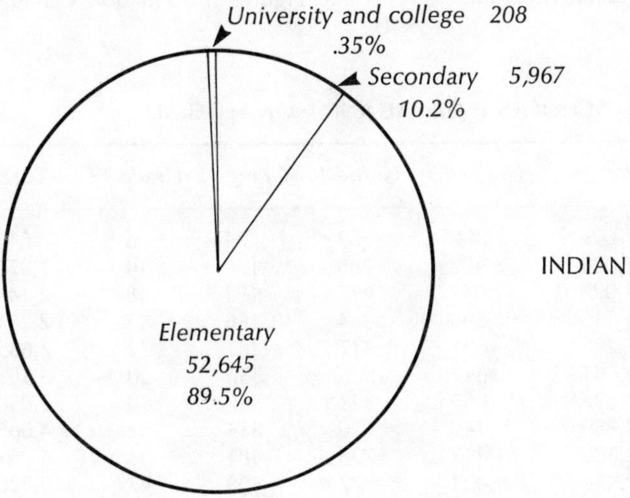

1967–68

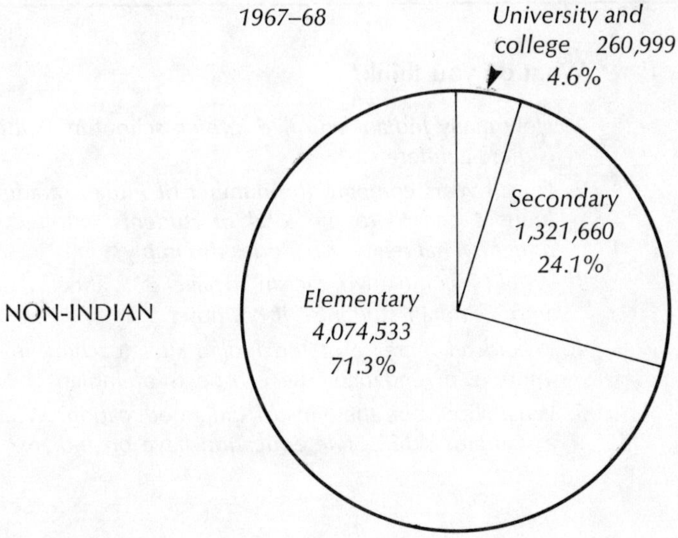

What do you think?

1. *There are approximately 240,000 registered Indians in Canada. How do the school attendance figures compare with those of the White population of Canada? How would you account for this?*
2. *What was the amount spent on Indian education in 1969 (see page 81)? Account for the poor showing of Indian students.*

5. INDIAN AND NON-INDIAN SCHOOL ATTENDANCE COMPARED

The Department of Indian Affairs and Northern Development provided a statistical accounting of Indian school attendance. This table has been taken from Indian Facts and Figures *(Information Canada, 1968).*

HIGH SCHOOLS (FEDERAL AND NON-FEDERAL)

	Grade 9	*Grade 10*	*Grade 11*	*Grade 12*	*Grade 13*	*Total*
1948–49	375	144	62	24	6	611
1957–58	1,024	472	288	176	10	1,970
1958–59	1,020	647	277	182	18	2,144
1959–60	1,115	599	384	166	17	2,281
1960–61	1,294	691	417	261	22	2,685
1961–62	1,681	817	503	350	30	3,381
1962–63	1,827	1,065	541	367	30	3,830
1963–64	1,959	1,140	620	314	32	4,065
1964–65	2,309	1,212	726	481	33	4,761
1965–66	2,474	1,423	777	499	47	5,220
1966–67	2,590	1,520	897	478	25	5,510

What do you think?

1. *How many Indians enrolled in high school in 1948? In 1966? Why is there a difference?*
2. *For all years compare the number of Indians graduating (add columns 4 and 5) to the total of students enrolled. What do you notice? What relationship does this imply?*
3. *Would "cumulative racism" (page 33) affect the dropout rate among Indian students? If so, how?*
4. *Would an increase in the Indian staff teaching in Indian schools improve or endanger the prospects of Indian children. Why?*
5. *What should be the aims of Indian education? What effects might a standard White-style education have on Indians?*

6. DIFFERING BACKGROUNDS IN CHILDHOOD

In 1967 the findings of a government-sponsored inquiry into Indian affairs, which came to be known as the Hawthorn Report, were released. This selection is taken from the report's study on Indian education. (H. B. Hawthorn, ed.: A Survey of the Contemporary Indians of Canada *[Information Canada, 1967].)*

PHYSICAL ENVIRONMENT	*Indian*	*Non-Indian*
Housing	Generally over-crowded; child sleeps with siblings in same bed; little or no privacy; scarcity of furniture; sometimes dirty house; often unattractive, unpainted and uncared for.	Seldom crowded; child may share room but not bed; possibility for privacy; furniture adequate, usually clean; house usually painted and not unattractive.
Food	Generally inadequate for good nutrition and often inadequate in amount; lack of diversity and poorly prepared; meals when hungry rather than scheduled and communal; school lunches often lacking.	Sometimes inadequate for good nutrition but seldom is child hungry; usually diverse and adequately prepared by an adult; always scheduled and usually social; school lunches available and adequate.
Clothing	Generally insufficient and in poor condition; often unclean or unironed; often hand-me-downs and obtained from poor quality bargain sales.	Usually adequate and in good condition; always washed and ironed; some hand-me-downs but in good condition and usually of good quality.
Objects	Few toys; sometimes T.V.; seldom books or magazines available for child to read; sometimes records available; seldom any use of scissors, crayons, and paste in making objects for play; meagre household furniture and objects useable for variety of experiences.	Often over-abundance of toys; usually child has own books, records and access to those of adults; considerable use of paste, scissors, crayons for constructing play objects; child uses own or household items such as egg-beaters, etc.

PSYCHOLOGICAL FACTORS	*Indian*	*Non-Indian*
Attitudes toward Child	At age of mobility child is considered a person and left relatively free to create and explore his own environment. He develops a sense of independence and autonomy. He has limited stimulation and feedback from adults.	Child is watched and controlled by parents and remains dependent on them throughout childhood. He is not autonomous and has little opportunity to become independent. He has constant interaction and feedback from adults around him.

PSYCHOLOGICAL FACTORS (cont.)	*Indian*	*Non-Indian*
Parental Interest in Learning	Parents have little background in formal education and are not oriented, nor do they have time to teach their children specific skills. Little time is spent on teaching the child to walk and talk; some time may be spent in encouraging child to imitate father or mother in activities related to life on the reserve.	Parents have usually completed high school and are oriented toward preparing the child for school. Time is taken to teach children skills which will help them in school. Time is spent urging child to walk early and to talk early and correctly. Time is taken to expose child to a variety of stimuli through expeditions, shopping and visiting.
Verbal Practice and Development	Conversations between children and adults limited; questions often answered in monosyllables; custom sometimes demands silence from children in presence of adults; English spoken by adults often inaccurate and limited in vocabulary. Some children have the opportunity to hear stories and folk tales which have colorful imagery and language. No one reads to the child.	Conversations often unlimited; detailed answers given as often as monosyllabic replies; child's speech and labelling may be corrected consistently. English spoken by parents usually correct and diverse; child is read to often and has books of his own.
Sanctions for Learning	Child is permitted to do things which interest him when he is ready. Seldom is he rewarded or punished for specific learning attempts although he receives approval when he does the task correctly after trial and error learning. Time is not a factor; he can take all morning to get dressed if he needs it. If child attempts a task and can't complete it, he is not urged to stay with it.	Child is urged to try things which are considered appropriate for him to know whether he has expressed interest, or not. He is rewarded for trying whether he learns task or not. Time is a factor: "see how fast you can dress yourself." Emphasis is placed on trying and on completing tasks undertaken.
Routines for Learning	Routines are flexible and often non-existent. Meals are served on demand; bedtimes vary with sleepiness and family activity. Life is adult-centred and child is fitted in.	Routines are rigid. Meals served regularly and bedtimes are stringently adhered to. Life is more child than adult-centred in sense that child's bed-time would not be disrupted for adult activities.

PSYCHOLOGICAL FACTORS (cont.)	*Indian*	*Non-Indian*
Discipline	Discipline is primarily protective and loose. Seldom is child punished. Age-graded behavioral expectations are minimal in early childhood; as child grows older, he is ridiculed if he fails to meet expectations but he has plenty of leeway. The concept of autonomy allows him his own decisions.	Discipline is relatively over-protective and rigid. Age-graded behavior is demanded; few decisions are permitted, routines are controlled by adults; punishment is meted out for failure to comply with adult demands.

MISCELLANEOUS FACTORS	*Indian*	*Non-Indian*
Economic Involvement of Children	Children often involved in economic routines and pursuits of parents which sometimes mean frequent mobility for seasonal labor, babysitting while mother works, helping on fishboats, and with fruit picking. Illness of mother often means older siblings care for whole family; economic level of reserve may involve children in wood and water-hauling and similar tasks.	Economic pursuits of parents seldom involve children; patterns tend to be stable and regular; mobility is low and participation of child in maintaining economic level is virtually nil; chores seldom disrupt routines of child; illness of mother and help with household chores usually handled by importing an adult.
General Family Patterns	Often unstable and father may be absent for long periods of time; in some cases, there is great deal of conflict and disruption within the home; drunken periods may mean children are left on their own for days at a time; care of children tends to diminish with periods of drinking.	Usually stable and father is usually at home more consistently than he is absent. Many homes have conflict but in most cases, there is an attempt to keep outbursts to a minimum and hidden from children. Children virtually never left on their own.

What do you think?

1. *Briefly describe what you feel is the type of education offered in most Canadian schools. What values does this type of education seem to represent? What values does it not, for the most part, approve of? What sort of behavior does it expect and demand from*

a child? What methods of learning does it enforce? What does it assume about a child's background?

2. *Under three headings—physical environment, psychological factors, and miscellaneous factors—outline the differences in background between Indian and White middle-class children. What sort of experiences do these differences imply for an Indian child who is being educated in a Canadian school? How can these experiences account for the dropout rate among Indian students?*
3. *By analyzing the background of Indian children, as seen above, suggest an alternative to the type of education offered by the average Canadian school which Indian children might find more suitable to their needs. To what extent do you think all Canadian children might benefit from such an alternative? Why?*
4. *How could the present school system be accused of assimilating Indian children?*

4

The Historical Roots

When the White man first arrived in North America he was both welcomed and aided by the Indians, who were aware of his pathetic helplessness in the face of a wilderness he was ill-equipped to deal with. The Indians, of course, were not aware that these first helpless guests were the advance guard of a powerful and expanding civilization.

Cartier desperately needed Indian help when his crew were dying of scurvy. Early fur traders required the knowledge and skills of Indians to survive and prosper in the alien environment. Yet by the mid-nineteenth century, the Indian was virtually at the mercy of the White man in many cases for food, land and medicine.

What were some of the events causing such a dramatic shift in Indian-White relationships? What attitudes accompanied this shift, and indeed still remain? What were the specific policies which contributed to these changes?

The following section provides a selection of materials grouped around four areas of concern: the history of government dealings with Indians, the part played by economics, the role of the churches, and finally the prevailing attitudes held by Whites and Indians towards one another through the years.

What insights, if any, do you feel this section, dealing with the historical roots of Indian-White relations, offers in providing a better understanding of present-day tensions? Does your analysis of this chapter affect the way you perceived the issue in the contemporary section? Does it affect your views regarding the future options which may be adopted in an attempt to resolve the tensions in today's Indian-White relations?

Government

Why was it that at one time the Indian was regarded by both the British and the French as a vital ally in war and trade, but before long, had become a "ward' of the crown, a pawn for politicians, a childlike figure to be given the same rights as criminals, lunatics, and women?

What caused this dramatic shift in government policy? How do the memories of this reversal, and the policies following upon it, affect present-day Indian attitudes towards the White man and his institutions?

1. SCOTT THE POET LOOKS AT THE INDIAN

Duncan Campbell Scott joined the Department of Indian Affairs as a copy clerk in 1879 and remained for fifty-two years, rising to the rank of deputy minister. It is interesting to note the connection between the attitude expressed in Scott's poems on the Indian and his public statements as an Indian Affairs official.

The poem here, "The Onondaga Madonna," is taken from The Poems of Duncan Campbell Scott *(Toronto: McClelland and Stewart, 1926).*

She stands full-throated and with careless pose,
This woman of a weird and waning race,
The tragic savage lurking in her face,
Where all her pagan passion burns and glows;
Her blood is mingled with her ancient foes,
And thrills with war and wildness in her veins;
Her rebel lips are dabbled with the stains
Of feuds and forays and her father's woes.

And closer in the shawl about her breast,
The latest promise of her nation's doom,
Paler than she her baby clings and lies,
The primal warrior gleaming from his eyes;
He sulks, and burdened with his infant gloom,
He draws his heavy brows and will not rest.

2. SCOTT THE CIVIL SERVANT

This article by Duncan Campbell Scott, written in his capacity as an official of Indian Affairs, appeared in the Proceedings of the Fourth Conference of the Institute of Pacific Relations *(Canadian Institute of International Affairs, 1931).*

The department is confronted with serious probems in the slow process of weaning the Indian from his primitive state. For some of the obstacles to progress the public must be held responsible. In the minds of the promoters of fairs, stampedes and affairs of the kind, particularly in the western provinces, the Indian is regarded as an asset when decked out in feathers and war-paint, and exhibited for the entertainment of the curious. In this way the Indians are induced to leave their reserves for considerable periods, and generally at times of the year when they should be engaged with their agricultural duties. In addition to the distractions provided by White show-men, there are the aboriginal ceremonies to contend with. Like all people living close to nature, the Indians perform rites at the time of the summer solstice; notable among these ancient native customs is the Sun Dance of the Plains. The Indian Act prohibits the appearance of Indians in native costume without the consent of the Superintendent General at pageants, and also dances or ceremonies involving mutilation of the body. It may seem arbitrary on our part to interfere with the native culture. The position of the department, however, can readily be understood, and it is pointed out that Indians will spend a fortnight preparing for a sun-dance, another fortnight engaging in it, and another fortnight to get over it. Obviously this plays havoc with summer ploughing.

Another picturesque native custom which the government has found it necessary to legislate against is the pot-latch of British Columbia. This in brief was the method followed by Indian tribes in the west coast region of visiting one another for the purpose of promoting social intercourse and the settlement of intertribal debts, arrangement of marriages and so forth. The giving away of gifts on a lavish scale was one of the most prominent features of the pot-latch. Before the advent of the White man this plan undoubtedly served a useful purpose and was adequate to the needs of the people. Obviously, however, with the introduction of the new money system of economics, the engagement of Indians as wage earners in industry, the effects of the pot-latch, if the practice were unchecked, would be disastrous.

These inherent difficulties are being overcome, and each new generation becomes noticeably more adaptable to modern conditions.

In the newer provinces where association of the Indians with Whites covers but a short period, the reserve system is undoubtedly the only satisfactory one.

It is intended to ensure the continuation of the tribal life and that of the individual as an Indian, and as well to render possible a continuous and consistent administrative policy directed toward civilization. If there were strict confinement to reserve limits, the system would have had many objectionable features, but neither officials nor Indians considered the reserve as more than a "pied à terre." The Indians wander away from it and return to it as the nomadic instinct prompts, no doubt bringing back much undesirable knowledge and experience. But this mingling with the outside world was less injurious than a strict confinement within boundaries would have been, even had such confinement been possible. In the older provinces. however, where Indians have mixed and intermarried with Whites for more than two centuries, the efficiency of the reserve system tends to weaken. In southern Ontario and Quebec there are communities of Indians who for the most part show little trace of their ancestry, either in their physiognomy, color or habits of life. There is no apparent reason why these groups should not take their place in the community and assume the responsibility of citizenship. In other words they should be enfranchised under the provisions of the Indian Act. As the Act stands, however, an Indian can only be enfranchised on his own application, and while a considerable number have taken advantage of this opportunity, the majority cling to wardship. This attitude is largely actuated by the exemption provided for Indians under the Act, such as freedom from taxation and the protection of propery, both real and personal on an Indian reserve from seizure for debt. The government on its part as a result of influences that have been brought to bear, is hesitant to enforce enfranchisement upon the Indians, even those whose Indian blood has been reduced to a small percentage through intermarriage.

* * * * *

It is the opinion of the writer, however, that by policies and activities such as have been outlined, the government will in time reach the end of its responsibility as the Indians progress into civilization and finally disappear as a separate and distinct people, not by race extinction but by gradual assimilation with their fellow-citizens.

What is meant by?

"the primal warrior"

What do you think?

1. *Referring to Scott's poem, describe what you think his attitude towards the Indian was. Take note of his diction and the imagery he uses.*
2. *Explain how the poem sheds light on Scott's official views. What sort of policy statement might George Ryga write?*
3. *How do Scott's arguments support the argument of many modern Indians that when the government says integration it means assimilation? To what extent do you think government attitudes have changed?*
4. *Could Mr. Scott's policy be called "paternalistic"? Why?*
5. *The Indian during the first half of this century has never been, before or since, so quiet or passive.*

(a) Does this document provide an explanation for this? How?
(b) What other explanation might there be?
(c) Have these conditions changed? Why?

3. BAD LAWS AND SAD CONDITIONS

This critical survey of Indian affairs is taken from Robert Sinclair's The Canadian Indian *(Ottawa: Thorburn and Abbot, 1911).*

1. The scope and basis of our Indian Act is wrong and injurious to the Indian.

It interferes with his enjoyment of natural and inherent rights.

2. Whilst the Crown sought Indian alliance for war purposes, it conceded every right enjoyed by other subjects and did much in addition to conciliate.

Since alliance for war has no longer been needed, Indian rights have been constantly restricted and encroached on and the attitude of conciliation has been replaced by either indifference or assumption of unwarranted or unneeded interference.

3. In negotiation for territory and possessions originally his, the Indian has always been treated as a free and independent man.

After such negotiations that treatment has been altered. He is no longer dealt with as being free and independent in the sense that other citizens are and the values of annuities and things given to him under treaty have been impaired by legislation.

4. The right to govern himself and the governing capacity of his chiefs was formerly fully recognized.

Both right and capacity have been interfered with by ill-considered legislation not enacted to correct abuses but at the prompting of official theorists.

5. It has always been intended to remove all lines of demarcation between Indian and White.

Instead of being removed they have been broadened and deepened.

6. Royal Commissions have after careful enquiry agreed in indicating a true policy.

Our Indian management has proceeded in directions diametrically opposed to the policy so indicated.

7. Our Indian affairs are dealt with exclusively by a bureaucracy of officials, whose interest it is to assume, and retain, complete control and who prompt all legislation to give them such control; the functions and duties the Indian once enjoyed have been transferred to officials.

The Indian has no voice whatever in such legislation, is often opposed to it and suffers from its deleterious effects.

8. There is hardly any matter that an Indian can undertake that is not dependent for its outcome on the whim of some official who probably has the most casual knowledge or no knowledge whatever of the circumstances to be considered.

This destroys forethought, freedom, initiative, responsibility and thrift.

9. The policy of the Indian department has led to a constant series of encroachments upon the natural rights of a man to manage his own affairs.

The effects must be disastrous to the man.

10. The Indian may have the usufruct of land but he cannot lease the same or fully enjoy the fruits of his industry upon the land, or devise them or give them to his family or reduce the usufruct into possession without the consent of the superintendent general, which means the dictum of a departmental clerk, dealing perfunctorily, signed by a minister who personally knows nothing of the matter.

He therefore has no real property in the reserved land he occupies nor in his buildings, fences or other constructions placed upon it.

11. An Indian cannot become enfranchised unless he occupies land on a reserve, or is a doctor, lawyer, clergyman or university graduate. If he occupies land on a reserve he has to pass through humiliating tests and a long probation.

What is most desired—early enfranchisement of the Indian—is impeded to such an extent that scarcely any have become enfranchised. Yet to enfranchise them is the prime object of maintaining the Indian service.

12. If an Indian claims to be entitled to share in the properties and annuities of his band, officials decide upon the claim and the decision is final.

He has no recourse to our open courts, as he once had. That has been taken away by law, though the properties and things claimed may be worth thousands of dollars.

13. An Indian annuitant cannot with his annuity money purchase anything that he can dispose of or give title to, no matter what his necessity or advantage.

He is so surrounded by the technicalities, prohibitions and exemptions of the Indian Act and its multifarious amendments that he is absolutely prevented from doing business or transacting the most ordinary affairs that daily, as a matter of course, are the incidents of the life of other people.

14. A Chinaman, a Hindoo, or the most ignorant or unsophisticated of new settlers can assume obligations or secure credit and may easily obtain the franchise.

The Indian can not.

15. Canada has encroached more and more upon Indian rights in

a way that no other civilized people that had a native race to deal with has ever done.

The United States, New Zealand, Africa, India, etc., have all acted differently, with excellent results, that have not been attained in Canada and can never be attained without complete change of treatment.

16. The matter is not a party one. It is a system grown up and perpetuated and made more difficult to emerge from ever since the year 1859. Since then no attempt has been made to deal with Indian matters except in the most perfunctory way.

The Indian has had disabilities piled on him and liberties taken from him until now he is, as never before, in a condition of complete subjection and tutelage; unparalleled in any free country now or in the annals of history.

17. The result of the system is that the White man, as well as the Indian, has imperceptibly adopted the view that the Indian is a man with no rights whatever except such as he derives from the Indian Act.

A Canadian attorney general pleaded that Indians had no right to sue.

18. The government seems to think that an obligation entered into with an Indian may be implemented as it pleases.

In one case a department pledged its "honor" fourteen years ago to do certain things without delay. Those things have not been done yet.

What do you think?

1. Compare Sinclair's views on the role of government in Indian matters to those of:
(a) Walter Currie (page 90),
(b) Harold Cardinal (page 78),
(c) Prime Minister Trudeau (page 71).
What do you notice?

2. "Judging by Sinclair's arguments, there appears to have been little change in the situation since 1911—more than sixty years ago." Is this assessment accurate? Support your answer. Give reasons why you think the situation has or has not changed?

4. THE MACDONALD FRANCHISE

Sir John A. Macdonald gave the vote to all Indians who could meet certain qualifications. This selection from Hansard is from the Commons debate of April 30, 1885.

MR. MILLS (Reformer): I rise to ask the hon. gentleman how we are to understand the word Indian. Does he use it in the sense of an Indian enfranchised under the Indian Act, or in the sense of Indians who are not enfranchised?

SIR JOHN A. MACDONALD (Conservative): I fancy that an Indian who is qualified would have a vote if he is a British subject. If an Indian has an income of $300 a year, he will have a vote the same as any other person.

MR. MILLS: What we are anxious to know is whether the hon. gentleman proposes to give other than enfranchised Indians votes.

SIR JOHN A. MACDONALD: Yes.

MR. MILLS: Indians residing on a reservation?

SIR JOHN A. MACDONALD: Yes, if they have the necessary property qualification.

MR. MILLS: An Indian who cannot make a contract for himself, who can neither buy nor sell anything without the consent of the superintendent general—an Indian who is not enfranchised.

SIR JOHN A. MACDONALD: Whether he is enfranchised or not.

MR. MILLS: Poundmaker and Big Bear?

SIR JOHN A. MACDONALD: Yes.

MR. MILLS: So that they can go from a scalping party to the polls. Why the honorable gentleman should be anxious to confer the electoral franchise upon a portion of the community who are not taxed, who are not subject to any burdens in the conduct of the government of the country, who are not permitted to buy or sell or to make contracts on their own behalf, who are dealt with by the government precisely as children are dealt with, and at the same time withhold the franchise from large numbers of the White population, a great many people will not be able to understand. That class of the community who are held to be wards of the government, utterly incapable of managing their own affairs are to be entrusted with the most important franchise that can be conferred upon a free people. I am opposed to placing in the hands of the administration a certain number of votes because that is precisely what this provision means. An Indian who is a ward of the government who can buy or sell nothing without a licence from the superintendant general, and who is less qualified to exercise the franchise than many a boy running through the streets of this city, is to have the franchise conferred upon him, while many a White man is denied that privilege.

MR. BLAKE (Reformer): The question before us is not one of sympathy with the Indians at all. I do not suppose any well-regulated mind can feel anything but sympathy with the original possessors of the soil of this continent. That is not the question. The question is, whether the Indian, in the sense in which the hon. gentleman uses that word is this clause, is it a fit subject for the exercise of the franchise? It is a symbol of the freedom of the party, and it is not upon any except a free man that you have a right to confer the power to elect the representatives who will make the laws. Freedom is essential to this right, and I maintain that under the laws as they exist there is sufficient evidence to show that the Indian—at any rate the Indian who is not enfranchised within the meaning of that word in the Indian Act—does not occupy that position in which it is safe to give him the franchise.

MR. PATTERSON: (Reformer) It (the Bill) confers no rights on the Indian. If his desire is to benefit the Indians let him give greater facilities for them to attain the full status of their rights and liberties, to emancipate them from the guardianship of the government of the day, to make them free agents with the right to manage their own affairs. The Act does nothing of the sort. It gives the Indians a right to vote, but the Indian and his vote are virtually controlled by the government of the day, and will be used by the government of the day, and will be used by the government as a means of retaining themselves in power.

What do you think?

1. *Why do you think Macdonald wanted to enfranchise the Indians? Why did the Opposition oppose him?*
2. *"By the nineteenth century the Canadian Indian had become the ward and pawn of the federal government."*
   (a) How does the wrangling between Macdonald and the Reformers prove or disprove this remark?
   (b) Compare the accusations levelled at the government in this document to those of Harold Cardinal on page 78.

5. BACKGROUND OF THE TREATIES

In their brief, Citizens Plus, *presented to the federal government in June 1970, the Indian chiefs of Alberta outlined their interpretation of the treaty agreements made in the nineteenth century. The brief prefaces its remarks about specific treaty agreements with a description of how the negotiations were carried on between the Indians and the treaty commissioners. We see here, accordingly, the Indian interpretation of the historical basis of the treaty agreements which dealt with, among other things, lands, reserves, medical care, and schools, as well as hunting, trapping, and fishing rights.*

The Indian commissioners for all the Treaties tried to call all the tribes of the affected area together for the negotiations. For most of the Treaties there were a few tribes who were not present. Some were hunting. Other tribes lived far away. The commissioners searched for those tribes and usually arranged supplemental agreements under which the Indians agreed to be bound as if they had signed the Treaty when it was made. These supplemental agreements are called Adhesions.

The men who signed the Treaties as the representatives of the tribes were chiefs, councilors, or headmen. When the negotiations for a Treaty began, the commissioners asked the Indians to point out their chiefs. These chiefs were usually the main spokesmen but in some cases "orators" spoke. The medallions, flags and suits of clothes which were presented to the chiefs and headmen were intended to symbolize the authority of the Queen's government and the special responsibility of the chiefs and councillors in teaching the children to respect the Treaties and maintaining law and order.

The Treaties were signed in utmost good faith by the commissioners and by the Indians. For example, at Treaty Six, Lieutenant-Governor Morris said:

> Again, I say, all we seek is your good; I speak openly, as brother to brother, as a father to his children, and I would give you a last advice, hear my words . . . My words, when they are accepted, are written down, and they last, as I have said to the others, as long as the sun shines and the river runs.

There is no doubt that the Treaties were necessary for the westward growth of the Dominion of Canada. The . . . truth is that the Dominion government acknowledged that the Indians held title to the land. In order to acquire lands to permit mining and homesteading, the province of Canada, and later the Dominion, acknowledged the necessity to deal with the Indians for their land. The Indians were regarded as the Queen's subjects—but special subjects, the owners of the land.

The land occupied by the Indians thus became part of the Dominion, not by conquest, not as the spoils of war, but through the honorable process of Treaties between the Queen and the aboriginal peoples. The benefits accruing to the Indians under the Treaties were to last forever—in perpetuity—"for as long as the sun rises and the river runs."

The making of the Treaties took the form of verbal discussion between the commissioners and the Indians. The written texts, with their very legalistic construction, were prepared later by government lawyers. The formal written treaties (small t) are therefore insufficient as reports of the Treaties (large T), of the verbal promises exchanged by Red men and White men. Indeed, it was necessary to revise Treaties Numbers One and Two because some verbal promises were not included in the written text.

The purpose of the Dominion in making the Treaties was to acquire the land of the Indians. The yielding up of most of their land was clearly the most important undertaking to which the Indians agreed in signing a treaty contract. The one extra undertaking, to abide by the law, was added at the end of the document. In Treaty Six it is written:

> The Plain and Wood Cree Tribes of Indians, and all of other Indians inhabiting the district hereinafter described and defined, do hereby cede, release, surrender and yield up to the Government of the

> Dominion of Canada, for Her Majesty the Queen and Her successors forever, all their rights, titles and privileges, whatsoever to the lands included in the following limits. . . .

These same words ". . . cede, release, surrender, and yield up to the Government of Canada . . ." also appear in Treaty Seven. And in Treaty Eight, it is written:

> And whereas the said Indians have been notified and informed by Her Majesty's said Commission that it is Her desire to open for settlement, immigration, trade, mining, lumbering, and such other purposes as to Her Majesty may seem meet the said Indians do hereby cede, release, surrender and yield up to the Government. . . .

The Indians yielded their land in return for the many promises made to them by the commissioners. The commissioners went to Indians from the Government with their minds made up. They listened to counter-proposals with seeming patience but soon forgot. The commissioners promised to send some Indian proposals back to the Queen's representative, but they forced the hand of the Indians by saying in effect, "Sign our treaty or we shall leave in the morning."

The Queen's negotiators believed that the Indians were in weak bargaining positions. The White settlers and surveyors and miners were too numerous to be excluded, even if the Indians had been willing to take up rifles. The slaughter of the buffalo had nearly exterminated the magnificent animals before Treaty Six was signed. Smallpox had killed the young, the old, and the weak. It was recognized that the Queen's Mounted Police Force were needed to keep out the whiskey and gun traders and to keep the peace between some tribes. Consequently the Indians were hoping to be "treated" but at the same time fearful that they would be confined to reserves, be required to abandon hunting, and to serve in front lines if war occurred.

This presumption of the weak bargaining position of the Indians was expressed in 1871 by Adams G. Archibald, the Lieutenant-Governor of Manitoba, who reported on the negotiations in Treaty Two:

> In defining the limits of their reserves, so far as we could see, they wished to have about two-thirds of the province. We heard them out and then told them it was quite clear they had misunderstood. . . . We told them that whether they wished it or not, immigrants would come in and fill up the country; that every year from this one twice as many in number as their whole people there assembled would pour into the province and in a little while would spread all over it, and that now was the time for them to come to an arrangement that would secure homes and annuities for themselves and their children. . . . We requested them to think over these propositions till Monday morning.

If they thought it better to have no treaty at all, they might do without one, but they must make up their minds; if there was to be a treaty, it must be on a basis like that offered. . . .

The settlement of the vast areas of western Canada was a prerequisite to full nationhood and proceeded quickly and peacefully. Never before had such a vast expanse of land been opened to settlement so rapidly with so few disruptive events. The Indians have conducted themselves as the good and loyal subjects of Her Majesty the Queen as they promised in the Treaties they would be.

What do you think?

1. *Why does* Citizens Plus *emphasize the fact that Indian lands were not won through conquest, but through treaty? Why does it emphasize the fact that the Indians were in a weak bargaining position?*
2. *What do you think the government's aim in making treaty with the Indians was? What sort of future for the Indian do you think the government had in mind?*

6. THE RESERVE SYSTEM

Alexander Morris, Lieutenant-Governor of the Northwest Territories and Keewatin, negotiated many treaties with western Indians. He was considered an authority on government Indian policy. The following selection from Morris's The Treaties of Canada with the Indians *(Toronto, Belfort, 1885) represents his views on the Indian future.*

[I wish also to speak of] the allotment of lands to the Indians, to be set aside as reserves for them for homes and agricultural purposes, and which cannot be sold or alienated without their consent, and then only for their benefit; the extent of lands thus set apart being generally one section for each family of five. I regard this system as of great value. It at once secures to the Indian tribes tracts of land which cannot be interfered with by the rush of immigration, and affords the means of inducing them to establish homes and learn the arts of agriculture. I regard the Canadian system of allotting reserves to one or more bands together in the localities in which they have had the habit of living, as far preferable to the American system of placing whole tribes in large reserves which eventually become the object of cupidity to the Whites, and the breaking up of which has so often led to Indian wars and great discontent even if warfare did not result. The Indians have a strong attachment to the localities in which they and their fathers have been accustomed to dwell, and it is desirable to cultivate this home feeling of attachment to the soil. Moreover, the Canadian system of band reserves has a tendency to diminish the offensive strength of the Indian tribes should they ever become restless, a remote contingency if the treaties are carefully observed. Besides, the fact of the reserves being scattered throughout the territories will enable the Indians to obtain markets among the White settlers for any surplus produce they may eventually have to dispose of. It will be found desirable to assign to each family parts of the reserve for their own use so as to give them a sense of property in it, but all power of sale or alienation of such lands should be rigidly prohibited. Any premature enfranchisement of the Indians or power given them to part with their lands would inevitably lead to the speedy breaking up of the reserves and the return of the Indians to their wandering mode of life, and thereby to the re-creation of a difficulty which the assignment of reserves was calculated to obviate. There is no parallel between the condition of the North-Western Indians and that of the Indians who have so long been under the fostering care of the government in the older provinces of Ontario and Quebec.

A very important feature of all the treaties is the giving the Indian bands agricultural implements, oxen, cattle (to form the nuclei of herds), and seed grain.

The Indians are fully aware that their old mode of life is passing away. They are not "unconscious of their destiny"; on the contrary, they are harassed with fears as to the future of their children and the hard present of their own lives. They are tractable, docile, and willing to learn. They recognize the fact that they must seek part of their living from "the mother earth," to use their own phraseology. A chief at Fort Pitt said to me, "I got a plough from Mr. Christie of the Company twelve years ago. I have no cattle; I put myself and my young men in front of it in the spring, and drag it through the ground. I have no hoes; I make them out of the roots of trees. Surely, when the Great Mother hears of our needs, she will come to our help." Such a disposition as this should be encouraged. Induce the Indians to erect houses on their farms and plant their "gardens" as they call them, and then while they are away on their hunts, their wives and children will have houses to dwell in and will care for their patches of corn and grain and potatoes. Then, too, the cattle given them will expand into herds. It is true that the number assigned to each band is comparatively limited, and the government is not bound to extend the number. This was done advisedly by the successive governments of Canada and the commissioners, acting under their instructions, for it was felt, that it was an experiment to entrust them with cattle owing to their inexperience with regard to housing them and providing fodder for them in winter, and owing, moreover, to the danger of their using them for food, if short of buffalo meat or game. Besides, it was felt that as the Indian is, and naturally so, always asking, it was better that if the government saw their way safely to increase the cattle given to any band, it should be not as a matter of right, but of grace and favor, and as a reward for exertion in the care of them and as an incentive to industry. Already, the prospect of many of the bands turning their attention to raising food from the soil is very hopeful.

I said "that their present mode of living is passing away; the Indians are tractable, docile and willing to learn." I think that advantage should be taken of this disposition to teach them to become self-supporting which can best be accomplished by the aid of a few practical farmers and carpenters to instruct them in farming and house-building.

This view was corroborated by my successor, Lieutenant-Governor Laird, who in 1878 reported from Battleford "that if it were possible to employ a few good, practical men to aid and instruct the Indians at seed time, I am of opinion that most of the bands on the Saskatchewan would soon be able to raise sufficient crops to meet their most pressing wants."

It is satisfactory to know, that the government of Canada, decided to act on these suggestions, at least in part, and have during the past summer sent farm instructors into the Plain [*sic*] country. It is to be hoped that this step may prove as fruitful of good results as the earnest desire of the Indians to farm would lead us to believe it may be.

What do you think?

1. *Morris gives eight or nine reasons why he favors the reserve system. What were the motives behind this policy?*
2. *What relationships did Morris envisage between the government and the Indian? Why?*
3. *Evaluate the role of these motives and policies in creating today's situation. Are some of these motives and policies still in action? Elaborate.*

7. OFFICIAL ROBBERIES

Grip *(published by the Toronto* Globe, *an anti-Macdonald paper) was a well-known humor magazine of the day. This cartoon is from the February 13, 1885 issue.*

What do you think?

1. *According to the cartoonist, the government while enfranchising the Indians was at the same time participating in "official robberies." What do you thing these "official robberies" were? Can you think of any similar situations today?*
2. *Though the treaties had received little public attention, there was a furor over the Macdonald franchise. Why? How would the knowledge of this type of incident influence the thinking of Indian leaders today?*

LO! THE POOR INDIAN

MACDOUGALL: For the honor of our country this Indian question ought to be settled at once.

SIR JOHN: The only Indian question that I'm interested in is, Have they got votes?

8. MANITOULIN ISLAND

This is the story of the Manitoulin Island Reserve created in 1836. The excerpt is from Nan Shipley's article "The Twilight of the Treaties," which appeared in Queen's Quarterly *in the summer of 1968.*

In 1836 Sir Francis Bond Head, Governor of Upper Canada, was most anxious to have all the Indians in that part of the country removed from what was then known as the Western frontier to make room for immigrants from the Old World. With this in mind, he arranged that Manitoulin Island be reserved exclusively for the Indians. They had always maintained that this beautiful island had been given to them by the Great Spirit, Manitou. Some fourteen hundred Indians settled there, and although the island covers about a million acres, some of it was good for farming and some only for hunting.

In 1861 the Indians on the island heard that the government was about to propose a treaty for surrender of their "exclusive" reserve. They held a council and agreed not to surrender Manitoulin Island. A few weeks later two commissioners arrived to make treaty. They failed. A second, and more generous offer was made, and this time a few Indians agreed to surrender. A treaty was hurriedly drawn up which would leave the eastern side of the island in the possession of those violently opposed to surrendering any part of the land.

For two years the government then made repeated attempts to gain control of all Manitoulin Island. In 1863 an armed police force arrived to arrest those who still resisted. These Indians were branded as rebels opposing the government and the law because they objected to their land being sold to White men. The editor of the Toronto *Globe* declared: "They [the Indians] cannot be permitted to stand in the way of civilization on this continent. A fine tract of land like the Manitoulin, cannot be permitted to remain uncultivated because it is Indian property. . . ."

What do you think?

1. *What events in Canada today are prompting opinions similar to those of the* Globe *editor above?*

9. SPECIAL COMMISSION, 1858

The Report of the Special Commission to Investigate Indian Affairs in Canada *was published in 1858. The purpose of the commission was to ascertain the "best means of securing the future progress and civilization of the Indian tribes in Canada," and to find the "best mode of so managing the Indian property as to secure its full benefit to the Indians without impeding the settlement of the country." The first selection from this report is the questions that the commissioners sent to various people who worked with Indians. What do these questions reveal about the direction of government policy at that time?*

Queries to the missionaries and others acquainted with the Indians.

1. How long have you had an acquaintance with any body of Indians?
2. What has been their improvement during that time in their moral and religious character and in habits of industry?
3. Do you find them improved in their mode of agriculture to any extent since you first became acquainted with them?
4. What progress have they made in Christianity?
5. Since their conversion to Christianity, are their moral habits improved? What effect has it had upon their social habits?
6. Do the Indians appear sensible of any improvement in their condition?
7. What number are still pagans?
8. What in your opinion is the best mode of promoting their religious improvement?
9. How many schools do you have upon your mission station? And what number of scholars?
10. What number of baptisms have taken place, or do take place at an average yearly, and into what church?
11. What in your opinion is the best mode of promoting the moral, intellectual and social improvement of Indians?
12. Can you offer any suggestion on the expediency and the best means of establishing schools of industry for the Indian youth, and the best system of instruction to be adopted in them?
13. Do the Indians show any aptness for mechanical arts and if so, to what does their genius most lead them?
14. Is the general health of the Indians good as contrasted with neighbouring White population?
15. Do the Indians increase?
16. Do many of them emigrate, and what is the cause of their doing so?

What do you think?

1. *Judging from the questions they asked, what do you think the attitudes of the commissioners were towards the Indians?*
2. *What matters were the commissioners most concerned about? How does this compare with government interests today?*
3. *Describe what you think the government policy was at the time this document was written.*

10. AN INDIAN LOOKS AT WARTIME ALLIANCE

This selection, another excerpt from the 1858 Report, *is the comment of an Indian who had fought with the British army during the War of 1812. He later became an Indian agent and so received the list of questions drawn up by the 1858 commissioners. In his reply he gave his view of the alliance system that the British set up with various tribes during the American Revolution.*

But a wise providence had not designed that so fine a country should remain a waste in the hands of those who could not appreciate its worth, and the "spirits who came in the big canoe with wings," were received with friendly feelings by these sons of nature, who had laid no scheme for self-aggrandisement, or secret plan to demoralize and enslave their visitors. But they were confiding, frank and honest, hence commenced their degradation; a trade was opened, and from that time to the present, the White man has over-reached and plundered them; both parties have coveted the others' goods. The Indian could procure furs without number, and was ignorant of their value, and as the magic production of fire from flint and steel was to him incomprehensible, he must have it; so one to ten beavers were freely given in exchange for a flint and steel or a pinch of vermillion. However, competition in trade soon gave them to understand that the White man's goods, as well as the skins of animals, commanded various prices, and they were taught to tell lies and deceive. White trappers went to hunt on their grounds, and the natives interfered with them, and the destruction of the Red man was contemplated. They had become so fond of "fire water" that even wives or children were not too great a price to pay for it, and their wise men became aware that their people were fading away like the falling leaves in autumn, and proposed driving the intruders back to where they came from. Wars then ensued, and the forests echoed the war yell, the scalp dance and the joyous song around burning victims. The Indians had now acquired wants which they themselves could not supply. The Whites had married some of their squaws . . . The "fire water" and other considerations combined prevented a federal union of the tribes, and they contented themselves by murdering, now and then a White family or an individual whom they might find unprotected.

Previous to this the White men had asked for small portions of ground, about the length of two spear poles to build their wigwams, then a little more to make a garden and so on, all of which were freely granted, with lands for farms and towns, and still they asked for more. In the meantime, the tribes were observed to decrease rapidly, the small pox annually committed its ravages while the White men came over in their "big canoes," and occupied the country, as if it belonged to them, and made the tribes subject to their will. They assumed the Government of their unlimited dominions. The grasping disposition of the French, Spanish, English, and Americans, have despoiled them of the inheritance of their fathers, and there remains to their descendants barely land enough to bury their dead.

When the country was filling up with White people, they disputed amongst themselves as to who should have the largest portion of the Indian lands. The French went to the north and settled in the vicinity of Quebec, and the English who had become very numerous removed along the shores of the "great salt lake." However they quarrelled with their friends on the other side of it, and the English king sent over many canoes full of his warriors to keep the settlers quiet, but they would not obey his voice, and his warriors threatened to enforce obedience. About this time a great English chief (Sir Wm. Johnson,) invited the head men of the tribes to meet him in council at the "Crooked Place." His chief and his officers were dressed in scarlet, a uniform much admired by the natives, and he made great presents to the Indians, giving silver medals and large Union flags to the chiefs, spreading before them the great wampum belt of friendship, and inviting them to take up the tomahawk and join the "Red Coats" in the struggle; on this belt is represented in black figures the head chiefs of each tribe, on one end, a vessel in England said to be loaded with Indian presents, and on the other end the City of Quebec, thus forming a link connecting the two countries. This "Red Coat" told them that the king of England wished to adopt them as his own children, that if they would become his true and faithful allies, he would continue to give them presents as long as water flowed, or trees grew. They accepted the proposal, and exchanged their pipe of peace for the English wampum belt of friendship. The war whoop rang through the woods, the scalpel was sharpened, and the war club fell heavily on the heads of many settlers. But the "Red Coats" were foolish, they would not stand behind the trees but in the open field, and we were beaten. The lands were thus divided, the English taking one portion and allowing the Bostonians or Big Knives to occupy the other. Part of the tribes preferred following the "Red Coats," settling amongst them, giving up their possession for that purpose to other tribes (though bound by the same treaty), and loving their English great father above all other White men. [Other tribes, however,] still thought it imprudent to abandon their vast possessions for that purpose, and therefore determined to remain in the country allotted to the "Big Knives." Before this the "Red Coats" had beaten the French at Quebec, and they had returned to their own country. The Tribes were thus separated, and have been since distinguished by the terms, the "Indians of the Red Coats," and the "Indians of the Big Knives." Their ancestors left them in possession of lands, and hunting grounds sufficient (as they supposed) to keep them and their descendants for ages to come.

The feelings of the remnant of this once numerous race, are expressed to the following effect. From the time of the great council at the "Crooked Place," we have considered ourselves bound to the "Red Coats" by the sacred ties of friendship. They have called us children and we have addressed them by the title "Father." Confiding in their promises we have obeyed their voice at all times, our blood has been spilt, and our warriors slain in their battles, and we are ready at any time to assist as becomes their allies when required.

Our great Father the King had been very kind to us and respected the promises made at the great council. But lately our presents have been stopped and our lands we have been induced to sell for small value, and we see it settled upon by our White brethren, a thriving rich and happy people. But they wish our great mother to take from us, the few acres that remains to our children. However we still trust that the Queen will take pity on us and secure for us at least a place for our graves. We have not been accustomed to labor, and though we see its advantages, we are incapable of farming to the same extent as the Whites. Of late years we have been advised to take the White man's religion, and learn the will of the Great Spirit from the Big Book, and many of our people have followed this advice, and have learned a little from the "Black Coats," but we cannot read. The government established schools all over the country for the White children whilst we are left to take money from our annuities for that purpose. Our children do not learn much. We were in hopes that instead of our presents, the money would have been applied in teaching us to live like our White brethren, but such is not the case, and we now hear that a greater evil is to befall us in the withdrawal of the protecting arm of our great mother by breaking down the Indian Department, through which we have so long enjoyed our privileges, and friendly intercourse with her. Should this bad news be true we are at a loss when to look for real friends in whom we can trust for assistance and counsel.

All of which is respectfully submitted.

Indian office,

Cobourg, 19th August, 1857.

What do you think?

1. *According to this author why did the Indians ally with the British? Why do you think the British sought the alliance?*
2. *To what extent were the terms of the alliance adhered to by later British authorities?*

11. INDIAN AS ALLY

This selection is from a proclamation issued by General Sir Isaac Brock during the War of 1812. (Cited in the Champlain Society's Select British Documents of the Canadian War of 1812.)

Be not dismayed at the unjustifiable threat of the Commander of the Enemies forces, to refuse quarter if an Indian appear in the Ranks. The brave bands of Natives which inhabit this Colony, were, like his Majesty's Subjects, punished for their zeal and fidelity by the loss of their possessions in the late Colonies, and rewarded by his Majesty with lands of superior value in this Province: the Faith of the British Government has never yet been violated, they feel that the soil they inherit is to them and their posterity protected from the base Arts so frequently devised to overreach their simplicity. By what new principle are they to be prevented from defending their property? If their Warfare from being different from that of the White people is more terrific to the Enemy, let him retrace his steps—they seek him not—and cannot expect to find women and children in an invading Army; but they are men, and have equal rights with all other men to defend themselves and their property when invaded, more especially when they find in the enemies Camp a ferocious and mortal foe using the same Warfare which the American Commander affects to reprobate.

This inconsistent and unjustifiable threat of refusing quarter for such a cause as being found in Arms with a brother-sufferer in defence of invaded rights, must be exercised with the certain assurance of retaliation, not only in the limited operations of War in this part of the King's Dominions but in every quarter of the globe, for the National character of Britain is not less distinguished for humanity than strict retributive justice, which will consider the execution of this inhuman threat as deliberate Murder, for which every subject of the offending power must make expiation.

Isaac Brock. Maj. Gen. and President.
God Save the King.
Head Quarters Fort George, 22nd July 1812.
By order of His Honor the President,
J. B. Glegg, Capt. A.D.C.

What do you think?

1. *According to Brock, why did the Indians join with the British during the war? Compare his views to those of the Indian agent on page 125. Account for the differences in their interpretations.*

12. BRITISH POLICY

George F. G. Stanley, in his article "Indian Background to Canadian History" (Canadian Historical Association Report, *1952), described the changes in British Indian policy towards the Indian from the sixteenth to nineteenth centuries.*

With the outbreak of the last long battle for the control of northern North America, it became essential for the Anglo-Americans to ensure the support of the Iroquois Indians. As a result, Sir William Johnson, whose intercourse with the Mohawk had been to say the least friendly, was appointed by the Commander-in-Chief as Superintendent of Indian Affairs, an appointment which was subsequently approved by the crown. Johnson was to be responsible for the conduct of relations with the Indians and it was largely as a result of Johnson's influence that the Mohawk played so important a part in the Seven Years War.

Friendly relations with the Indians had been imposed upon the Anglo-Americans by military necessity. But military necessity did not impose upon the British authorities any policy beyond the traditional promises and presents which were periodically doled out to the Indian nations. There was no real appreciation of the problems arising out of the increasing pressure upon the Indians by the expanding White settlements. Johnson saw the war-clouds gathering but his warnings went unheeded until Pontiac lighted the torches of warfare along the whole of the western frontier. In October 1763 George III took steps to deal with the situation. A proclamation was issued which, among other items, set aside a large western Indian territory and promised that the native peoples would not be "molested or disturbed in the Possession of such Parts of our Dominions and Territories as, not having been ceded to or purchased by Us, are reserved to them, or any of them as their Hunting Grounds". The Proclamation strictly prohibited all royal governors from making grants of land beyond the boundaries of their individual jurisdictions and forbade all private land purchases from the Indians. In effect the Proclamation laid down three main principles: that the Indians possessed rights of prior occupancy, although not of sovereignty, over all lands not formally surrendered by them; that all land surrenders to be legal must be made to the Crown alone; and that all persons unlawfully occupying Indian lands should be expelled by authority of the Crown. These principles constituted a great step in advance in dealing with the Indians. The Proclamation was the first serious attempt made by the British government to deal with the Indian problem and it laid the foundation for the treaty system which was to become the corner-stone of British, and later Canadian, Indian policy.

What do you think?

1. *Outline changing British policy towards the Indians drawing on your knowledge of the early fur trade, the Seven Years War, the Proclamation of 1763, the 1858 Report. Compare the official attitude of today with these policies. What do you think is the main factor determining White-Indian relations in each era? economics? race? religion? war? Do these factors change in importance from era to era? If so, why?*

The Churches

The first missionary to the Indians came out with Simon de Monts in 1604 on the insistence of King Henry IV of France who was determined that the Indians be converted to Christianity. Henry granted a trading monopoly to de Monts only on the condition that de Monts transport missionaries to New France. Thus began the informal alliance between religion and commerce which was to characterize the European invasion. The Jesuits and others were to accompany the fur traders, while in later years Methodists, Anglicans, and Baptists became active as White settlements expanded.

What impact did this peculiar relationship have on the teaching of Christianity to Indians who could see a little distinction between preacher, trader, and farmer? How did the missionaries perceive the Indian? What effects does this still have on the relations between Whites and Indians?

1. TURN-OF-THE CENTURY MISSIONARY

The Reverend Thomas Ferrier, a Methodist missionary, wrote an article for the Methodist Mission Rooms entitled "Our Indians: Their Training for Citizenship" in 1905.

THE METHOD OF ISOLATION IS BAD. GIVE THE INDIANS THE SAME CHANCE AS WE GIVE OUR IMMIGRANTS.

Use the same method of isolation with the immigrant as we use with the Indian and the Canadian nation would soon be destroyed. Use the same methods of distribution, association and opportunity with the Indian as we do with the immigrant and in a few generations our Indians will become a real part of our country's life blood. Any policy would be recognized with serious apprehension that compelled all Germans to locate in a district by themselves, all Swedes in another, all Poles in another, all Norwegians in another, all Russians in another, all Doukhobors in another, all Bukowinians in another, all Galicians in another, all Japanese in another and all Chinese in another; very soon we would have within our borders a German empire, a Swedish kingdom, a Polish principality, a Russian monarchy, Doukhobor, Bukowinian and Galician provinces, a Japanese empire, a Chinese republic. Such results are made impossible from the fact that each settler is free to locate where he pleases with the natural consequence that the Germans, Swedes, Poles, Russians, Doukhobors and Galicians become lost in the influences surrounding them, and they become Canadians, because perforce they speak the English language, observe the country's customs and submit to its laws.

INDIAN RIGHTS. THE RIGHT TO MAKE A MAN OF HIMSELF IS HIS GREATEST RIGHT.

Take any body of civilized people, place them under restrictions similar to those which surround the Indians on the reserve, render it impossible for them to provide against their own necessities, feed and clothe them, compel them to live apart from all elevating influences, give them sums of money for which they have not labored, set a premium upon idleness, make it difficult for them to observe the simplest hygienic laws, appoint an agent over them to see that they do not get away, and in a few years they would degenerate to exactly the condition of an Indian reservation. I do not believe in Indian rights any more than I do in German rights or Irish rights. There should be no special rights. The Indian has the same right to make a man of himself as the White man. He has the same right to live a decent, honest, and industrious life, to become a good citizen with a clean, moral character, and there his rights end. The government owes him more because he is a human being than because he is an Indian.

MANUAL TRAINING OF GREAT IMPORTANCE.

The Indian is accustomed to exercise, but his energies have not been directed to useful channels. Manual training is of the utmost importance. It does not mean teaching the boy a trade but it does mean giving him a training which enables him to get a living and thus become self-dependent and independent. I believe that this is one of the best methods of civilizing the Indian. This feeling of self-dependence will appeal deeply to his manhood, and he will soon begin to realize that he has the ability within himself to compete with his White brother and thus imbibe civilization.

THE INDIAN IS CONSERVATIVE.

The Indian is naturally suspicious of the White man. He clings to the ways of his ancestors, insisting that they are better than ours, and many resent every effort of the government to educate their children or teach them to earn an honest dollar in any way other than their grandfathers did. But they have no objections to appropriations from the government treasury.

SOME OF THE DIFFICULTIES OF BOARDING SCHOOLS.

The difficulty in carrying on the work in a boarding school is often greater. We have cases where the boarding school tends to pauperize the people; the parents and friends come and feed at the school, some go so far as to beg for food for those at home, and sometimes threaten to keep their children at home if such favors are not bestowed upon them. Such constant visitation on the part of the parents provides an opportunity for the pupils to make complaints. This fault finding is usually found to be more in harmony with the fertile imaginations of the child than the facts in the case. The keeping of good order and discipline in these boarding schools is a much greater problem than in a non-reservation school, for often the parent, as well as the child, must be dealt with, and when a parent must be disciplined the task is more difficult. Experience teaches that visits of boarding school pupils to their homes should be as brief and as infrequent as possible.

What do you think?

1. *What appear to be Ferrier's chief concerns? What does this reveal about the role of the missionary during this period? In what ways does this document lend weight to the arguments of James Dumont page 97)?*

2. *How do you think the attitudes expressed by this author about the boarding schools contributed to the Indian education situation today?*
3. *"There should be no special rights." Where have you seen the modern-day equivalent of this assertion? Compare the reason that this author would give for his views to that that the contemporary would give.*

2. THEN AND NOW

This song taken from an 1894 Anglican missionary bulletin, Aurora, *speaks eloquently of the nature of the missionary impulse. It was to be sung by Indian students in mission schools to the tune of "God Bless the Prince of Wales."*

In days of old our fathers, bold
In arts of war must chase
To bend a bow, or scalp a foe,
Gave *strength* the highest place.

Chorus

Then let us praise the peaceful days
Of that Queen Mother's rule,
Whose kindly laws must give us cause
To love our Indian school.

A lawless life, unrest and strife,
Lone graves among the trees;
But heart and brain find higher gain
In nobler crafts than these.

Then let us praise the peaceful days, etc.

'Tis ours to learn the thoughts that burn
In Christian hearts, to train
Both head and hands in heathen lands
From *work* true strength to gain.

Then let us praise the peaceful days, etc.

What do you think?

1. *According to this song why is "work" better than "strength"? Why was the White way of life said to be superior to the Indians?*
2. *Does the fact that Indian children could recite such a song confirm the opinions of James Dumont (page 97) and Howard Adams page 101)? Why?*

3. What implications were there in having Indian education allied to a religion alien to the Indians? What were the effects? Would secular education have benefited the Indian more? Why or why not?

3. FATHER LACOMBE AND THE RIEL REBELLION

The peace-making activities of Oblate Missionary Father Lacombe during the Riel uprising in 1885 are not, perhaps, well known. (Paul Emile Breton: The Big Chief of the Prairies: The Life of Father Lacombe *[Edmonton: Palm Publishers, 1955].)*

In the West the tension continued to increase. Alarmed after a visit to Prince Albert, Saskatchewan, the bishop drew his own conclusions in a letter to the prime minister.

> I have seen the principal Métis of the place," he wrote, "those whom we might call the ringleaders; and I am grieved to realize that they are not the most culpable. They are pushed forward and excited not only by the English half-breeds but by inhabitants of Prince Albert, persons of some prominence and opposed to the government, who hope without doubt to profit by the regrettable steps of the Métis. . . .
>
> It will surely be easy for your government to suppress this sort of revolt which might later have painful consequences, because the Métis can do as they please with the Indians.
>
> How many times have I not addressed myself in letters and conversation to Your Honour, without being able to obtain anything but fine words? . . . I have written at their dictation the complaints and demands of this discontented people; I send them to you again under cover with this. . . .
>
> I implore Your Honour not to be indifferent to this and to act so that this evil may be checked.

Writing in September 1884, the bishop had accurately gauged the situation. The Métis, grieving over their wrongs, were further unsettled by the plaints of English half-breeds and Eastern immigrants. The Indians, warned against the Whites by Sitting Bull's Sioux warriors (The Sioux had moved north into Canada to escape the American army after the Sioux victory at Little Big Horn.) began to sound the drums of alarm. But it was the Métis who acted first, drawing the Indians and some Whites after them. They sent for Riel.

* * * * *

On March 27, 1885, the news sped to Calgary: "War in the Saskatchewan district!" Riel had driven off the North West [Mounted] Police from Batoche the day before.

Excitement reached its climax in the little town that night. People gathered in agitated groups digesting the news. Armed patrols guarded the town; a home guard of 104 men received its orders, and women and children huddled behind locked doors.

Riel's supporters and couriers travelled to neighboring Indian tribes urging them to rise against the government. The Crees had joined the rising. What would the Blackfeet do? The White settlers of Calgary, threatened and isolated, turned to Lacombe for help.

"At that time the Blackfeet were well armed with rifles and they had plenty of cartridges," Lacombe later recalled. "Among the Indians of the North-West there was a kind of general feeling, among the old and the young, that the time was at hand to finish with the White police. Many influential Indians were at that time fomenting the fire of rebellion.

" 'If we are to be mastered by the Whites,' they said, 'and to receive only the crumbs of their tables, it is better for us to be killed by bullets than to starve ignominiously.' Such was the position and such the state of minds when the message of the Cree tobacco reached Crowfoot [the Blackfoot Chief]."

Quickly the priest rushed to the side of his old friend. As usual the wise old leader was listening to the counsels of his people; some wanted peace, others were for war. Crowfoot, more than the other leaders, realized that the days of rebellion and Indian supremacy were past. He wanted to live in peace with the Whites. Lacombe added his warning against the Cree emissaries.

A few days after the brief meeting between Lacombe and Crowfoot, the Indian Commissioner, Edgar Dewdney, arrived from Regina. He sought out Lacombe and arranged for a meeting with the restless Blackfeet. Again Lacombe went to Cluny taking the commissioner with him.

They were met at Cluny by a hundred mounted Indians with Crowfoot at their head. The war-painted braves led the Whites to the Roman Catholic mission, where a grand council of the tribe had been called.

During the council the Indian Commissioner was at pains to assure the Blackfeet that the government intended to protect them, as well as the Whites, from any incursion of the Crees.

"You must shut your ears to all rumors you may hear about the Crees coming to fight you for not joining in their rebellion," he said. "Many soldiers are coming into the country not to hurt you, but to punish the bad Indians for killing the Whites. You have nothing to fear so long as you remain faithful to your treaty."

Crowfoot sat calmly with his people, listening to the words of the

Queen's representative. Not a flicker of emotion crossed the chief's face as he heard the reassuring words. Some of the Blackfeet grumbled, others muttered discontentedly. One word from their chief and dozens of turbulent young warriors would wipe out the Whites in seconds, spreading war westwards to the Rockies.

But Crowfoot was a man of wisdom. He smoked the pipe of peace and then, Blackfeet fashion, he shook hands with his guests.

"We never regretted following the advice of the missionaries," he spoke at last. "Today they want us to be peaceful and not to take part with the Crees. Our great White chief is here with us; so is our agent and all those who take an interest in our welfare. Therefore I say that we must stand on the side of our true friends, and I say that we will stand. Let the Crees and the half-breeds fight against the Whites; as for us, we will be peaceful. I give my word today, in my name and in the name of my people, that nothing need be feared on the part of the Blackfeet, that we will remain loyal."

The same day, Lacombe sent a telegram to the Prime Minister: "I have seen Crowfoot and all the Blackfeet. All quiet. Promised me to be loyal no matter how things may turn elsewhere."

What do you think?

1. *Why do you think Crowfoot realized that the days of Indian supremacy were over?*
2. *How would you describe the relation between the missionaries and the Canadian government, judging by this story?*
3. *Missionaries were usually present at treaty discussions, acting as advisers and interpreters. How do you think Indians saw the relationship between the churches and government? How would this influence their thinking?*
4. *Would this past relationship affect the attitudes of Indians today towards the churches and church schools? How, and to what extent?*

4. OUR HOME, OUR TOMB

In the summer of 1867 a group of Grey Nuns from Quebec made a 10-week, 910-mile journey from St. Boniface (near present-day Winnipeg) to Fort Providence on the Mackenzie. This selection is an excerpt from the journal of one of the nuns, Mother Ward, describing the last part of the journey. (Reverend Father P. Duchaussois: The Grey Nuns in the Far North *[Toronto: McClelland and Stewart, 1919].)*

We should have liked well to stay for a while at Salt River, whether to rest, or to enjoy what was so pleasing and edifying. But it was our duty to go forward still. Two more days and nights brought us to St. Joseph's Mission, Fort Resolution, Great Slave Lake. There the Rev. Father Gascon gave us a thousand welcomes in his humble abode. The poor Father had been a long time alone, and had wondered what the meaning could be of our long delay in coming. There were tears in his eyes, as he kept looking from the Bishop to us, and from us to the Bishop, seemingly not quite sure whether he was awake or dreaming. He would have wished us to make a long stay at Fort Resolution, but the Bishop wanted to move on, as the weather was fine. It must have been Father Gascon's prayers and tears, like those of St. Scholastica, which brought on a storm. The Lake was so rough that we were obliged to remain two days at St. Joseph's Mission.

We were now in the last stage of our journey, and it was with pleasure that we set sail once more. Great Slave Lake is an inland sea, and a veritable cave of all the winds. We had to plough through its waves very slowly. Sometimes after sailing for a couple of hours, we had to put into land, and to remain for a whole day waiting for the storm to go down. These forced delays were all the more trying because we knew that we were so near our destination, so near the end of what seemed a never-ending journey. On August 27 we sailed for many hours, though the wind was not favourable. Towards evening it turned, and, in the hope of getting to La Providence the sooner, we decided to spend the night on board. An unlucky decision it was, for the wind soon changed again, the clouds gathered thick and black, and we soon were stranded. All night we remained exposed to the rain and the cold. Sleep was out of the question. Fortunately, this was the last of our many arduous adventures.

The light of the morning star was enough to show our guide where we were. He called up the boatmen, and in a short time we landed for breakfast on a little island, where the waters of the Great Lake rush out to form the broad Mackenzie. *Deo Gratias!* A few hours more, and we shall be at home!

Yet those hours seemed long, and it was only at three o'clock in the afternoon that we saw a flag flying on the Bishop's house. Gradually, other obstacles stood out quite clearly, and soon we saw on the bank a crowd of Indians and others, cheering our arrival, and firing off volleys in the gaiety of their hearts. We responded by intoning the *Magnificat*, and it was whilst we sang our Lady's hymn that we were welcomed by the Rev. Father Grouard, Brother Alexis and Brother Boisramé, and all the people. We were ashore, in a strange, though longed-for, land in our new country, our home, our tomb.

And now, dearest Mother General, is there anything more that I have to say? Never, since our arrival, have we regretted coming: never for a moment have we been unhappy. That does not at all mean that we have all that we can wish for! There are, in truth, many sacrifices to be made. But it was in order to make them that we came here. We find it rather hard to get used to the coarse food, which is always the same. We never taste bread.

Adieu, dearest Mother! This paper, happier than ourselves, will find its way into the bosom of our loved community. We can only follow it in spirit. Or, rather, we shall go before it, for our thoughts fly back more quickly there. Adieu, good and dear Sisters all! Most probably, we shall never see one another again in this world. Adieu, until the blessed day of our meeting in a happier land! Please to remember us, day by day, at the foot of the altar, in our own old home, and again near the shrine of our venerated Foundress, Mother d'Youville."

What do you think?

1. *From the description of Father Gascon, and from the thoughts of Mother Ward herself, describe the life that new missionaries saw themselves entering, and the life that awaited them. What sort of people do you think these missionaries were? What attitudes might the Indians have had towards them?*

5. THE CREE ALPHABET

In 1841 at Norway House, four hundred miles north of present-day Winnipeg, James Evans, an English Methodist missionary, transcribed the Cree language into a phonetic alphabet. (John Maclean: James Evans: Inventor of the Syllabic System of the Cree Language *[Toronto: Methodist Mission Rooms, 1890].)*

When James Evans had got settled down to his work, he began with his accustomed energy to study the Cree language, conscious of the increased influence wielded by the missionary when able to speak to the natives in their own tongue. He found two efficient and willing helpers in Mr. and Mrs. Ross, the factor and his wife. An old Hudson's Bay employee who went to Norway House nearly fifty years ago, informed the writer that Mrs. Ross rendered the chief help to the missionary in studying the language. It was a comparatively easy task for James Evans to master the Cree tongue, as he was thoroughly conversant with the Ojibway language, and as these belonged to the Algonquin family of languages, their grammatical construction was similar. Possessing this advantage added to his natural aptitude for studying philology, he was not long in gaining knowledge sufficient to enable him to carry on a short conversation, and with the help of an interpreter, translate accurately and with force portions of the Scriptures and hymns.

Quick to observe the principles of language, and ever desirous of utilizing his knowledge for the benefit of others, he beheld with joy the recurrence of certain vowel sounds, which when fully grasped might prove of great service in simplifying language and preparing a literature for the people. The wandering bands of Indians which visited Norway House aroused the sympathies of the missionary, and he longed for some method by which he could send to distant camps of red men the knowledge of Christ and His salvation. Pondering deeply, working meanwhile and praying to the Most High for assistance, at last in the year 1841, the Cree syllabic system was completed, the alphabet distributed among the Indians, and placed in the school, and instruction given in its arrangement. In less than one year from his advent to Norway House, he had devised and perfected the syllabic system upon which his enduring fame rests.

When the invention had been made, the first thought was how to utilize it for the benefit of the Indians. There was no printing press, type or paper, and it was impossible to get any. Naturally enough, the Hudson's Bay Company officials objected to the introduction of a printing press, lest that mighty censor of modern times, the newspaper, should find a location within the domains of the Company, and a powerful antagonist to its interests arise. The missionary, ever fertile in resources, whittled his first type from blocks of wood with his pocket-knife, made ink from the soot of the chimney, and printed his first translations upon birch-bark. Afterward he made moulds, and taking the lead from the tea chests, and old bullets, cast his first leaden type from these. In January, 1889, the writer called upon the Rev. Dr. Evans of London, Ontario, who informed him that his brother, before leaving Norway House for England, burned nearly all his manuscripts. Dr. Evans was in England in 1841, attending missionary meetings under the auspices of the Wesleyan Missionary Society, when a letter came from his brother from Norway House with rough castings of the Cree syllabic characters. The letter asked the Wesleyan Missionary Society to call on the Hudson's Bay Company authorities to obtain permission to have a printing press sent into their territory. Dr. Evans worked hard in conjunction with Drs. Alder and Elijah Hoole, to secure this permission, and a press and font of type were sent to James Evans. These were allowed to go into the country after Dr. Evans and the missionary authorities had given a pledge that the materials would not be used for any purpose but religious instruction. The aged minister has now in his possession in his home in London, Ontario, some of the original type made by James Evans, from tea lead and bullets. He has also some old books made of birch-bark, and others made of paper, printed in the Cree syllabic characters, and bound by the inventor himself.

The invention was in a very short period understood by the Indians, who were able to master it in a few days. The writer has heard Steinhauer and Young repeatedly state that a clever Indian, on being shown the characters in the morning, was able to read the Bible by their use before the sun went down the same day, and that one week was all that was necessary for the average Indian to master thoroughly all the characters, and to use them accurately. A careful writer like Semmens has said that, "One month was all the time considered necessary to enable even the dullest to read for himself the words of life and liberty."

What do you think?

1. *On page 100 Bishop Watton of Moosonee said that missionaries were responsible for giving Indians the opportunity to have a written culture.*
   (a) Was this James Evans's goal?
   (b) Would modern Indians construe Evans's invention as an interference with Indian culture? Why or why not?
2. *What do you think was the position and power of the Hudon's Bay Company in the North at this time? Would the Company help or hinder missionary work? Would the missionary work help or hinder Company business? Explain.*

6. BROTHER! LISTEN TO WHAT WE SAY

Indian oratory was justly renowned. This speech, delivered in 1805, is taken from an article entitled "Great Indian Orators" which appeared in The Outdoorsman, *July-August 1968.*

Brother, our seats [lands] were once large, and yours were small. You have now become a great people, and we have scarcely a place left to spread our blankets. You have got our country, but are not satisfied; you want to force your religion upon us.

Brother, continue to listen. You say that you are sent to instruct us how to worship the Great Spirit agreeable to his mind; and if we do not take hold of the religion which you White people teach, we shall be unhappy hereafter. You say that you are right, and we are lost. How do we know this to be true? We understand that your religion is written in a book. If it was intended for us as well as you, why has not the Great Spirit given to us—and not only to us, but to our forefathers—the knowledge of that book, with the means of understanding it rightly? We only know what you tell us about it. How shall we know when to believe, being so often deceived by the White people?

Brother, you say there is but one way to worship and serve the Great Spirit. If there is but one religion, why do you White people differ so much about it? Why not all agree as you can all read the book?

Brother, we do not understand these things. We are told that your religion was given to your forefathers, and has been handed down from father to son. We, also, have a religion which was given to our forefathers, and has been handed down to us, their children. We worship in that way. It teaches us to be thankful for all favors we receive; to love each other, and be united. We never quarrel about religion, because it is a matter which concerns each man and the Great Spirit.

Brother, we do not wish to destroy your religion or take it from you; we only want to enjoy our own.

What do you think?

1. *Compare the comments of this 1805 Indian leader to those of James Dumont.*
2. *Would this speech be more attractive or less attractive to a modern White audience than to one in 1805? Why or why not?*

7. THE CATHOLIC MISSIONARY DRIVE

The French government was primarily interested in converting the Indian. Lescarbot, author of the 1618 History of New France *is quoted in* Native Rights in Canada *(Indian-Eskimo Association, 1972).*

And as the over-conscientious make difficulties everywhere I have at times seen some who doubted if one could justly occupy the lands of New France, and deprive thereof the habitants; to whom my reply has been in few words, that these people are like the man of whom its is spoken in the Gospel, who had wrapped-up in a napkin the talent which had been given unto him, instead of turning it to account, and therefore it was taken away from him. And therefore, as God the Creator has given the earth to man to possess it, it is very certain that the first title of possession should appertain to the children who obey their Father and recognized Him, and who are, as it were, the eldest children in the House of God, as are the Christians, to whom pertaineth the division of the earth rather than to the disobedient children, who have been driven from the House, as unworthy of the heritage and of that which dependeth thereon.

But I would not have these tribes exterminated, as the Spanish has those of the West Indies, taking as pretext Commandments formerly given to Joshua, Gideon, Saul and other warriors of God's people. For we are under the law of grace, the law of gentleness, piety and pity, wherein our Saviour hath said: "learn of me, for I am meek and lowly in heart," and likewise "come unto Me, all ye that labor and are heavy laden, and I will give you rest"; and not, "I will route you out." Moreover, these poor Indian tribes were defenseless in the presence of those who have ruined them, and did not resist as did those people of whom the Holy Scripture makes mention —and further, if it was intended that the conquered be destroyed, in vain would the same Saviour have said to his Apostles: "Go ye into all the world, and preach the Gospel to every creature." The earth, pertaining, then, by divine right to the children of God, there is here no question of applying the law and policy of Nations, by which it would not be permissible to claim the territory of another. This being so, we must possess it and preserve its natural inhabitants, and plant therein, the name of Jesus Christ and of France, since today many of your children have the unshakeable resolution to dwell there with their families. The inducements are great enough to attract men of valor and of worth, who are spurred on by goodly and honourable ambition to be the first in the race for immortality by this action, which is the greatest men can set before themselves.'

What do you think?

1. *On what basis does Lescarbot justify the taking over of Indian lands? Do you agree with his arguments? Why or why not?*
2. *Indian citizenship was conditional on their conversion to Christianity. What sort of conditions are imposed on Indians today for them to achieve full "citizenship"?*

Economics

How powerful a factor is economics in determining events? What differences in life-style and values did the coming of a Western economy impose on the Indian? To what extent did the developing economy of Canada create the changes in government policy which influence Indian-White relations to this day?

This section has been designed to encourage you to probe some of the questions.

1. THE HONEST ACTIVITIES OF CIVILIZATION

In February 1891 the editor of a Methodist mission paper The Canadian Indian *made a suggestion for aiding the Indians.*

The Indian, constantly driven away from experience and back upon himself, will remain his old self or grow worse under the aggravations and losses of the helps to his old active life, in the destruction of game and the buffalo; and unless opportunities are forced upon him, must either disappear or die out. Any policy which invites the Indian to become an individual and brings him into the honest activities of civilization and especially into the atmosphere of our agricultural, commercial and industrial examples, assures to him mental, moral and physical development into independent manhood. An Indian boy, placed in a family remote from his home (and it is better distant from the school), surrounded on all sides by hardworking; industrious people, feels at once a stronger desire to do something for himself than he can be made to feel under any collective system, or in the best Indian training school that can be established. His self-respect asserts itself; he goes to work, behaves himself, and tries in every way to compete with those about him. For the time he in a measure forgets the things that are behind, and pushes on towards a better life.

What do you think?

1. *What is this author proposing for the improvement of the Indian condition? What brought the Indian to that condition?*
2. *"Once the economic foundation of a culture has been destroyed, the culture must disappear." Does this document support this comment? To what extent is this general statement true for the Indian people today?*

2. THE OPENING OF THE WEST

Robert Ignatius Burns, S.J., in Jesuits and the Indian Wars of the West *(New Haven: Yale University Press, 1966), relates the history of the Oregon Territory Indians after the coming of the fur trade. The book was written from an American point of view, but its insights hold true generally for Canada's western Indians.*

The important event for the Interior Indians was the penetration of their region by the British and Americans. In 1805 Lewis and Clark, the most famous of the land explorers here, made their way over the Rockies and down to the sea. Fur companies of both nations came hard upon their heels, inaugurating a brief era of cutthroat rivalry. After 1821 the Hudson's Bay Company by merger and maneuver became supreme; Americans continued to trade in the mountains, especially up to 1837. From Fort Vancouver, located at the mouth of the Columbia River, the Company began its quarter-century career as the major White presence in the Oregon country Interior.

The tiny posts of the Company were physically an insignficant addition in this vast region, but they were to mark the Indian way of life deeply. Firearms, blankets, fishhooks, tobacco, knives, utensils, cloth, and trade goods of all kinds now became common. The Company persuaded various bands to start vegetable plots, then taught them beekeeping, herding, and other elementary disciplines. The Indians, taking a giant stride away from their immemorial isolation, were excited by the ways of these fantastic strangers and were conditioned to accept the White presence. They soon came to respect the Company and prize its trade. The militaristic tribes among them were especially enthusiastic; they were desperate for guns, because their encroaching Plains enemies had them. They could now recover the offensive, and even indulge more effectively in intramural raiding. In a hunting economy the gun complemented the horse. Forty Flathead hunters, for instance, could bring down three hundred deer in a day. Eventually this new efficiency was bound to diminish both game and furs, but for a blissful interim period cultural development accelerated.

Hudson's Bay employees, mostly French Canadians and Iroquois with Scots overseers, could travel anywhere in comparative safety. They married into the many tribes, subtly influencing tribal habits and psychology. By this time many of the nameless Interior "tribes" answered to French names, chosen by the traders for reasons trivial or fanciful or erroneous. These appellations the later Whites usually retained either in an English version (Snakes, Kettles, Flatheads) or in badly pronounced French (Nez Percés, Coeur d'Alenes).

The eventful years to about 1840 were generally happy for the Interior Indian. He hardly realized that a Pandora's box of trouble had been unlocked. Yet the White man's diseases were spreading recurrently through the tribes, taking a toll more terrible than any Black Death known to Europe's history. Over two-thirds of the Indians of the Pacific Northwest simply disappeared. In 1780 there were perhaps 75,000 in the future American portion of the Oregon country (exclusive of the Plains area); after 1830 there may have been less than 20,000. In 1782 it was smallpox, in 1831 fever and ague, in 1835 smallpox again, and so on. The smallpox of 1846, the measles of 1847, and the smallpox of 1852–53 were terrible killers in the Interior. Tuberculosis and venereal diseases ravaged the coastal Indians.

On the Coast these disasters were compounded by another kind of plague. Tribal morals disintegrated under the impact of bad example; the Indian was fatally attracted to the worse elements of the frontier population. Wholesale prostitution and ruinous alcoholism were one stage of his descent into misery. So painful was the spectacle that some sympathetic Whites felt it a mercy when disease swept away almost whole tribes. Catholic missionaries were later to remark upon the rapid decline of the Indian character as White settlement increased.

Like the arrival of the first ants at a picnic, the trading ships and fur posts were only an advance guard. The White invasion had begun. Ironically, the coming of the first missionaries in 1834 was to swell the invasion to proportions that the Indians could no longer tolerate. The time was the period just before and after 1840. The crucial place was the final stretch along the Oregon Trail.

* * * * *

The 1840s were to be as much a turning point in the Interior Indians' history as the era following the acquisition of the horse had been, a century before. Protestant and Catholic missions were active there. Indian society was split into antagonistic levels—pagan and Christian, Protestant and Catholic, friends of the Americans and traditionalists. Some Indians would have nothing to do with the White man's religion. Others were attracted superficially, or were greedy for status or advantage, or simply curious. Conversions had the effect of slowly altering the folkways and Indian personality. And ominously, all this time, the great stream of American wagon trains kept rolling up the Oregon Trail and out to the Coast. The Indian looked upon the Trail's great swath with its litter and could hardly believe that any Whites were left in the East. Then, before 1850, political control of the whole Interior passed by treaty from the deft management of the Hudson's Bay traders into the brasher hands of American pioneers.

The general appearance of the country remained much the same. The timeless face of the Interior bore only the scar of the Oregon Trail. But many tribesmen could discern an oppressive change of atmosphere. The masters were arriving. These were not the "French" but the "Bostons," who mistrusted the inferior Indian, a multitudinous people who meant to settle everywhere and take over the land. Already the pelts and game were less plentiful. Already disease and liquor had worked their deadly ravages. Agitators, some of whom had been educated in White towns and shrewdly read the future, were stirring up the Interior tribes. Soon war parties began riding. Just before 1850 came the Whitman Massacre at the Presbyterian mission, with the concomitant Cayuse War. Protestant missionary work in the Interior ceased. Catholic work was disturbed for a decade.

There ensued a quarter century of Indian retreat. The government labored to immobilize the tribes, proposing separate treaties with them and relegating them to reservations. Government promises were broken again and again; those fulfilled were capriciously timed. Indian affairs were now conducted by a civilian Indian bureau rather than by the army. Agents robbed the tribes. Towns came and the game fled. Out on the Plains the buffalo disappeared. Waves of miners took the Indian lands. Squatters interfered with the communal Indian fishing rights, and stripped Indian holdings of their timber. Despite the availability of better lands elsewhere, settlers hurried westward like lemmings.

Ugly incidents multiplied. Wars erupted and ran their course. Garrisons sprang up close at hand. The reservation Indian, deprived of his traditional economy, living in a tribal framework no longer very functional or meaningful, was a man exploited, insecure, and hopeless. Native apathy intensified to a maximum. By 1880 the Indian was a despised inferior in his own country, caught between two ways of life and thought. In the southwestern corner of the Interior, where this evolution began earlier, a Catholic missioner saw the process far advanced by 1862. The "Americanized Indians" on their "melancholy" reservations, he wrote sadly, were not the same kind of men he had encountered at his arrival fifteen years previously.

In some ways the country still had not changed. The absolute number of Whites in the Interior was absurdly small. One might ride far without encountering a road or a house. But consider a chief just seventy-five years old, born at the time Lewis and Clark penetrated the Interior, already a young warrior when the Hudson's Bay Company built its first posts, a mature chief when the pioneer missionaries came, and a man of fifty years when government treaties were signed with the powerful Interior tribes. To such a chief these declining twenty-five years of his life had been the end of his world.

What do you think?

1. *What characteristics of White civilization did the fur trade introduce to the Indian? With what effects?*
2. *(a) What was the traditional economy of these Indians? Why did its loss endanger their culture, life-style, and social structure?*
   (b) How can modern Indians strengthen these modes without the traditional economy?
3. *How are the reasons for Indian alcoholism in the nineteenth century paralleled today? Explain.*
4. *What areas of Canada are now undergoing the process described in this document? What are the similarities and differences, if any?*

3. DISLOCATION OF DISEASE

David Thompson, explorer and map-maker, came to Canada in 1784 at the age of fourteen to work with the Hudson's Bay Company as a clerk in the fur trade. In 1788 Thompson wintered with Saukamappee, a seventy-five-year old Peigan Indian who told the young adventurer his life's story. The old Indian described the smallpox epidemic that had ravaged his people just a few years before. The disease was unknown to North America before the Europeans arrived so the Indian had no immunity or protection against it. Its effects were so far-reaching that the once stable economy and life-style of the Indian was drastically disrupted. This excerpt is taken from David Thompson: Travels in Western North America *(Toronto: Macmillan, 1971) edited by Victor G. Hapwood.*

We thus continued to advance through the fine plains to the Stag [probably the Red Deer] River, when death came over us all, and swept more than one half of us by the smallpox, of which we knew nothing until it brought death among us. We caught it from the Snake Indians. Our scouts were out for our security, when some returned and informed us of a considerable camp which was too large to attack and [had] something very suspicious about it. From a high knoll they had a good view of the camp, but saw none of the men hunting or going about; there were a few horses, but no one came to them, and a herd of bisons [were] feeding close to the camp, with other herds near. This somewhat alarmed us as a stratagem of war; and our warriors thought this camp had a larger not far off, so that if this camp was attacked, which was strong enough to offer a desperate resistance, the other would come to their assistance and overpower us, as had been once done by them and in which we had lost many of our men.

The council ordered the scouts to return and go beyond this camp, and be sure there was no other. In the meantime we advanced our camp. The scouts returned and said no other tents were near, and the camp appeared in the same state as before. Our scouts had been going too much about their camp and were seen; they expected what would follow, and all those that could walk, as soon as night came on, went away.

Next morning at the dawn of day, we attacked the tents, and with our sharp flat daggers and knives cut through the tents and entered for the fight; but our war whoop instantly stopped; our eyes were appalled with terror; there was no one to fight with but the dead and dying, each a mass of corruption.

We did not touch them, but left the tents, and held a council on what was to be done. We all thought the bad spirit had made himself master of the camp and destroyed them. It was agreed to take some of the best of the tents, and any other plunder that was clean and good, which we did, and also took away the few horses they had, and returned to our camp.

The second day after this, dreadful disease broke out in our camp, and spread from one tent to another as if the bad spirit carried it. We had no belief that one man could give it to another, any more than a wounded man could give his wound to another. We did not suffer so much as those that were near the river, into which they rushed and died. We had only a little brook, and about one-third of us died, but in some of the other camps there were tents in which every one died.

When at length it left us, and we moved about to find our people, it was no longer with the song and the dance, but with tears, shrieks, and howlings of despair for those who would never return to us. War was no longer thought of, and we had enough to do to hunt and make provisions for our families, for in our sickness we had consumed all our dried provisions. But the bisons and red deer were also gone; we did not see one-half of what was before; whither they had gone to we could not tell; we believed the Good Spirit had forsaken us, and allowed the bad spirit to become our master. What little we could spare we offered to the bad spirit to let us alone and go to our enemies. To the Good Spirit we offered feathers, branches of trees, flowers, and sweet-smelling grass.

Our hearts were low and dejected, and we shall never be again the same people. To hunt for our families was our sole occupation and [to] kill beavers, wolves, and foxes to trade [for] our necessaries; and we thought of war no more, and perhaps would have made peace with them [the enemy], for they had suffered dreadfully as well as us, and had left all this fine country of the Bow River to us.

What do you think?

1. *Why were the Indians particularly susceptible to the ravages of smallpox?*
2. *What changes do you think such an epidemic made in the Indian economy and life-style?*

4. FLING ALL THESE THINGS AWAY

Canadian historian W. J. Eccles in The Ordeal of New France *(CBC Publications, 1965) quotes the message Pontiac sent around to his people on the eve of his extremely effective campaign against the English colonists in 1763.*

Why do you suffer the White men to dwell among you? . . . Why do you not clothe yourselves in skins, as your ancestors did, and use the bows and arrows, and the stone-pointed lances, which they used? . . . You have bought guns, knives, kettles, and blankets, from the White men, until you can no longer do without them; and, what is worse, you have drunk the poison firewater, which turns you into fools. Fling all these things away . . . And as for these English . . . you must lift the hatchet against them. . .

What do you think?

1. *Why did Pontiac instruct his followers to "fling all these things away"?*
2. *What were Pontiac's reasons for going to war?*
3. *In what way could it be said that the Indian-White wars were based on a conflict of economies? How far would you care to take this theory of economic conflict? Explain.*

5. THE FUR TRADE

Baron de Lahontaine, a French visitor to the New World, in his New Voyage to North America, *dating back to the eighteenth century, described the early trading with the Indians. (Lahontaine, Baron de:* New Voyage to North America *[Chicago: McClurg, 1905].)*

As soon as the French Ships arrive at Quebec, the merchants of that City who have their Factours in the other Towns, load their Barques with Goods in order to transport 'em to their other Towns. Such Merchants as act for themselves at Trois Rivières, or Montreal, they come down in Person to Quebec to Market for themselves, and then put their Effects on board of Barques, to be convey'd home. If they pay for their Goods in Skins, they buy cheaper than if they made their payments in Money or Letters of Exchange; by reason that the Seller gets considerably by the Skins when he returns to France. Now, you must take notice, that all these Skins are bought up from the Inhabitants, or from the Savages, upon which the Merchants are considerable Gainers. To give you an instance of this matter. A Person that lives in the Neighbourhood of Quebec, carries a dozen of Martins Skins, five or six Foxes Skins, and as many Skins of wild Cats, to a Merchants House, in order to sell 'em for Woollen Cloth, Linen, Arms, Ammunition, etc. In the truck of their Skins, the Merchant draws a double profit, one upon the score of his paying no more for the Skins, than one half of what he afterwards sells 'em for in the lump to the Factours for the Rochel Ships; and the other by the exorbitant rate he puts upon the Goods that the poor Planter takes in exchange for his Skins. If this be duly weigh'd, we will not think it strange that these Merchants have a more beneficial Trade, than a great many other Tradesmen in the World. In my seventh and eighth Letter, I related the particulars of the Commerce of this Country, especially that which the Inhabitants carry on with the Savages, who supply 'em with the Skins of Beavers, and other Animals. So that now it remains only to give you an Inventory of the Goods that are proper for the Savages. . . .

Powder.
Ball and cut Lead, or Small-shot.
Axes both great and small.
Knives with their Sheaths.
Sword-blades to make Darts of.
Kettles of all sizes.
Shoomakers Awls.
Fish-hooks, of all sizes.
Flint Stones.
Caps of blew Serge.
Shirts made of the common Brittany Linnen.
Woolsted Stockins, short and coarse.
Brazil Tobacco.
Coarse white Thread for Nets.
Sewing Thread of several colours.
Pack-thread.
Vermillion.
Needles, both large and small.
Venice Beads.
Some Iron Heads for Arrows, but few of 'em.
A small quantity of Soap.
A few Sabres or Cutlasses.
Brandy goes off incomparably well.

What do you think?

1. *Why was the fur trade a sound business venture?*
2. *Why were there only a few arrowheads sold to the Indians? What were the economic implications of this, particularly in the West?*
3. *"Brandy goes off incomparably well." Why? What did this liquor trade mean for the life-style of the Indian?*

4. What effect would the acquisition of these Western gadgets have on the way Indians make their living? How would this in turn influence their culture? Are there any parallel developments today in our country or in other countries?

6. ECONOMIC IMPACT ON THE CREES

E. Palmer Patterson II in his The Canadian Indian: A History Since 1500 *(Toronto: Collier-Macmillan of Canada, 1972) discusses the changes experienced by the Cree Indians through their involvement with the fur trade.*

In many cases, as we have seen, the impact of the new culture on the Indians had proceeded westward ahead of the actual physical presence of the White men. In the Eastern Woodlands, and along the edge of the Prairies, we have already noted the role of the Ojibways and Ottawas as transmitters of elements of the new influence. Still another people, to the north and west of them, had begun to experience this impact by the late seventeenth century. These were the Crees. The ramifications of White impact are perhaps nowhere better illustrated in Canada than in the case of the Crees. Their northern and western migrations, which eventually led to their occupancy of land from Ontario to the Rockies, saw them change into two groups—Woodland and Plains, brought them into sharper and fiercer conflict with their neighbours, the Blackfoot and the northern Athabascans, and through their contact with the white man led to the creation of a large Cree-White population of Métis which is so important to later events in the history of Canada.

The Crees are divided into two main subdivisions, the Woodland Crees and the Plains Crees, but in the seventeenth century they were not yet differentiated, and lived in the area south and southwest of Hudson Bay, in the Lake Nipigon area and along the Eastmain River, roughly the area occupied by the Woodland Crees in 1900. By mid-seventeenth century some of the Crees were already involved in the fur trade. They rendezvoused in the summer with middlemen such as the Ottawas and the Nipissings. In their practice of coming to the shores of the lakes in the summer and returning to the interior in the winter, they followed a pattern like that of the eastern Algonkians and northern Athabascans, a pattern which was to continue for some Indians of northern Ontario until the twentieth century. The Crees were eager to get trade goods, and by 1670 some of them were dependent on traders for part of their food supply. The commodity desired and available at posts like the Sault was corn; it was nutritious and easily transported.

The coming of the Hudson's Bay Company in 1670 altered the situation of the Crees. Not only did they now have a choice of French or

English goods, but they became middlemen as well. From having been on the extreme western edge of the trading relations they were, after 1670, in direct contact with their European source of goods. . . . The pattern of power and influence which had passed thus far across the continent with the acquisition of certain European trade items was now to work on the Crees. The Crees quickly became allies of the Hudson's Bay Company and entrenched as middlemen in the trade with more remote peoples. This position they guarded jealously, as had the Ottawas in their situation earlier and the Hurons and Algonkians before them. David Mandelbaum asserts that they readily adapted to new weapons, tools, and utensils, and the trading trip to the Hudson's Bay Company post became an important annual event.

Armed with guns and seeking furs, they pushed out gradually into the Prairies, where they formed an alliance with their Assiniboine neighbours, a Sioux-speaking people, to fight against the Dakota Sioux. They also fought with their Athabascan neighbours, especially the Chipewyans, whom they tried to keep from first-hand contact with the Hudson's Bay Company. For a time they succeeded in pushing these northern neighbors farther northward, but by the end of the eighteenth century a general peace seems to have been established.

The extension of French posts into the Prairies in the eighteenth century, especially due to the efforts of La Verendrye, again provided the Crees with a bargaining position between French and English competitors. N. M. Crouse does not specify any particular Indians when he asserts that the French were preferred to the English; on the contrary, he states: "The English did not permit them to come within their fortifications, but held them at arm's length and selected what they wanted from their stock of furs, giving them in return what they though was a fair price." This looks like poor business practice on the part of the Hudson's Bay Company in a competitive situation. Another writer, however, concluded that on the basis of information gained from accounts of traders, no important difference existed between the English and the French in their tolerance, understanding, or rapport with the Indians. Nor is there evidence, according to Lewis Saum, that the French or English traders were themselves aware of any differences between themselves regarding their relations with Indians.

The conflicts between Crees and other groups did not foster the best trading conditions and both French and English prevailed upon the Crees, with varying degrees of success, to end their hostilities with adjacent peoples. Fighting between the Plains Crees and their enemies was due mainly to raiding for horses rather than for territory or trade advantages. In addition to local trade, Crees served as guides for English exploration and also carried furs as far as Montreal.

David Mandelbaum, in his classic monograph on the Plains Crees, sums is up thusly:

Within one hundred years after the arrival of the Whites the Crees moved westward. The fur trade impelled the movement, the gun enabling them to push other people before them. They were brought to the fringes of the prairie country in their quest for fresh fur-trapping areas. Because of their function as middlemen in the trade, they traveled into the plains to carry goods to distant tribes. Their superior armaments enabled them to gain a foothold in the plains.

By the 1730s some of the Crees were permanently out on the Prairies. Their wealth and power due to the trade made them a popular people for others to adhere to. Thus, by the late eighteenth century, they seem to have attracted adherents from several other peoples including Assiniboines, Ojibways, Dakotas, and Athabascans. The Crees probably first acquired horses in the 1770's, the more westerly bands getting them before those to the east. Their main sources were most likely the Blackfoot and Assiniboine.

An increase in population was drawing them westward. This is to be correlated with their deep involvement in the fur trade, exhaustion of nearby sources, and the desire to open up new areas or exploit more thoroughly existing sources which made expansion desirable and, indeed, a necessity. By the mid-eighteenth century they were in "economic subservience" to the European economy. Their livelihood was in the grip of European fashions for fur garments as a stylish item of apparel. The pattern already noted for the more easterly Indians was being repeated. Their expansion served as a continued source of irritation to their neighbours, producing the threat of clashes already noted.

What do you think?

1. *Describe the effects on the Crees of their involvement with the fur trade. What were the effects on their neighbours?*
2. *What was the role of the Hudson's Bay Company in establishing the Crees as a powerful, imperialistic nation?*
3. *"By the mid-eighteenth century they were in 'economic subservience' to the European economy." What was the significance of this position for the future of Cree-White dealings?*

7. THE HURON-IROQUOIS WAR

Some historians say that the Huron-Iroquois War of the mid-seventeenth century, which ravaged Huronia and almost destroyed the Huron nation, was a direct result of the fur trade. According to this theory, the Iroquois were anxious to control the water routes to the West which were in Huron-held territory. The Hurons were backed by the French, the Iroquois by the British. This selection from a Jesuit report is from Edna Kentor: The Indians of North America *(New York: Harcourt Brace Jovanovich, Inc., 1927).*

But of these matters I will write more fully at another time. For, in truth, our Hurons are distressed not only by war, but by a deadly famine and a contagious plague; all are miserably perishing together. Everywhere, corpses have been dug out of the graves; and, now carried away by hunger, the people have repeatedly offered, as food, those who were lately the dear pledges of love,—not only brothers to brothers, but even children to their mothers, and the parents to their own children. It is true, this is inhuman; but it is no less unusual among our savages than among the Europeans, who abhor eating flesh of their own kind. Doubtless the teeth of the starving man make no distinction in food, and do not recognize in the dead body him who a little before was called, until he died, father, son, or brother. Nay, more, even the dung of man or beast is not spared. Fortunate are they who can eat the food of swine,—bitter acorns, and husks,—innocent food, and indeed not without relish, to which hunger adds a sauce; to these, the scarcity of this year has given a value far higher than, formerly, was usually placed upon Indian corn.

This calamity of our people was, though destructive to their bodies, salutary to their souls,—for, up to this time, our labors have not yielded greater fruits; never before has faith gone more deeply into hearts, or the name of Christian been more glorious, than in the midst of the disasters to a stricken people. We count more than three thousand savages baptized this last year. . . . At present there remain in this mission thirteen Fathers, four coadjutors, twenty-two donnes, eleven other domestics (to whom alone are paid very modest wages), six soldiers, and four boys,—sixty souls in all; to these, heavenly things have so sweet a savor that they render those of earth insipid. . . .

For the future, the Lord will provide. . . . Nevertheless, there are two sources of possible destruction to this mission, which we greatly dread,—first, the hostile Iroquois; second, the failure of provisions; and it is not clear how these dangers may be encountered. Our Hurons, last year, were forced not only to leave their homes and their fortified villages, but even to forsake their fields, because they were harassed by warfare, and crushed by unceasing disaster. We, the Shepherds, followed our fleeing flock, and we too have left our dwelling place—I might call it our delight—the residence of Sainte Marie, and the fields we had tilled, which promised a rich harvest. Nay, more, we even applied the torch to the work of our own hands, lest the sacred House should furnish shelter to our impious enemy; and thus in a single day, and almost in a moment, we saw consumed our work of nearly ten years, which had given us the hope that we could produce the necessaries of life, and thus maintain ourselves in this country without aid from France. But God has willed otherwise; our home is now laid waste, and our Penates [household goods] forsaken; we have been compelled to journey elsewhere, and, in the land of our exile, to seek a new place of banishment.

Within sight of the mainland, about twenty miles from that first site of Sainte Marie, is an island surrounded by a vast lake (which might better be called a sea). There the fugitive Hurons checked their flight—at least most of them; there also we must abide; there, where lately were the dens of wild beasts, we were obliged to build new homes; there the forest, never touched by the axe since the creation, had to be cleared away; there, finally, not only we, but the savages, had to construct fortifications, a task pertaining to war. This was our occupation, this our unceasing effort—winter and summer alike—that we might at last render ourselves safe, in this respect, and quite prepared to receive the common enemy. We surrounded our position, not merely with a wooden palisade, as hitherto had been the custom, but with a closely-built stone wall, as difficult to scale as it is easy of defense—which defies the enemy's torch, or a battering ram, or any engine of war which the Iroquois can employ.

But a far more laborious task remains, in pulling out trees, and preparing the ground for cultivation, that its yield of grain, roots, and vegetables may be sufficient to prevent famine—for on such food we live here; we have no other beverage than cold water. We have almost no covering save the skins of beasts, which nature furnishes without labor on our part. We saved ten fowls, a pair of swine, two bulls, and the same number of cows—enough doubtless to preserve their kind. We have one year's supply of Indian corn; the rest has been used for Christian charity. However, the small amount which I have mentioned has been saved, because charity does not act blindly, and ought not to be so lavish, especially in saving bodies, as to leave nothing for our sustenance who must devote ourselves to the cultivation of the faith, and to securing the salvation of souls. But, though everything should fail, never, God helping us, shall courage, hope, and patience fail; for love can do all things, and endure all things. This solemn assertion I can make as regards all the Fathers living here. Their hearts are ready for all things. . . .

Your most Reverend Paternity's
Most humble and obedient son,
Paul Ragueneau.

From the Residence of Sainte Marie,
in the Island of Saint Joseph, among the Hurons
in New France, March 13, 1650.

To our Very Reverend Father in Christ,
Vincent Caraffa,
General of the Society of Jesus, at Rome.

What do you think?

1. *Why were the water routes so important?*
2. *Why would the number of converts to Christianity increase during disastrous times? What does this document reveal about the Jesuits? About their relation with the Indians? Did this relationship enhance or diminish the economic opportunities of secular Europeans? Explain.*
3. *Describe the changes in the Huron life-style that the war created.*

8. LIQUOR TRAFFIC

The Catholic Church in New France was alarmed at what the brandy trade was doing to the Indians. But Colbert, the French finance minister under Louis XV, was afraid that the fur trade could go to the English should the liquor trade be stopped. The following are Colbert's remarks to an Intendant, Duchesneau, cited in J. H. Stewart, Kenneth McNaught and Harry S. Crowe, eds.: A Sourcebook of Canadian History *(Toronto: Longman's Green and Co., 1959).*

I see that the Count de Frontenac is of opinion that the trade with the savages in drinks called in that country intoxicating, does not cause the great and terrible evils to which Mgr. de Quebec takes exception. . . In this matter, before taking sides with the bishop, you should enquire very exactly as to the number of murders, assassinations, cases of arson, and other excesses caused by brandy . . . and send me the proof of this. If these deeds had been continued, His Majesty would have issued a most severe and vigorous prohibition to all his subjects against engaging in this traffic. But, in the absence of this proof, and seeing, moreover, the contrary in the evidence and reports of those that have been longest in this country, it is not just, and the general policy of a state opposes in this the feelings of a bishop who, to prevent the abuses that a small number of private individuals may make of a thing good in itself, wishes to abolish trade in an article which greatly serves to attract commerce, and the savages themselves, to the orthodox Christians.

What do you think?

1. *Should the liquor trade have been stopped? Defend your answer.*

As Whites Saw Indians

The previous sections dealing with the history of Indian-White relations have shown that no policy—governmental, economic, or religious—remained constant over the years. Naturally, shifts in policy were accompanied by corresponding changes in the attitudes held by Whites. The following readings show some typical White attitudes prevalent during various parts of our history.

Do the attitudes of Whites in the past correspond to those of today? What is the relationship, if any, between the policies that a majority implements for a minority group and the *attitudes* of the majority? How would the knowledge of such a relationship affect plans for the future?

1. THE MARTYRDOM OF BRÉBEUF AND LALEMANT

C. W. Jefferey (1869–1951) was a famous illustrator of scenes from Canadian history. This drawing is taken from Canada's Past in Pictures *(Toronto: Ryerson, 1934).*

What do you think?

1. *Jefferey's pictures were reproduced in numerous textbooks. What effect would this one have on a student's attitudes and actions towards Indians?*

2. BRÉBEUF AND HIS BRETHREN

F. R. Scott, a Canadian teacher and writer co-edited in 1957 The Blasted Pine, *an anthology of "satire, invective and disrespectful verse." His poem "Brébeuf and his Brethren" was included in the anthology.*

When de Brébeuf and Lalemant, brave souls
Were dying by the slow and dreadful coals
Their brother Jesuits in France and Spain
Were burning heretics with equal pain.
For both the human torture made a feast
Then is the priest savage, or Red Indian priest?

What do you think?

1. *Compare the views of the Indian projected by the Jefferey's illustration and Scott's poem.*

3. ON THE INDIAN CHARACTER

Francis Parkman was a popular nineteenth-century American Romantic historian who saw "Progress" as the most important criterion by which men and their acts ought to be judged. Parkman's works were republished in 1962 by Collier Books in New York.

Of the Indian character, much has been written foolishly, and credulously believed. By the rhapsodies of poets, the cant of sentimentalists, and the extravagance of some who should have known better, a counterfeit image has been tricked out, which might seek in vain for its likeness through every corner of the habitable earth; an image bearing no more resemblance to its original, than the monarch of the tragedy and the hero of the epic poem bear to their living prototypes in the palace and the camp. The shadows of his wilderness home, and the darker mantle of his own inscrutable reserve, have made the Indian warrior a wonder and a mystery. Yet to the eye of rational observation there is nothing unintelligible in him. He is full, it is true, of contradiction. He deems himself the center of greatness and renown; his pride is proof against the fiercest torments of fire and steel; and yet the same man would beg for a dram of whiskey, or pick up a crust of bread thrown to him like a dog, from the tent door of the traveller. At one moment, he is wary and cautious to the verge of cowardice; at the next, he abandons himself to a very insanity of recklessness; and the habitual self-restraint which throws an impenetrable veil over emotion is joined to the unbridled passions of a madman or a beast.

* * * * *

Nature has stamped the Indian with a hard and stern physiognomy. Ambition, revenge, envy, jealousy, are his ruling passions; and his cold temperament is little exposed to those effeminate vices which are the bane of milder races. With him revenge is an overpowering instinct; nay, more, it is a point of honor and a duty. His pride sets all language at defiance. He loathes the thought of coercion; and a few of his race have ever stooped to discharge a menial office. A wild love of liberty, an utter intolerance of control, lie at the basis of his character, and fire his whole existence. Yet, in spite of this haughty independence, he is a devout hero-worshipper; and high achievement in war or policy touches a chord to which his nature never fails to respond. He looks up with admiring reverence to the sages and heroes of his tribe; and it is this principle, joined to the respect for age springing from the patriarchal element in his social system, which, beyond all others, contributes union and harmony to the erratic members of an Indian community. With him the love of glory kindles into a burning passion; and to allay its cravings, he will dare cold and famine, fire, tempest, torture, and death itself.

These generous traits are overcast by much that is dark, cold, and sinister, by sleepless distrust, and rankling jealousy. Treacherous himself, he is always suspicious of treachery in others. Brave as he is—and few of mankind are braver—he will vent his passion by a secret stab rather than an open blow. His warfare is full of ambuscade and stratagem; and he never rushes into battle with that joyous self-abandonment, with which the warriors of the Gothic races flung themselves into the ranks of their enemies. In his feasts and his drinking bouts we find none of that robust and full-toned mirth, which reigned at the rude carousals of our barbaric ancestry. He is never jovial in his cups, and maudlin sorrow or maniacal rage is the sole result of his potations.

Over all emotion he throws the veil of an iron self-control, originating in a peculiar form of pride, and fostered by rigorous discipline from childhood upward. He is trained to conceal passion, and not to subdue it. The inscrutable warrior is aptly imaged by the hackneyed figure of a volcano covered with snow; and no man can say when or where the wild-fire will burst forth. This shallow self-mystery serves to give dignity to public deliberation, and harmony to social life. Wrangling and quarrel are strangers to an Indian dwelling; and while an assembly of the ancient Gauls was garrulous as a convocation of magpies, a Roman senate might have taken a lesson from the grave solemnity of an Indian council. In the midst of his family and friends, he hides affections, by nature none of the most tender, under a mask of icy coldness; and in the torturing fires of his enemy, the haughty sufferer maintains to the last his look of grim defiance.

His intellect is as peculiar as his moral organization. Among all savages, the powers of perception preponderate over those of reason and analysis; but this is more especially the case with the Indian. An acute judge of character, at least of such parts of it as his experience enables him to comprehend; keen to proverb in all exercises of war and the chase, he seldom traces effects to their causes, or follows out actions to their remote results. Though a close observer of external nature, he no sooner attempts to account for her phenomena than he involves himself in the most ridiculous absurdities; and quite content with these puerilities, he has not the least desire to push his inquiries further. His curiosity, abundantly active within its own narrow circle, is dead to all things else; and to attempt rousing it from its torpor is but a bootless task. He seldom takes cognizance of general or abstract ideas; and his language has scarcely the power to express them, except through the medium of figures drawn from the external world, and often highly picturesque and forcible. The absence of reflection makes him grossly improvident, and unfits him for pursuing any complicated scheme of war or policy.

Some races of men seem moulded in wax, soft and melting, at once plastic and feeble. Some races, like some metals, combine the greatest flexibility with the greatest strength. But the Indian is hewn out of a rock. You can rarely change the form without destruction of the substance. Races of inferior energy have possessed a power of expansion and assimilation to which he is a stranger; and it is this fixed and rigid quality which has proved his ruin. He will not learn the arts of civilization, and he and his forest must perish together. The stern, unchanging features of his mind excite our admiration from their very immutability; and we lock with deep interest on the fate of this irreclaimable son of the wilderness, the child who will not be weaned from the breast of his rugged mother. And our interest increases when we discern in the unhappy wanderer the germs of heroic virtues mingled among his vices—a hand bountiful to bestow as it is rapacious to seize, and even in extremest famine, imparting its last morsel to a fellow-sufferer; a heart which, strong in friendship as in hate, thinks it not too much to lay down life for its chosen comrade; a soul true to its own idea of honor, and burning with an unquenchable thirst for greatness and renown.

What do you think?

1. *Parkman wrote this passage to correct "a counterfeit image" of the Indian that was prevalent at that time. Evaluate his own analysis of the Indian "character." Explain why Parkman felt the way he did.*

2. *How would this attitude towards the Indian affect the way Whites treated Indians?*
3. *"Parkman saw Progress as the final judge." Does this passage on the Indian support this contention?*

4. THE WHITE MAN'S BURDEN

The next selections are revealing remarks made about the Indian by nineteenth-century people. The first snippet is from the 1877 Algoma Missionary News, *the second from a Regina missionary paper,* Progress, *dated 1896.*

It has been said, "We have enough to do with our White population, let the Indian go," but in a family, is it only the fair and promising who are considered, perhaps, less favored by nature, and were prone to stray, to be left to the dictates of their own evil inclinations? Rather should our hearts turn with pity and strong compassion towards the poor wanderer.

The Indian can not resist the fatal effects of drunkeness. The spirituous poisoning creeps into this blood, and rendering him a beast, it enters the veins of his children in another form, transmitted by his tainted blood, and they died by the thousands from that dread disease, consumption, the direct inheritance from their drunken fathers.

What do you think?

1. *In what ways does the UNESCO statement explain the beliefs revealed in the passages above?*
2. *Explain how the second statement could be accused of contributing to "cumulative racism" (page 33)?*
3. *If these items are examples of racial Darwinism, how would you define it? What sort of policies would such a belief give use to? Cite some modern examples of racial Darwinism. Why could the excerpt from the textbook on page 38 be used here?*

5. THE NOBLE SAVAGE

Daniel Harmon, a New Englander, joined the Northwest Company in 1800 for a salary of twenty pounds a year as an itinerant fur dealer. The journal he kept from 1800–1816 provides this selection. (W. Kaye Lamb, ed.: Sixteen Years in Indian Country: The Journal of Daniel Harmon *[Toronto: Macmillan and Co., 1957].)*

The White people have been among the above mentioned tribes, for about one hundred and fifty years. To this circumstance it is probably to be attributed, that the knowledge of these Indians is more extensive, than that of the other tribes. But I very much question whether they have improved in their character or condition, by their acquaintance with civilized people. In their savage state, they were contented with the mere necessaries of life, which they could procure, with considerable ease; but now they have many artificial wants, created by the luxuries which we have introduced among them; and as they find it difficult to obtain these luxuries, they have become, to a degree, discontented with this condition, and practise fraud in their dealings. A half-civilized Indian is more savage, than one in his original state. The latter has some sense of honor, while the former has none. I have always experienced the greatest hospitality and kindness among those Indians, who have had the least intercourse with White people. They readily discover and adopt our evil practices; but they are not as quick to discern, and as ready to follow the few good examples, which we set before them.

What do you think?

1. *What is this author saying about relations between Indians and Whites?*
2. *Explain the meaning of the term "the noble savage"? How does this document illustrate this term? What effect would such a belief have on the White treatment of Indians?*

As Indians Saw Whites

Indians were not passive observers of the invasion of North America. Their views of the White man were spoken often, and in strong and eloquent terms. Do you see any similarities between the attitudes of Indians in the past to those of present-day Indians?

1. A PROPHETIC LAMENT

Mohawk princess Pauline Johnson, or Tekahionwake as she called herself, who has been called the voice of Canada's Indians. When she died in 1913, she left behind a legacy of poetry, some lyric, some harsh, on her people and her country. Below is an excerpt from her poem "The Cattle Thief" a critical look at the White man's religion. The poem is from Flint and Feathers *(Toronto: Hodder and Stoughton, 1967), an anthology of Pauline Johnson's poetry.*

You have stolen my father's spirit, but his body I
 only claim.
You have killed him, but you shall not dare to
 touch him now he's dead.
You have cursed, and called him a Cattle Thief,
 thought you robbed him first of bread—
Robbed him and robbed my people—look there, at
 that shrunken face,
Starved with a hollow hunger, we owe to you and
 your race.
What have you left to us of land, what have you
 left of game,
What have you brought but evil, and curses since
 you came?
How have you paid us for our game? how paid us
 for our land?
By a *book*, to save our souls from the sins *you*
 brought in your other hand.
Go back with your new religion, we never have
 understood
Your robbing an Indian's *body*, and mocking his
 soul with food.
Go back with your new religion, and find—if find
 you can—
The *honest* man you have ever made from out a
 starving man.
You say your cattle are not ours, your meat is not
 our meat;
When *you* pay for the land you live in, *we'll* pay
 for the meat we eat.
Give back our land and our country, give back our
 herds of game;
Give back the furs and the forests that were ours
 before you came;
Give back the peace and the plenty. Then come
 with your new belief,
And blame, if you dare, the hunger that *drove* him to
 be a thief.

What do you think?

1. *What was the attitude of the Indian woman in the poem towards the White man? Why did she feel the way she did?*
2. *"Go back with your new religion, we never have understood Your robbing an Indian's body and mocking his soul with food." Explain.*
 (a) Did the White man ever use a religious justification for his

treatment of the Indian? If so, what were his arguments, and why did he use them?

(b) Are there any modern counterparts to this sort of justification? If so, describe them.

2. THEY HAVE NO HONESTY

Big Bear, one of the most famous Indians in Canadian history, was a Cree Indian who was involved in the Riel Rebellion. His remarks here were spoken at the 1884 Indian Council at Duck Lake where he pleaded for a common Indian front against the Whites. (Public Archives of Canada. Cited in G. F. G. Stanley: The Birth of Western Canada *[Toronto: University of Toronto Press, 1960] and T. C. McLuhan:* Touch the Earth *[Toronto: New Press, 1971].)*

I have been trying to seize the promises which they [the Whites] made to me; I have been grasping but I cannot find them. What they have promised me straight way, I have not yet seen the half of it.

We have all been deceived in the same way. It is the cause of our meeting at Duck Lake. They offered me a spot as a reserve. As I see that they are not going to be honest, I am afraid to take a reserve. They have given me to choose between several small reserves but I feel sad to abandon the liberty of my own land when they come to me and offer me small plots to stay there and in return not to get half of what they have promised me. When will you have a big meeting? It has come to me as through the bushes that you are not yet all united; take time and become united, and I will speak. The government sent to us those who think themselves men. They are not men. They have no honesty. They are an unsightly beast. Their faces are twisted from the appearance of honest men.

What do you think?

1. *Compare Big Bear's attitudes towards treaty-making with those of the chief on page 165.*
2. *What caused this change in attitude?*
3. *Compare Big Bear's view of the reserve system to that of Alexander Morris's (page 120). Why do you think Big Bear felt the government to be dishonest?*
4. *Are Big Bear's views paralleled by modern Indian leaders? Explain.*

3. INDIANS TALK BACK

The next article is taken from the Algoma Missionary News *of 1877. It deals with part of the dialogue which took place at a parley in July 1877 between the bishop of Algoma and four chiefs in his diocese. There was present a half-breed interpreter.*

His lordship endeavored to impress them with the importance of embracing the Christian religion, but to all he said a deaf ear was turned. These Indians had already weighed the matter according to such opportunities as they had of judging, and had come to the conclusion that the religion of their forefathers was better than the new religion of the White people. Blackstone especially spoke in very boastful terms of the superiority of his own religion. "We Indians," he said to the bishop, "are good, the Great Spirit loves us, he has prepared happy hunting grounds for us after death,—but you White people are only half of you good, the Great Spirit has made two places for you to go to, a good place and a bad place. We Indians don't need gaols to be locked up in like White people. My people are all honest and good, it is the White people that teach them to be bad."

What do you think?

1. *What was Blackstone's attitude towards the White man's religion?*
2. *How do you think the missionaries would regard such attitudes? Why?*

4. NO ONE CAN COMMAND BUT THEY

In 1864, Sanaindi, the head chief of the Dog-Ribs on the Lower Mackenzie, complained of the missionary Father Petitot's continued stubborness. (Marius Barbeau and Grace Melvin: The Indian Speaks *[Toronto: Macmillan, 1943].)*

Eh! Menounlay-ya-tree!

The French prayer men are rash and unbearable. No one can command but they, not even in our country. Here is one of them, the one whom we have summoned to baptize us. We long desired his coming, we greeted him as a dear relation, we listened to his words, we loved him, we sheltered him and fed him.

Now then, can we get anything out of him in return, we, the chiefs? No more than could those children yonder. He is alone in this land of ours, without relatives, without protection. But this does not keep him from defying us all. He knows nothing but his own will, and wants everybody to bow his head before him. Yet, I am a chief, I, Sanaindi! My hair is white with age.

Why does he not obey me, like our Déné witch doctors? If I bid them, "Sing for us!" they obey. If I say, "Attend to this patient!" they attend to him. This little French priest is the only one who will say, "No!"

If we offer to pay him for baptism, he flashes with indignation. He pours the water of baptism on the head of the evil because he knows not their bad heart, and withholds it from the good, whom he mistakes for the evil.

No sooner do we ask him to stay, than he takes his leave. If we dismiss him, he stays! He thinks he is the only man on earth, Kay-odeha, and he will never submit to anyone, not even to me, the chief, while he lives in my tent and in our forests, the forests we have occupied since the beginning of time!

What do you think?

1. *What was the Indian chief's reaction to the missionary? Why did it change? Was he afraid of the priest? Defend your answer.*
2. *"He thinks he is the only man on earth . . ." Why would the chief have this attitude?*
3. *How does this story support the explanation offered by James Dumont (page 97) about the changing attitudes of Indians toward Christianity?*

5. INDIANS TENACIOUS OF INDEPENDENCE

Robert "Gadfly" Gourlay, an early adventurer-entrepreneur, cited these remarks by an unknown Upper Canadian in his Letters from an American Loyalist in Upper Canada to an English Friend. *The date of publication is not exactly known, but it was probably around 1807.*

The Indian tribes, even those who live in the midst of settlements, have always been treated by the British government as independent nations, and not considered as subject to our municipal laws; except in the case of a murder committed upon a White man. No race of men are more impatient of control, or more tenacious of personal and national independence. Any interference with these they would consider as the highest "injury," and such interference would indeed tend to disaffect them effectually.

What do you think?

1. *Compare the attitudes of these 1807 Indians to those of Big Bear in 1885 (page 163). Did Alexander Morris agree (page 120)? Explain.*
2. *How does Francis Parkman support the view of the Indian given in this document? What does he say that Indian pride would inevitably lead to? Do you agree? Why or why not?*

6. BURY THE HATCHET

In the late eighteenth century the British signed a peace treaty with the Five Nations Indians. For such events the Indian custom was to bury a gaily decorated tomahawk and to plant a young tree over the same spot. The speech given by the Indian chief at this treaty-making with Britain makes reference to this custom. (Egerton Ryerson Young: Stories from Indian Wigwams and Northern Camp-Fires *[Toronto: Wm. Briggs, n.d.].)*

We are happy in having buried under ground the red ax that has so often been dyed with the blood of our brethren. Now is this spot we inter the ax and plant the tree of peace. We plant the tree whose top will reach high up into the sunlight, and its branches will soon spread abroad, that it shall be seen afar off. May its growth never be stifled and choked, but may it continue to flourish until it shades both your country and ours with its leaves. Let us make fast its roots and extend them to the utmost of your settlements. If enemies should come to shake this tree we would know it by the motion of its roots reaching into your country. May the Great Spirit allow us to rest in tranquillity upon our mats beneath its shade, and never again may the ax be dug up to cut down this tree of peace. Let the earth be trod hard over this ax which we have buried on its edge, so that if ever it moves it may only sink down the deeper. Let a strong stream like that which rushes by wash the evil thoughts and deeds of war out of our sight and remembrance. The war-fire that has so long burned is now extinguished. The bloody bed on which our wounded tossed, breathing vengeance, is now washed clean as are their hearts, and the tears are wiped from their eyes. Brothers, we now renew the covenant chain of friendship. Let it be kept bright and clean as silver, and never again may its beauty be tarnished by contact with any rust. As now it unites us in the bonds of friendship, may not any one pull away his arms from it.

What do you think?

1. (a) *"May its growth never be stifled and choked, but may it continue to flourish until it shades both your country and ours with its leaves."*
   (b) *"Brothers we now renew the covenant chain of friendship" How did the Indian see his relationship with the White man at this time? Did the White man have the same opinion of this relationship? Defend your answer.*

7. DIVINE INTRUDERS

The first Europeans were often regarded by the Indians as almost god-like creatures. Daniel Harman a "gentleman adventurer" with the North-West Company from 1800–1819, recorded his experience with this phenomenon in his Journal of Voyages and Travels in the Interior of North America *which was published in 1904 in Toronto by the George N. Morang Company.*

The Carriers are so very credulous, and have so exalted an opinion of us, that they firmly believe, though I have often assured them of the contrary, that any of the traders or chiefs, as they call us, can, at pleasure, make it fair or foul weather. And even yet when they are preparing to set out on an excursion, they will come and offer to pay us, provided we will make or allow it to be fair weather, during their absence from their homes. They often inquire of us whether salmon, that year, will be in plenty in their rivers. They also think, that by merely looking into our books, we can cause a sick person to recover, let the distance which he may be from us be ever so great. In short, they look upon those who can read and write, as a kind of supernatural beings, who know all that is past, and who can see into futurity.

For a considerable time after we had been among them, they were fully of the opinion, that the White people had neither fathers nor mothers; but came into the world in a supernatural way, or were placed on the earth by the sun or moon.

As a further specimen of their limited conceptions, they now firmly believe that a watch is the heart of the sun, because it is ever in motion, as they say, like that great body of light. They add further, that unless a watch and the sun were nearly related, it would be impossible for the watch, considering the distance which there is between them, to point out so precisely the minute when the sun is to make its appearance and to leave us. In short, they say that the one must know perfectly well what the other is about, and that there must be the same connexion between them, as between the members of the human body.

What do you think?

1. *Account for the Indian deification of the White man. What misconceptions of the Indian did the first Europeans entertain?*
2. *How does this early Indian feeling about the White man help to explain the impact that Western technology and religion was to make on the aboriginal people?*

5

The Future: Assimilation, Integration or Separation?

The preceding chapters have provided you with the opportunity of examining the contemporary issues and the historical conditions of Indian-White relations.

But what of the future? Where do we go from here? Should future relations between Indians and Whites be one of assimilation, integration or separation?

Since the question of the preservation of an Indian cultural identity is central in any attempt to understand the implications of these three options, this chapter is introduced by a selection of documents which deal with the interaction of the Indian and White cultures. Following these are documents which outline the current debate about assimilation, integration and separation. The insights gained from this discussion should enable you in the next section to better assess, in relation to the three options, the 1969 White Paper of the federal government on Indian policy and the Indian reaction to it. There is a final section giving an indication of some programs that have already been put into practice. Which of the three options do each of these programs illustrate, and what successes have been achieved through them?

The Indian Culture

The Indian has been in contact with European civilizations for over four hundred years. During this time, as demonstrated by the historical documents you have seen, his culture has been under constant threat. Yet, despite this, pieces of the ancient Indian culture have survived to form the basis of Indian ambitions for the future.

How strong a sense of uniqueness or "Indianness" do the remnants of this culture give the native people? How do these remnants influence the Indian relationship with White society? What could they mean for future relations between Indians and Whites? What can White society learn from the Indian culture?

1. TIME, SAVING, WORK

Dr. Ben Neifel, the author of the following article, which appeared in Indian Education, *April 15, 1957, briefly outlines a few points of comparison between the values of the Indian culture and those of White society.*

Time, saving and work—we find them popping out at us in everything that we do; . . . Those of us of Indian descent, who have become habituated to the values of time, work, and saving in the American way of life are no longer culturally Indian in the sense of living by the values of old Indian life ways.

1. In the American way of life, those of us who are carried along in its social stream are future-oriented. In contrast, those whose lives are governed by the values of the Indian life are oriented to the present. The Indians had no need to be apprehensive about the future, from a material standpoint. It is reliably estimated that not more than one million people inhabited what is now the United States and Canada at the time that Columbus discovered this part of the world. Nature's bounty did not require modification for the survival of this handful of humans. The Indian, in his societies those thousands of years when he was fashioning his way of life, found he could have all that he required in the way of food, clothing, and shelter by living in harmony with nature. This meant that the essence of life was found *in being* and not in *becoming* something we are not today.

2. Time, in the sense of measuring duration by clocks and days-of-the-week calendars as we do, is not important in the Indian way of life. In our economic and other social relationships it becomes essential to schedule most of our activities in accordance with a commonly accepted system of timing if we, as personalities, are to attain a satisfying sense of achievement in the

complex way of life in which we find ourselves today. In the economically simple life of the old Indian system there was never any need to co-ordinate the efforts of the group except in some general way around the natural objects, such as the sun, moon, and seasons.

3. Saving as a means to achieve economic development has not been a part of the life of the Indian in his nomadic state where he lived largely by hunting and food gathering. We have been taught to forego present use of our time and money for anticipated greater satisfactions at a later date. We are encouraged to put any extra income we have into bonds, insurance, property, and other types of savings for use in later years when our earning power might be lost.

With the Indians there was no reason to be constantly thinking of the future. To them the necessities for living were nearly as free as the air we breathe. Air is necessary for life but we seldom think of saving it up for future use except in unusual conditions such as high-altitude flying, or to aid a very sick person with extra oxygen. The things essential to life in those early times, like air to most of us today, has no economic value and therefore there was no need to act in terms of saving for this purpose.

4. Habituation to hard work, including drudgery for over a period of years, if necessary to earn a living, was not in the Indian system, particularly for the men. Sociologists explain that this is an inheritance of Western European origin. The forefathers of the emigrants to this country from Europe were taught to work. There developed a pride in work for work's sake.

The Indian culture did not make provisions in its social system to develop like habits of work among the men of the tribes. It fell to the lot of women to do the tedious tasks such as the tanning of skins, the care of children, the preparation of the food: Indian women were the "hewers of wood and the carriers of water." In the Indian life of that earlier day, the able-bodied men of the tribes could not be permitted the luxury of doing these jobs that came to be regarded as "women's work."

They had an equally important role to perform. They had to keep themselves ever ready to guard their camps against the possible attack of enemy tribes and be prepared to yield up their lives if that supreme sacrifice was necessary to the accomplishment of the job. Theirs was the more rigorous task of hunting so that the people would have food, clothing, and shelter. If the men did otherwise, their people would either become slaves or perish.

What do you think?

1. *Describe specific instances where Indian cultural values would be in conflict with those of White society? How can cultural differences contribute to discrimination?*
2. *How does the article explain certain types of White prejudice? (See "Lo! The Poor Indian," page 34.)*

3. Are there any groups today who have adopted a life-style closer to the values of the Indian culture than to the traditional values of White society? If so, why are they doing this?

2. NON-INTERFERENCE

Differing notions of the degree to which we should intrude on others' lives causes much misunderstanding between Indians and Whites. This article, "American Indians and White People," by Rosalie Wax and Robert Thomas appeared in Phylon *in the winter of 1961.*

In every human relationship there is some element of influence, interference, or downright compulsion. The White man has been and is torn between two ideals: on the one hand, he believes in freedom, in minding his own business, and in the right of people to make up their minds for themselves; but, on the other hand, he believes that he should be his brother's keeper and not abstain from advice, or even action, when his brother is speeding down the road toward perdition, death, or social isolation due to halitosis. The Indian society is unequivocal: interference of any form is forbidden, regardless of the folly, irresponsibility, or ignorance of your brother.

Consequently, when the White man is motivated as his brother's keeper, which is most of the time when he is dealing with Indians, he rarely says or does anything that does not sound rude or even hostile to the latter. The White, imbued with a sense of righteousness in "helping the downtrodden and backward," does not realize the nature of his conduct, and the Indian cannot tell him, for that, in itself, would be "interference" with the White's freedom to act as he sees fit.

In a general sense, coercion has been and is a fundamental element in the social orders of the Western world. Social theorists have characterized the state as that national institution that effectively claims that legitimate monopoly of violence. Lesser institutions utilize a variety of corporal and spiritual sanctions to effect cooperative action, and the economy prides itself on utilizing the lash of need and the lure of wealth. These characteristics of Western social structure have stimulated the more idealistic to the proposal of new communities in which the elimination of brute compulsion would ensure the release of the creative energies of man; but so deeply entrenched is this system of hierarchial and enforced organization that these are ridiculed as "utopian." In contrast, many of the Indian societies were organized on principles that relied to a great extent on voluntary cooperation and lacked the military or other coercive instrumentalities of the European.

The Indian defines all of the above behavior, from the gentlest manipulation to the most egregious meddling, as outside the area of proper action. From earliest childhood he is trained to regard absolute non-interference in interpersonal relations as decent or normal and to react to even the mildest coercion in these areas with bewilderment, disgust and fear.

We have noted that most White people who have a tolerably good relationship with Indians consciously or unconsciously subscribe to the notion that White men ought to keep their noses out of Indian matters. However else they may behave seems to make little difference. Thus, one of the finest field workers known to us is an anthropologist of so gentle and unaggressive a nature that one sometimes wonders how he can maintain himself in the modern world. When he is in the field, the Indians spend a good deal of their time seeing that he comes to no harm. Another White man has no tact at all and breaks some rule of Indian decorum in almost every sentence he utters. Both men, however, subscribe to non-interference in Indian matters and both are admired and liked by Indians.

What is meant by?

"coercion"
"corporal and spiritual sanctions"
"utopian"

What do you think?

1. *According to the author what is the source of misunderstanding between Whites and Indians? If they are correct, how would bringing up children differ between Indian families and White families?*
2. *Discuss the pros and cons of the "ethic of non-interference." How applicable is it to your own life? How would it change family, school and business?*

3. SOME ASPECTS OF THE INDIAN CULTURE

William B. Newell outlines contributions made by Indians to White culture, and dispels a few myths about the Indian "character".

Within recent months a few scientists have become intensely interested in the science of acculturation and have selected the American Indian as a subject for study. These men are interested in learning to what extent the American Indian has been affected by contact with European peoples and to what extent he has become a "White man." In contrast to this phase of research your writer has been studying the subject from the other way around and has sought to determine to what degree the European has become an "Indian" since there is unquestionably an even exchange, more or less, of culture traits between the European people and the American Indian since the advent of the White man to the New World some four or five hundred years ago. We often hear it said that the White man taught the Indian only evils and none of the White man's virtues. Perhaps the time will eventually come when we can honestly say that the American Indian "taught the White man only his virtues and no evils."

The socio-culture of the American Indian was not as complex as that of the European peoples and due to its simplicity and intense stability was the stronger of the two, and was little affected by the very small groups of Europeans who first met the Indians, who were living in much larger communities, where they were forced to accept the order of the day and imitate so far as possible those with whom they resided. In other words "When in Rome do as the Romans do." If we were to decide on a trip to the land of the Eskimo we most certainly would have to learn to eat raw fish and endure hardships and conditions with which we would be totally unacquainted. A culture such as existed in the life of the American Indian was sacred and lasting. On the other hand, civilization is a highly complex mixture of culture and is less stable and less influential in its ability to ingratiate itself permanently into the life of a primitive group such as existed among the American Indians. Cultural change takes place more easily in a complex civilization than in a more simple cultural group.

This fact is emphasized in that the American Indian today, after hundreds of years of contact, still retains a large percentage of his native culture even after struggling against strong forces which have sought to break down his culture and inculcate into his personality European cultural traits.

In spite of the concentrated efforts and close proximity of European peoples in their endeavor to force upon the American Indian their culture the result has been failure to a very large extent. This is again emphasized by the fact that today over half of the six thousand Iroquois Indians living in the thickly populated state of New York still retain their ancient religious concepts and beliefs. . . .

The real purpose of this paper is to point out a few of the definitely established sociological and economic contributions which have been accepted by the best authorities on the subject. A discussion of the moral and ethical values of Indian culture would require a volume in itself. Indian political theories as embraced in the League of the Iroquois are important and stand out in marked contrast to the European theory of "the divine right of kings," which flourished in Europe at the time of the discovery of America. The individual rights of man were recognized in America long before the Europeans awakened to this political philosophy. Ideas of freedom, liberty, and equality existed and were engraved in the hearts of the Indians when Europeans were "boiled or roasted" for daring to speak against the state or church. One of the outstanding differences between the European and the American Indian was the fact that in America the Indian was permitted freedom of thought while in Europe an individual's thinking was done for him by autocratic and dogmatic leaders. A similar situation still exists today in some European countries and even in America there are those who would shape our opinions if they could.

It was from the Iroquois League that we first learned the meaning of true democratic ideals. It was here in America that we learned what freedom of speech, freedom of worship, equal representation, and constitutional government really meant. It was from these ancient political philosophers that the world first knew democracy. It was here that real statesmen served their constituents faithfully, without any other pay than the honor, respect and esteem of their people. Governor Cadwallader Golden who wrote the first American history in 1727, some fifty years before the Revolutionary War, tells us that these men "were elected on the basis of their merit, because of their honesty and integrity, and that they were usually the poorest men in the nation, never keeping anything for themselves, but distributing all annuities and monies equally among the people." It was in this first history that the early colonists were informed that there existed a "true democracy." In order to illustrate further how the Indian lived under an order such as this I will list in the following paragraphs some customs which were a part of the everyday existence of these people; and at the same time call the attention of the reader to the fact that present day "Americans" are doing these same things which were strange to them before coming to the land of the free and the home of the "brave."

DICTATORS were unknown among the Iroquois. No man could tell another what he should do. Every man was allowed to decide for himself what he should do. Even the Sachems and "Chiefs" suggested but never commanded or insisted too strongly. To do such a thing would immediately lower them in the estimation of the people and cause their removal from office. "We counsel together" was a famous phrase of the Iroquois and every man was allowed freedom of expression.

GOVERNMENT had a central seat where representatives of the several nations met to discuss state matters and where unanimous decisions only were rendered. A single dissenting vote defeated legislative action. There was "absolute harmony and the greatest decorum observed in their great councils."

HUMANE: Indians were gentle and kind. They never whipped their children but still retained the love and respect of their children all through life. . . . They cared for their old people and among the Iroquois an elderly person was never heard of who did not have a home and food to eat. It is unknown for young Indian boys and girls to torment or tease elderly persons. Father Pierre Biard, the first Jesuit priest to reach America in 1611, said that if it had not been for the kindness and hospitality of the Indians they would have perished the first three winters they lived in America. The Pilgrim Fathers were welcomed and cared for and nursed back to health by the same Indians who had been pillaged and plundered by adventurous Europeans for over seventy-five years before the arrival of the Pilgrims. It was these same Indians who had lost their sons, fathers, and grandfathers to marauding kidnappers from Europe who took their human cargo to Spain and sold them as slaves. It was actually one of these young Indians who greeted the Pilgrims in "excellent" English, who had escaped from Spain, and who had lived in England for seven years after his escape, that approached the Piligrims upon their arrival in the New World and asked them what they wanted. The fact that these Indians would go to the trouble to ask their enemy what they wanted when they already knew from seventy-five years' experience, only goes to show that the Indian was just, reasonably tolerant, and always willing to give the benefit of any doubt to the other fellow. These people were not savages who were so tolerant, so generous, so forgiving and ready to extend to these Whites a home in America. There is not a single early explorer who was not extended the helping hand by the American Indians upon their arrival in America.

QUARRELING: All the Jesuit writers inform us, was never seen in Indian homes, towns, or communities. Even today . . . one hardly ever sees two Indians quarrel unless they may perhaps be intoxicated. When Indians living in New York City, or any other city for that matter, are arrested for "celebrating" or arrested for any other reason it is significant that deadly weapons are never found on their persons. They do not carry guns, daggers or blackjacks. They are not cowards.

BULLIES are unknown among the Indians. It is unknown for an Indian to take an unfair advantage of an adversary. There is not a record of an Indian war that was not first of all announced to the enemy. There is no place in history where any Indian nation was the first to start a war between the White and the Indians. Among children the common school bully is unknown.

CHARACTER: Sir William Johnson, British Indian agent, after thirty-five years' association with them, said "they are only beginning to deceive in their transactions with us." In another of his documents he states that he has even tried to make an Indian steal but failed. Lying was punished by death.

FREEDOM OF WOMEN: Women received the honor and respect that no other people gave their women. There is not a single court record in the State of New York showing that an Iroquois has ever been arrested for insulting or assaulting a woman, be she Indian or White. In all the lying, militaristic propaganda written about the Indians during the Revolutionary War, or any other war, for the purpose of arousing hatred in the hearts of the people against the Indian, no single writer has dared say that the sanctity of womanhood was ever desecrated by an Indian warrior. The writer has known at least fifty teachers who have taught on Indian reservations and they all state that they have no fear from the Indian men, be they drunk or sober. The respect that the Indians gave their women, and all women, is characteristic of the Iroquois Indians. Indian women enjoyed equal rights with men and, in some cases, were even considered superior to men. In some parts of the world women were not even supposed to have souls.

BIRTH CONTROL was practiced among the Iroquois, and the family was not larger than three or four children.

TRIAL MARRIAGE: The Jesuit priests inform us that trial marriage was also practised.

HEALTH habits practiced by the Iroquois have since been adopted by Europeans. People nowadays dress lightly. Boys no longer wear hats; heavy red woolens are no longer worn, and it was only ten years ago that the first women dared wear a pair of silk hose through a whole winter season, against the advice of physicians who stated that all women would die from pneumonia, if they did such a thing. Bathing has become more or less common now a days among White people. When America was first discovered Europeans did not bathe the body because it was considered a mortal sin to make the body beautiful by cleaning it. This accounts for the numerous skin diseases brought to America by Europeans. Measles, smallpox, chicken pox and all skin diseases were non-existent in America. On the other hand the Jesuit priest tell us that every Indian village had several turkish baths. Some Indian tribes had a bath cult, where it was part of their religion to bathe and keep clean. Sunlight and bathing have become the order of the day and exposing the body to the sun and fresh air, like the Indian did, is making America healthy and strong, like the Indian used to be. . . . Fresh air while sleeping was an Indian custom which twenty-five years ago was considered unhealthy by White people. Hiking clubs and soldiers were taught to walk like the Indian. George Catlin, who lived with the Indians, informs us that "the Indians have a peculiar way of swimming. Instead of shooting both hands out from the chin (the breast stroke) they use the overhand stroke." Today we all swim like the Indian swam.

CRUELTY: Our American Indians learned how to be cruel from the Europeans. Burning at the stake was a European custom introduced to Indians by the Spanish, French and English. Joan of Arc was burned alive sixty-one years before Columbus discovered America. The Apache Indians had never heard of scalping until it was first introduced by our own soldiers back in 1881. When America was first discovered it was believed by Europeans that anyone who knew not Christ was an infidel and it was the duty of these "dark age" Christians to burn all infidels. It meant one step nearer heaven to do this so that when the Indian was discovered many poor Indian victims suffered at the hands of these ignorant believers.

EQUALITY: It is told by many explorers that no one Indian had more than his fellow man and that when one was hungry they all were hungry. It is also said that they always shared their food equally among their captives and with strangers.

GAMBLING: Indians loved to gamble but strange as it may seem, at the end of the game it was customary to return all winnings to the losers. They had no desire to possess in the sense that we moderns do.

RESPONSIBILITY: Irresponsibility such as we have in America today could not and did not exist. Today we hear on all sides the philosophy of "let the other fellow take the rap," "Get away with it if you can," and many other attitudes of like nature. This was not Indian. The White man has not fully accepted this culture from the Indian. He has always been under the yoke of some overlord who has dominated him. In other words, he has never been fully free and it is only as these individuals become free that they will cast out greed and assume their positions as free men in a true democracy. When we learn to work for each other and not against each other we will have a true democracy. Such conflicts were practically unknown.

BROTHERHOOD OF MAN: The Indians always called the White man "brother" in all his dealings with him. He never called him "master," "Your Majesty," or any other title which in any way would indicate that he considered him a superior or lesser being. Every man was trusted and deceit was never looked for in a fellow man. White people first coming to America were given a place to build their lodge but never under any circumstances did the Indian give or sell outright to him land which was suppose to be free to all human beings.

Not only did the American Indian teach us our ideas of social democracy but also he contributed vastly to our economics.

The following list of food plants, and economic contributions are only a few of the many that exist. There are hundreds of others not mentioned here. The fact to bear in mind is that these were unknown to the Indian, and used by the Indian, long before the Europeans discovered America and eventually took it.

Corn is a culture as well as every other economic product or plant taken up by the White man. When Indian corn was accepted it meant taking the whole culture: husking pins, cribs, husking bees, "barn dances," and the forty or fifty ways of preparing corn for eating. The following are only a few such articles which involved hundreds of minor culture traits: potatoes, tomatoes, pumpkins, squashes, lima beans, kidney beans, peppers, coca (cacao), pineapples, nispero, strawberries, persimmons, papaws, guava, oca, cashew nut, pacay, jocote, star apples, mate tea, alligator pear, sour sop, sweet sop, custard apple, cassava, cucumber, peanuts, maple sugar.

Tobacco (a culture taken up by nearly everybody), quinine (important medical contribution), cocaine (important drug used extensively by Indians in pre-Columbian days), cotton (Indians first wore cotton clothing in the world), henequen (hemp), rubber (Indians first invented rubber), copal (an important varnish), Peruvian balm, sunflower, parica (in South America only).

Flavors: vanilla, chocolate, pineapple, maple and strawberry.

Under potatoes, it should be noted that among the Aymara Indians no less than 240 different varieties of potatoes were cultivated. Under cassava, it should be noted that it was first necessary to remove the deadly prussic acid from the plant before it became edible. This poison was sometimes used as a preservative to prevent putrefaction of meat.

Aseptics. The Indian was the first to use boiled water for cleansing and dressing wounds. Trephining. An important surgical operation whereby a section of the skull bone is removed to relieve pressure on the brain, was frequently performed by the Indians of Peru. The Indian was the first to cause a person to withstand pain and submit to amputation or other surgical operations.

In the field of science the Indians were especially clever. Zero was invented a thousand years before the Arabians came out with it in the Old World. The calendar system of the Maya was far superior to our own system and much more accurate. The first people to develop the decimal system represented in the Quipu of the Peruvian were Indians. This hundreds of years before the White man.

Metallurgy. They worked gold, silver, and bronze better than any of the ancient civilizations of the Old World. They were the first to use and work platinum. Arts and Crafts. The famous textiles of the Peruvians have been recognized by authorities as being the best the world has ever seen. Authorities claim that no race on earth made baskets as well as the Poma and other Indian tribes of California. Their beauty and technique excelled all others.

Agriculture. Irrigation, fertilizers, crop rotation, and many other so-called modern farming methods were practised by the intensive agriculturists of the Southwest in the United States, and in Peru.

Masonry. The stone walls of Cuzco are still as great a mystery to us today as they ever have been. We do not know how the stones were quarried and so well fitted together. Modern apartment buildings are much like the Pueblo buildings of the Hopi and Zuni Indians.

Chewing Gum.

Shaking hands is a good old Indian custom.

What do you think?

1. *Do you feel that we are very knowledgeable of the contribution made by Indians? If not, why not?*
2. *Evaluate the contributions made by the Indian culture to the survival of the Western European in North America. Cite examples.*
3. *"Cultural change takes place more easily in a complex civilization than in a more simple cultural group." Is this thesis sufficient to explain the tenacity of the Indian culture?*
4. *"It was from the Iroquois League that we first learned the meaning of true democratic ideals." Discuss.*

4. COMPARISON BETWEEN WHITE AND INDIAN CULTURES

This selection is from an article by D. G. Poole.

How then, can a useful comparison be drawn between White and Indian cultures?

As with all cultures, the Indian and the White were each particular answers to identical psychological drives and needs, but again, as with all cultures, responses differed greatly and according to a host of environmental factors, resulting in two configurations of custom, of practice, of belief, of tradition, greatly at variance. We will confine ourselves to those dominant differences which seem most pertinent.

White culture was nationalistically rather than communally oriented; capitalistic rather than communistic (in the non-political sense of the word); individualistic rather than tribal in the material and social sense. Usually, the two went hand in hand. The essential purpose was not that of self-improvement, but rather that of improving one's position in society. One went forth into the world to "gain one's fortune." One's greatest aspiration was to "rise in the world." The White brand of rivalry is best described by saying that a fall in the esteem in which one was held by one's contemporaries was justified and more than offset by a simultaneous rise in one's monetary fortunes. One could afford to lose ethical face; one could not afford to lose either money or the money game. These were dominant features of White culture.

Indian culture is more difficult to delineate because the Indian continental race was made up of hundreds of isolated societies representing many languages and a surprising variety of customs. In the entire tribal mosaic it is now possible to discern some customs and beliefs which were clearly antithetical to others. There were, however, many cultural features common to nearly all, if not all Indian societies, so that they may be regarded as representative of the entire race. For example, if one looks for the central meaning of Indian life, one finds that the most widespread definition of this resided in the vision quest and the religious beliefs and practices surrounding it. The primal purpose of Indian life could be realized only through the vision experience. Thus, each individual, at the appropriate time and in the prescribed ritualistic manner, sought to become possessed by a spirit, greater, wiser, more powerful than the ego-self. Success in any undertaking, achievement in all of life depended upon this displacement and this surrender. This was the dominant feature of Indian culture.

It is evident that in the essential sense of the meaning or purpose of life, the Indian and White cultures were not merely divergent, they were thoroughly opposed. There were, however, not a few customs common to both cultures and it was along these paths of practice that relating proceeded. Both cultures, for example, entered easily and readily into trade.

Both were traditional traders. Trade, indeed, continued as the most common means of communication between the two races, so far as it went, but the Indian was not a merchant. He had no cumulative concept of wealth, no monetary system, and thus, no real concept of purchase. The White mind was unable to appreciate the difference. Split on the rock of divergent customs, trade never did succeed in developing into commerce.

As with trade and commerce, so with work and employment. The Indian was quite accustomed to work, but for him, work was regarded with achievement rather than monetary recompense. His gains were in personal areas of satisfaction—physical and psychological. Except perhaps for certain tribes of the Pacific Coast, no Indian could have understood incentives which could only be satisfied by material gains valued not in terms of "enough," or even "more," but "more than." The Indian response to need-filling was a direct application to self, to the resources of environment and above all, to the powers of life and growth. He could conceive of making weapons, artifacts, tools, but making money was beyond his ken.

But the greatest breakdown in relations occurred as a result of the divergence of White and Indian customs with regard to the land. To the Indian, the concept of owning the land was as foreign as was that of owning the atmosphere to Whites. But it was more than this. The Indian had no tradition of castles, moats, and drawbridges. In the whole of America there was no "private property," no sign threatening trespassers with prosecution. The Indian lived in the world as an ecological participant rather than an economic competitor. He identified himself with environment. He was with nature rather than at war against her. He shared the land, the water, and the atmosphere with his brothers and other forms of life. The land was neither owned nor managed by man. It was possessed by a Great Spirit and it managed itself with innate wisdom, for the earth was not a dead thing. It was vibrant with a life peculiarly and vibrantly its own. It blossomed with life-forms as the wild plum bloomed with flowers, and judging from such records as exist, it would appear that the Indian was quite happy to *share* the land and its resources with his White brethren.

But to the European, the traditional relationship of man to land resulted in alienating him from a total environment and insulating him against nature. To the descendants of feudal serfs and lords, private ownership of land was the key to security, to freedom, to life itself. Without private land a man was at best, an indentured servant, at worst, a homeless vagrant. With it, he was a respected citizen with defined rights. It was psychologically impossible for the European immigrant to accept the impersonal and unpossessed land as a comfortable definition of home. He could be comfortable only with titled land—a specialized fragment cut from the corporate body of nature, personalized by fences and possessed by the right of private use.

Since it was impossible for the Indians to sell something which they had no conception of owning, land was ceded to the Whites. The basis of these transactions was trade rather than purchase and they were consummated and legalised after the European pattern of "treaty." It is certain that the intent of the initial treaties was not understood by the Indians. It is likely that until they found themselves forcibly ruled off of ceded lands they had no realization of loss. Subsequently, they obstinately resisted the ceding of land and submitted to treaties only under duress.

What is meant by?

"visionary experience"
"ecological participant"

What do you think?

1. *Using two columns draw up a list of the differences and likenesses between Indians and Whites. What do you find appealing about the Indian culture? Unappealing? Why?*
2. *How do these differences explain what has happened between Whites and Indians?*

5. HOW JOHN GOULD WENT TO SEE INDIAN LIFE AND FOUND PEACE

The late Wendy Michener, daughter of Governor General Roland Michener, was a well-known film critic. Her review of an N.F.B. film by artist John Gould appeared in the February 3, 1968 issue of the Toronto Globe and Mail.

The first place Toronto artist John Gould went when the ski-plane settled down at the Ojibway reserve was the Hudson's Bay store. "Here were these people standing like statues," he remembers. "They would pick up an object and just hold it. They weren't going to buy. They just wanted to feel it. I felt like I was watching slow motion."

A month later Gould left Pikangikum with enough drawings for a short National Film Board feature, and found himself wondering, like the Indians, why everybody was talking so much.

Gould is one of the few free-lancers to earn a commission from the National Film Board. He started in movies as a result of watching his drawings from Spain on a television show. "What knocked me out was the quality of the reproduction, a very selfish motive," he said.

On his next trip, to Mexico, he set out to cover his subject like a reporter, then made a film using the drawings. *Little Monday* was shown in Venice, earned back its money, and convinced the N.F.B. that Gould deserved a chance. But the N.F.B. doesn't just hand out films like that. They have to find a way of financing them. It was decided that Gould could easily fit into the program of Indian films, "Challenge for Change."

What Gould expected to find was poverty and unhappiness. Instead he found an enviable peace. "In many ways they are much better off than we are," he said. "We spend all this dough trying to achieve what they've got. "They can just sit and say nothing and appreciate what's around them. They dig nature. They are integrated with the surroundings and with people."

There are no roads at Pikangikum. No traffic, except for the rare skimobile or plane. Just one great lake, snow, a few huts, a store, a school, a nursing centre, three churches, and a lot of space. There are no radios, no movies, no newspapers, no alcohol (the tribe voted to be dry), no community hall, and a lot of silence. "It might drive some people crazy," said Gould. Him it drove peaceful.

Still, the message must have got through somehow because the Indian children soon named Gould, a good-guy-looking 38-year-old, "United States Marshow."

Gould spent a lot of time in the nursing centre where two nurses did everything—pulled teeth, delivered babies, looked after frost-bite. He went to church, and found he was not the only one to take in all three services on a Sunday. But according to the United Church minister John James Everett, "They don't act like Christians. They go to church, they pray, they sing the hymns and they say they are Christians. But the sun is their God—the sun, the stars, the rocks, everything." Gould was more struck by how much of Indian tradition the churches has done away with. Only the old men can do the drum dances, and he had trouble finding one who would. As one old man says in the film: "The old times have all gone by. The days gone by we'll never see again."

Gould also spent some time in the school. "The education is a laugh," he said. "They go to Grade eight and get about a Grade two level."

The film, *Pikangikum*, starts and ends in school. On screen, drawings of children bent over desks; off screen, their voices reciting 81, 82, 83, in a sing-song.

The space and silence of the reservation are reflected in Gould's drawings. His black lines have a stark quality against the glowing white screen. And the sound-track gives a parallel feeling of the silence surrounding the life. A few voices speak out quietly and briefly. The wind howls. In between there's stillness. It's an odd combination: drawings with documentary sound. The separation of the two makes you strangely more aware of each. It's neither a documentary, nor a film about art, but an extension of the artist's concerns into film. Gould is celebrating the beauty of people. What's important are faces, postures, and the look of a man's eyes as he reacts to the world around him.

There is almost no information in the film. You won't find out that Pikangikum is sixty miles from the nearest raw frontier town. You won't be told that these four hundred Indians are living as Indians on central reservations did fifty or one hundred years ago. But if you look closely, it's all there to be seen in the faces and heard in their soft statements.

Gould has put a lot into eleven minutes of film. School. Church. Birth. Work. The Bay. Transportation. But most of all people. What he is saying, though he never puts it into words, is that we have something to learn from them.

What do you think?

1. *"They are integrated with the surroundings and with people." Explain.*
2. *"We have something to learn from them."*
   (a) What might we learn?
   (b) Why did Gould not put it into words?

6. THE TWO-WAY STREET

This selection is, again, from an article by D. G. Poole.

The essential difference between Indian and White consciousness is that the Indian has never become alienated (individuated) from his tribal brothers and from his environment. To him, the earth has never been a lifeless and static lump separate and apart from humanity. Where White science is now achieving an intellectual appreciation of the relatedness of all of life which it has named ecology, the Indian has never lost his emotional-realization-identification, his intuitive knowing of the same thing. To him, the planetary environment has always been permeated with a certain indefinable but *valued* quality. To him, wealth has always been inherent in the self, and one can be wealthy only in one's experience and recognition of quality, never in one's possession of quantity. . . . Wealth can never be in the wallet or the bank. The dollar represents the attempt of a[n] . . . commercial society which has lost sight . . . of quality, to invent value. But the invention can never be of value in exactly the same way that a wax apple can never be an apple nor a plastic rose a rose.

In the Western world, the meaning of life, the traditional purpose and central source of respectability for almost everyone, has been that of preparing for a job, getting a job, earning a living and accumulating possessions. For hundred of years a great deal of virtue has been attached to this particular definition of work as the dominant custom affecting human activity. In consequence, earning has come to be regarded not merely as an economic necessity but as a moral achievement. It follows, of course, that those individuals who do not conform to this definition of "life's purpose" are classified as good-for-nothings. It also follows that such nonconformity is regarded as a vice. Such is the Western tradition, indeed, that in the minds of a surprising number, leisure is still associated with sin, as is also pleasure.

There is no intent here to quarrel with this narrow tradition, but it must be realized that during the past twenty years a major shift has been inaugurated at the very base of White commercial culture. Twenty years ago, the active individual in society was evaluated in terms of production. He was referred to as a producer. Today, the shift has proceeded far enough so that the same individual (though he may still be a producer) is evaluated in terms of consumption. He is referred to, with every increasing frequency, as a consumer. For this to have happened in the short pace of twenty years is hard to believe, yet it is nothing compared to the changes which the next twenty years can be expected to bring. Interpreted realistically, this shift in value and emphasis can only mean: (1) that there has been a decrease in the need for the productivity of human labor, and (2) that there has been an increase in means, other than earning (social welfare, unemployment insurance, etc.), whereby non-producers may still function as consumers.

It is the expressed opinion of a number of reliable economists and sociologists that in the next twenty years (perhaps much sooner) Western society will be forced to find a definition of meaning and purpose other than the traditional one of education-for-earning, job-holding, earning-a-living and accumulating possessions. These people warn that the above-mentioned shift is already much further underway than is popularly realized and that it will continue until automatic machines and computer complexes have removed seventy-five, perhaps eighty per cent of today's job opportunities and probably ninety per cent of the necessity for human beings to continue producing what cybernated machines can produce better, faster, and cheaper. In the face of these developments many of the features of traditional Indian culture are going to appear saner and more attractive.

Confronted with predictions of this sort, it would seem both wise and timely for the White community to ask itself questions such as these:

Before Columbus, what sort of people lived here? Who inhabited these continents? Men who worked hard but went to no job; who were purposefully active but never employed; who made adequate provision but earned no money—and having no money, accumulated (by White standards) no possessions. Where did they find meaning in life? What motivated them? What goals? What purpose? How could they have been so lacking in industry as never to have fought back the forest and cleared the land for erosion? How could they have been so delinquent in initiative as never to have possessed the land and divided it into fenced properties so that a civilized basis might have been established for communal and inter-communal conflict in perpetuity? How could they have been so blind as to invest their energies in an endless round of ritualistic ceremonials rather than to the object of converting all of the chemistry of Nature into more and more Indians and more and more gadgets and gismos for more and more Indians? How could they have been so naive in their relation to environment as to have rendered only that which they could use into necessities rather than that which could be seized into personal wealth? How could they have been content to live in nature rather than manage her—as if, indeed, they belonged to the earth instead of the earth to them?

The great fact of Indian culture is that long ago it discovered and devised means of sustaining a visionary experience of life. The central feature of traditional Indian culture was its open, exploring, inclusive heart. The astounding achievement of Indian people has been their preservation (in the face of unrelenting and terrible persecution) of faith in their vision; a faith in the feeling of self and environment as a single, flowing phenomenon. This visionary realization of life through feeling, as compared to the visual understanding of life through intellectual speculation might be called emotional curiosity. The result of emotional curiosity is that the seed-meaning of life has survived. It has not been sold in the market place. It does not lie, rotting and ignored in the garbage dumps of civilization. It has suffered no alienating, intellectual freeze-out. It lives on, unharmed and unscathed in those native Americans who, like their uncivilized forebears, are neither strangers in the earth nor aliens under the sun. The great fact of White culture is that it has repeatedly succeeded in bursting the limitations of its own intellectual customs, the structures of its own cultural beliefs. The outstanding feature of White culture has been, and is, its consistently open, exploring, inquisitive mind. The world has been alternatively blessed and cursed with the results of this insatiable curiosity but the benediction or the curse has never resided, intrinsically in any invention of itself, but in its application—the use or misuse to which it was put. The world is now faced with the ultimate effects of intellectual curiosity. It is possessed of the means of utmost construction and cultivation or, alternatively, utmost spoliation and destruction.

Symptomatic of White insensitivity is the blasé assumption that science can and will solve all problems, including that of human irresponsibility. But it will take far more than science (which by present definition, can never be more than the ultimate projection of reason), more than the abilities of sociologists, biologists and resource managers. It will require an infusion of poetic intuition; a transfusion of the ancient Indian way.

This is what White culture has to gain from integration with Indian culture. This is why it is more urgent and needful that the predominant flow of integration be from White to Indian, rather than the other way about. But it is unlikely that it will happen this way unless the need becomes so desperate as to be felt directly and in personal agony by every individual. It is infinitely more difficult for the passive non-aggressive way of intuitive knowing, of realizing through feeling, to invade and influence the practical, reasoned way of intellectual understanding than for the reverse to happen.

What is it that the Indian can expect to gain from White culture? The most significant positive aspect of White commercial culture is the sustained impetus it has provided for creativity, especially in the field of invention. It is to this particular culture and to the people who have erected a civilization upon it that the world owes almost all of its technological advance and the resultant *potential* of freedom and *promise* of security made possible by limitless reserves of energy and limitless automatic means of production and service.

Since he has not done so to date, it is pretty unlikely that the Indian will now accept White civilization *in toto*. It is to be expected that he will attempt to select from White culture those techniques and customs which seem most practical and useful. Again, as he has always sought to do. Always the Indian has evinced a respectful admiration for White techniques, White ingenuity, White industry and White audacity, but this has been tempered with a whimsical patience. One has the feeling that Indians have always observed the upstart White man as a sage might observe a child. Recently, an Indian friend remarked to me (while we watched one at work) "the bulldozer is, truly, a mechanical marvel, but the trees it uproots and smashes are living miracles."

Does the Indian want bulldozers? Yes, he has them now. But he does not want to smash up his homeland with them. Does he want modern plumbing? Yes, so long as the communal effluvium is not dumped into the rivers of his homeland. Does he want outboard motors? Yes. Aircraft? Yes. Television? Yes. Automobiles? Yes. Electric power? Yes. But he will probably draw the line at power-driven tooth brushes and motorized carving knives.

Does he want White medicine? Yes. But many Indians hold still to the primitive ways of folk medicine and folk health. The healing herbs and plants have not been forgotten. Does he want White education? Yes, so long as he feels it will help him, as an Indian, to realize Indian objectives. What about religion? Here again, the old traditions are not so much forgotten as overlaid. Given a choice, he will probably take what he values from Christianity, combine it with what he has saved from his own religious traditions, and let the rest go. And government? Yes, so long as he feels that government is representing him without prejudice, rather than merely manipulating him with condescension and managing him for its own obscure objectives. Is he interested in business? Yes, an increasing proportion of Indians will probably become involved in some form of commercial enterprise or one or another of the professions, as many have already done. The proportion may be expected to increase in ratio to the inclination of Whites to relinquish their narrow insistance upon commercial preoccupation as the only meaningful mode of existence.

Obviously, the Indian has a great deal to gain from White culture. But he also has a great deal to lose. If the price of acquiring the benefits of White civilization is that of relinquishing the Indian tradition and heritage, the Indian will forego the former and cling to the latter. Indeed, this is largely what he has done these four hundred years.

This is no accident, much less a recalcitrant posture. It is an instinctive reaction which has its roots in life-preservation. Spelled out it means that while he respects the techniques, accessories and know-how of White civilization, he has a profound distrust of its motives and objectives. It means that the Indian instinctively senses an unprecedented danger in White technology—a danger which threatens all of planetary life so long as White society remains incapable of transcending its present paranoic motivations and persists in its predatory practice of commerce.

What is meant by?

"alienated"
"ecology"
"intuitive knowing"
"communal"
"visionary experience"
"intellectual speculation"

What do you think?

1. *According to the author, Indians experience life through "visionary knowing." Whites experience life through "intellectual speculation." Explain the difference in your own words. How does a White man see a tree? How does an Indian?*
2. *How do the life-styles of Indian and White societies reflect the differences between their ways of looking at life?*
3. *According to the author what will future changes entail for modern society? What can Whites learn from Indians to help them adjust to this new life? What can Indians find in White culture that might be beneficial to them?*

Assimilation, Integration or Separation?

A number of options have been suggested to alleviate social tensions and to improve the conditions under which Indians live. These suggestions are often based on a particular view of what the native people's future relationship with White society should be. These views fall into three reasonably distinct patterns: assimilation into White society, integration with it, or separation from it.

The next few pages carry articles advocating versions of the three possibilities. Can you define each of the three terms? Can you identify which of the options each article is advocating? Can you assess the desirability and possible impact of each suggestion?

1. ONE NON-INDIAN SOLUTION

An editorial from the Orillia Packet and Times *was quoted in the* Kingston-Ontario Whig Standard, *July 24, 1967.*

Anyone who has ever driven through an Indian reservation in Canada must have been struck by the contrast between the all-pervading listlessness of the adult community and the restless energy of the bright-eyed Indian youngsters, as sharp and quick as so many chipmunks. The forces which transform the bright promise of childhood into the resigned and abject apathy of adulthood stem from the tremendous inertia implicit in reservation life, which makes no demands upon individual enterprise or initiative and confers no rewards beyond a basic subsistence. No amount of well-meant paternalism can alter the fact that reservation life is completely alien to today's concept of a competitive society, in which individual exertion brings its own rewards; no benign bureaucracy can compensate for the complete isolation of reservation life from the mainstream of Canadian society.

Canada in fact practices the very apartheid it professes to deplore in other multi-racial states, operating two parallel and supposedly equal societies in isolation from each other. It must be apparent to the most casual observer that the system has now become unworkable as the rapid growth of material affluence in Canadian society contrasts ever more glaringly with feudal institutions and subsistence standards of reservation life.

One must distinguish here between the highly-organized "sedentary" Indian nations, such as the Six Nations of the east and the Haida of the west, who adapt readily to a settled society, and the nomadic tribes who traditionally subsisted by hunting and fishing over wide areas of land. It is the latter who have suffered most severely from the enervation of reservation life; they live today in a society which has no use for their traditional skills, and whose values are completely alien to those engendered by tribal life in the wilderness. In the highly-industrialized Ontario heartland, there exists no frontier to sustain the hunting and fishing way of life, yet the descendants of generations of nomadic tribesmen do not take readily to life at the lathe or the plow.

Surely the answer to this increasingly serious problem lies in the phasing out of the reservations and the integration of Indian children into the educational and social structure of Canada. This must obviously be done over a considerable period, so that older generations are allowed to shelter in the security of reservation life to which they have become accustomed, and to which they are entitled. But the horizon of the youngsters must be lifted beyond the reservation limits. As Canadians they are entitled to share in the full measure of Canada's rewards and opportunities. It may be that such integration may mean the virtual disappearance of the Indian identity, as simply another blood strain in a truly Canadian people, but surely such an eventuality is infinitely preferable to the maintenance of an Indian "fact" which has grown quite unacceptable to a prosperous and enlightened twentieth-century society.

What is meant by?

"inertia in reservation life"
"paternalism"
"benign bureaucracy"
"feudal institutions"

What do you think?

1. *(a) What is your reaction to this article? Why?*
   (b) What do you think Indian reaction would be to this article? Why?
2. *What does the author propose in place of what he refers to as a present state of "apartheid"? What does he see as the possible consequences, and how does he feel about them?*
3. *Is this author advocating assimilation or integration? What are its disadvantages? advantages?*

2. AN OFFICIAL VIEW

The following statement is taken from the June 1967 edition of Citizen, *a publication of the Canadian Citizenship Branch in Ottawa.*

Canada is an excellent example of a country in which recognition of cultural diversity has led government and people alike to speak of the "integration," rather than the "assimilation" of groups and individuals. Integration, in contrast to assimilation encourages the newcomer in a society to retain what he regards as best in his own cultural background and tradition with the expectation that he will contribute them to the enrichment of Canadian life.

The fact that every Canadian is a member of an ethnic minority group has no doubt persuaded us, both collectively and often as individuals as well, that the "melting-pot" concept is not feasible for Canada. We have accepted the fact that the population of Canada represents an impressive array of cultural and social backgrounds; that there is no cultural mould into which people can be squeezed and from that they will emerge as "typical Canadians." We have in fact learned to live with cultural diversity and to recognize its advantages in developing a level and stimulating country in which to live.

In summary, integration of any newcomer into a community whether he be from another land or province, is a two-way street. It requires the newcomer to adapt himself to new circumstance and surroundings, to accept what he cannot change and contribute his talents and skills whenever he has an opportunity to do so. It demands as well, that the community itself be adaptable to change and active in providing opportunities for newcomers to share equally in community life—retaining at the same time their personal integrity and self-respect.

What is meant by?

"the melting pot"
"cultural diversity"

What do you think?

1. *How does the writer distinguish between integration and assimilation? Which does he favour? How do you know?*
2. *(a) According to this view what does integration require of the newcomer? Of the general community?*
   (b) What would this mean for Indians? for the White community?
3. *From your observation what happens to recent immigrants to this country as far as integration goes? What does this mean for Canadian society? For the Indian in particular?*
4. *Does Canada have a genuine cultural mosaic? Justify your answer.*

3. INTEGRATION: IS IT ASSIMILATION?

In 1971 Information Canada commissioned eight reports on the problem of communication between governments and residents of local communities. Here is an excerpt from the report on Schefferville, Quebec, a sub-Arctic community where 3,500 Whites and 750 Montagnais and Naskapi Indians live.

A member of Treasury Board has described an unofficial policy for Indian Affairs and Northern Development:

Along with the objective of providing the Indians with a choice as to their way of life, I believe that it is also fair to say that there has been an unspoken desire on the part of the federal government to encourage—

but not force—the maximum degree of integration of Indians into Canadian communities.

It is difficult to reconcile "choice as to their way of life" with the desire to encourage "maximum" integration but, to Schefferville people who are familiar with Indian Affairs, there is little doubt that government considers integration of the Indians more important than their freedom of choice.

As one ex-member of the department stated: "Indian Affairs wants total assimilation, but they call it integration."

It is interesting to examine the reasoning behind certain proposals that Indian Affairs has put forward. A departmental brief on the Block 16 (housing) project, for instance, explained the importance of sanitary conditions for the Schefferville bands with the following three references to the advantages of cleanliness among Indians:

1. Although electricity is available, there are no water or sewer services (at John Lake). It is impossible, therefore, for the Indians living in the John Lake settlement to maintain themselves and their clothing in a degree of cleanliness acceptable to the non-Indians at Schefferville with whom they have daily contact in respect of school attendance, employment and recreation. . . .

2. Almost from the commencement of the arrangement, however, complaints have been received from the local school boards concerning the lack of cleanliness of the children attending the schools. The concern expressed by the school boards includes complaints that many of the children are infested with lice. . . .

3. It is obvious, therefore, that the present difference in the living standards of the two groups (White and Indian) is so great that the presence in the schools of Indian children who are not reasonably clean is most distasteful to the school boards and the general public whom they serve. . . .

Not one of these observations expresses the slightest interest in the health risks to Indians that result from the lack of proper sanitation. The paramount concern is only the possibility that Whites may reject unclean Indians. That is, the life style of the Indians could retard "maximum integration."

A counselling service, to be operated by Indian Affairs, reflects the same interest in getting Indians to accept White values to smooth the way towards integration. The chief counselling concerns (translated from French) were as follows:

1. Problems of family drinking.
2. Lack of cleanliness of children at school.
3. Hygiene, or lack of hygiene in general.
4. Employment.
5. Understanding of the need for discipline in order to live with non-Indians.

6. Acceptance of the Indians by the non-Indians.
7. Irresponsibility of parents vis-à-vis their children (drinking, education, etc.)

These points unquestionably underscore some serious problems; but why is it that, in point 2, the lack of cleanliness among the children becomes a problem only when they are at school? Hospital statistics, as we've seen, clearly indicate the prevalence of gastroenteritis among pre-school Indian children, and this malady is directly related to unsanitary conditions.

Why is it that, in point 5, counsellors would encourage discipline not because of any intrinsic value it may have but, again, "in order to live with non-Indians"?

Point 6 is self-explanatory, but who needs the counselling? If the problem is lack of acceptance of the Indians by the Whites, then why not give some counselling to the Whites? Preferably by Indians.

What do you think?

1. *Does the departmental brief on housing and the counselling service's list of concerns contradict the definition of integration given by the Department of Citizenship and Immigration on page 191? Justify your answer.*
2. *How do you think the Indian concept of integration would differ from the concept of integration revealed in the above document?*

4. A REACTION TO THE OFFICIAL VIEW

This selection has been taken from an article by D. G. Poole entitled "Integration."

In the present case integration engineers should understand before they make any recommendations the extent to which the American continent is still populated with European colonials who conceive of themselves as governing and administering a lesser "native" populace—a fantasy which spawns condescension and defeats any worthwhile purpose.

It is not at all sure that engineered integration will work. If its object is that of perceiving, honoring and preserving the real, life values in any and every culture, its efforts will probably meet with cooperation and goodwill. The result will unquestionably be that of enriching and enhancing the entire human heritage, but if its object is that of coercing or enticing the members of a less dominant culture to desert their own good, humane (but differing) customs to become the expedient converts of a more dominant culture, it is likely that it will fail in all but the creation of further ill-will and misunderstanding.

By any honest definition, the official policy of integration means processing Indians, just as any honest definition of modern education means processing children. Integration is concerned principally with Indian children and has the object of transforming them from wards of government into dark-skinned–White-encultured civilians. The primary means to this end is education; standard public school education, where possible under the normal circumstances of any average community. Efforts are being made and will continue to be made, to draw the children and young people away from the reservations, to involve them first, in the school curriculum (with emphasis on technical studies) and second, in routine employments, with the hope that they will eventually settle in Canadian communities and live as normal, self-supporting, Canadian citizens. There is also the realization that the old people who cannot or will not change, will eventually die off.

It is perhaps understandable that to the bureaucrat or the social engineer this mode of integration seems not only practical but also humane. Thus, the sincerity of the architects of this policy is not here in question. But one must question the assumptions upon which it seems to rest. Namely, that Indians ought to be attracted to the White way of life; that Indians once processed, will not want to return to the reservations and will be equitably accepted into White communities; that integration is a one-way street.

If it is to work, integration must be a two-way street paved with the enduring macadam of equality. Which is to say that the White community must look for and discover something to admire and desire in the Indian way and the Indian as a human being—just as it is presently assumed that the Indian ought to be attracted to White culture and ought to find something to aspire to in the White human being. And insofar as this is not the present state of affairs, then it would seem that there must be an interim step in the integration program with a switch in emphasis, from White acculturation to Indian cohesion. It would seem that a program should be devised which will help the Indian rehabilitate himself as an Indian, regain his old-time self-respect and discover a degree of integration with Indians which he has never known.

Finally, let us take a brief look at the word, integration. It means the process of combining parts, or making a whole. In the psychological sense of the individual or in the sociological sense of community, the word integrity means wholeness. The word whole in turn, in its root meaning, is one and the same as health or hale. A man with integrity, then, is one who is consistently able to resist the divisive strains and pressures of environment and remain whole—undivided, uncompromised and in good health. He remains true to his own innate nature; he is himself; he plays his own part, his own role; he stands on his own reputation. The individual is not only accepted into the community, but valued for himself, in the degree that he demonstrates this definition of integrity. Just so, races are accepted into the world community on the same basis.

Thus, before they can accept the present bureaucratic proposal of integration into White society, the Indians themselves can scarcely escape the prior necessity of seeking and achieving a purely Indian integrity, inclusive and continental in scope. It is of the utmost importance, not only to Indians but also to Whites, that every Indian feel and know himself to be a number of an ancient and noble American race; that every Indian remember and honor the exploits of his forebears; that every Indian know and value the Indian tradition, the racial heritage which he alone can preserve for the enrichment of all mankind. It is important that every Indian, though proud of his status as a Canadian or American citizen, should first, hold up his head and be proud of his Indian blood.

Only thus can it be hoped that the White community may discover and value those features of the Indian tradition, so lacking in White culture and in which White society stands in such extreme need.

Only thus will the Indian be respectfully approached by his White neighbor and respectfully invited to live and work as an equal in a truly Canadian community which has itself achieved an integrity capable of transcending the petty differences in color, race or religion, represented in its individuals.

Only thus can we be assured that there will never be an Indian ghetto.

What is meant by?

"European colonials"
"processing"
"macadam"
"White acculturation"
"innate nature"

What do you think?

1. *What does the writer feel the official policy of integration means for Indians? What does he feel it should mean?*
2. *Describe and explain how D. G. Poole would see integration achieved?*
3. *Discuss how you think the White community might react.*
4. *Do you think Poole has refuted the editor of the* Whig-Standard *(page 189)? Justify your answer.*

5. SIDE BY SIDE WITH THE WHITE MAN

William I. C. Wuttunee, in his book Ruffled Feathers *(Calgary: Bell Books, 1971), discusses his views on the future relationship between Indians and Whites.*

There have been veiled threats by Red Power advocates against the establishment in Canada. Negative attitudes against White society are prevalent across Canada and they do untold damage. Many young Indians who are struggling to gain an education get caught up in the rat race of condemning Canadian society. The advocacy of an administration which is to be run by Indians for Indians, without the participation of the White man, destroys the initiative of those young Indians who are trying to educate themselves and trying to fit into Canadian society as a whole. The over-all effect of the anti-White bombardment is for the young Indians to drop out of Canadian society and suffer the usual affliction of excessive use of alcohol.

Present-day Indian leaders acutely dislike anyone who will stand up to them. They are very anxious to maintain their exclusive power over the Indian people, and they resort to attacking their own people by every corrosive method. They exercise their power from big offices in the cities, and because most Indians are still humble, the leaders can, without much objection from their own people, step upon them as they wish.

If Indians are going to see a different form of development which is more conducive to their welfare and general well-being, then they must form counter organizations which will promote integration of the Indian into the White man's society. There are many Indians who wish to integrate and who wish to have the opportunity of making a decent living side by side with the White man. There are many who are not perpetual alcoholics and who are prepared to become taxpayers. The establishment of Indian organizations opposed to Red Power—thereby forming a two-party system among the Indian people—would then enable Indians to use the democratic process within their own ranks. They would be able to stand up to people like Harold Cardinal, and obtain their own form of participation in Canadian society. They would be able to state freely that they are not reactionaries forever tied to the history of the 1800s and the treaties of that era.

This mulcting of the White man and the White man's government is an extremely negative policy. Current Indian leaders are not prepared to do their share; they are not prepared to tell the Indian people to get an education and to pull their share of the load in Canada.

Where is the dignity of the Indian people that they were once so proud of? Have they completely lost it? Or is there still some vestige of pride left in them? If so, they should immediately get rid of every dictator in their ranks; they should dispose of every racist and make sure they muzzle them adequately so that bitterness and hatred will not be further spread. Too often Indians spend their time criticizing and blaming the White man for their problems. Is it not possible that they are themselves responsible for the creation and the perpetuation of these problems? Is it not possible that they, too, can do something about them?

If we are to solve this dilemma there has to be a complete overhaul of the system of grants by government to Indian organizations. There has to be a toughening up of government attitude towards autocratic Indian associations. Indian people must stand up to the Red Power advocates and develop a new approach to the situation. There must be a sense of adulthood by the non-Indian people who are administering programs relating to Indians. Weak "love" or pity for Indian people is not going to improve their lot. There must be hard-headed programs designed to increase the participation of Indians in a non-Indian society. Sociologists and anthropologists can't spend their time in apologizing for Indian people, thereby encouraging an ethnic division which will perpetuate the problem for several more generations. Their studies must be done from a positive point of view, rather than by re-affirming a separation of the two races. There is certainly something good to be said about the value of people living together peacefully, mutually, for the benefit of one another. It is time to blast the arguments against integration and to speak in favor of it.

Integration doesn't have to mean forced integration, rather it can be a gradual process which will develop Indian men and women into independent, contributing members of Canadian society. It doesn't mean the wholesale displacement of Indian people, but individual attention to individual Indians and their problems. It means giving assistance to those Indians who are now helping themselves, rather than only helping the rebellious few.

When we have re-examined our approach with a sincere desire to assist and to develop, it is possible that "the Indian situation" can be solved within the next generation. Let the next century be one of development and self-fulfillment for Indian people. Let us establish a society within which an Indian and a White man can look each other in the eye, with mutual trust. Red Power advocates must rechannel their energy and efforts, not away from the White man, but, rather, toward helping all the poor of our land. They can join forces with the poor people of Canada, now numbering approximately 5 million, and thus form an invincible army of "people power" against neglect, oppression, and despair. . . .

What do you think?

1. *Is Wuttunee proposing assimilation, integration, or separation? Defend your answer.*
2. *Why does Wuttunee accuse Red Power of being anti-democratic, racist, and reactionary? What does he think the effects of Red Power are on Indians? on Whites? Do you agree with him? Why or why not? How might a Red Power advocate refute his arguments?*
3. *"Sociologists and anthropologists can't spend their time in apologizing for Indian people, thereby encouraging an ethnic division which will perpetuate the problem for several more generations."*

Explain this assertion. Do you agree that such studies encourage ethnic division? Why or why not? Would Vine Deloria (page 42) agree with Wuttunee? Explain. What do you think Wuttunee's views are on the importance of the survival of the Indian culture?

4. *Compare Wuttunee's views on integration to those of D. G. Poole. Where do they differ and why? Whom do you agree with and why?*

6. RACIAL INTEGRATION: A REMOTE POSSIBILITY

This is another excerpt from the Adams-Warnock interview which appeared in the Canadian Dimension, *April-May, 1968.*

Well, at this point I think that I would say that I am a separatist and I have been labelled as a separatist because I do believe that it is necessary to organize on the basis that we are Indian and Métis separate from the White culture, the White society, and the White people. Now, I am a little different here than some of the more militant, in that I feel in the long run, in the years to come, that once we have really revitalized our culture and that we have developed certain skills—social, psychological skills—that we may be able to move into the White society, but by that time we would want to dictate some of the terms on which we move in.

You see, really what we have to do is that the White man in Regina or Ottawa who owns or controls or has the power—we really have to adopt and learn his tactics and learn his concepts of power and move in. And these are things that are foreign to us.

. . . The thing is that we see ourselves and have been taught to see ourselves truly as Indians, and this becomes very confusing, and many of us want to move towards the White ideal. This—again typical of colonial people—there are so many jealousies and divisions, and, of course, the establishment of the society wants to keep us divided simply by Indian and Métis, Cree and Saulteux, Catholic, Anglican—and all these divisions, they exploit them as much as possible.

Well, I think that I would have to say that the strongest opposition at the moment is from the Uncle Tomahawks and the puppets. You see, generally, the chiefs on the reserves and the councillors, in most cases, are puppets, and so they are very definitely opposed to me and any member of a group which I represent or any militant organization who move toward changing the reserve system.

What is meant by?

"Uncle Tomahawks"
"puppets"

What do you think?

1. *Why does Adams describe himself as a separatist? What role does he see separatism fulfilling?*
2. *Compare Adams's views to those of William Wuttunee (page 195), D. G. Poole (page 193), and Kahn Tineta Horn (page 95). Account for any similarities or differences in their views.*

7. RACIAL INTEGRATION: AN IMPOSSIBLE DREAM

This is part of an address, "Education the Key to an Indian Identity," given by Lloyd Caibaiosai on October 26, 1968.

This brings me to a proposition which is the key to my understanding of the situation. I offer it tentatively even though I am convinced it is valid. If it is, it makes all of our present difficulties trifling and we have before us a problem in statecraft whose dimensions cannot now be imagined.

The proposition is that racial integration in Canada is impossible.

I set forth this proposition without qualification. There are no hidden unlesses, buts, or ifs in it. I shall not deny that in some remote future, integration may come about. But I do not see it resulting from the actual present trends and attitudes in Canadian society. It can only be produced by some event overturning these trends. There is no denial of this proposition that there will be a steady betterment in the material situation of Indians. This is even likely. My proposition does, nevertheless, contradict the words of Prime Minister Trudeau that "the just society shall be extended to all peoples in the nation's slums."

My proposition is sad. My proposition in short smashes the liberal dream. It eliminates the democratic optimistic claim that we are finding our way to a harmonious blending of the races. It changes the words of the marching song to "We Shall Not Overcome," (or was that "Overrun"?), for what was eventually to be overcome was hostility and non-fraternity, between Indian and White. My proposition dynamites the foundations of the IEA [Indian Eskimo Association], and similar organizations. It asserts that Indian Reserve, Canada, and Whitetown, Canada, for all practical purposes and with unimportant exceptions, will remain separate social communities.

I am not sure, but it may also mean that Indian Reserve will become a separate political community.

The proposition would seem to place me in the camp of the bigots and locate me with the hopeless, also probably the racists. It puts at ultimate zero the efforts of the tough and high-minded who are giving their lives to the dream of equality among men.

Yet I am convinced that integration in Canada is a sentimental, not a doctrinal idea. We came to the idea late in Canadian history and it disappears readily from the rhetoric of politics—though not from the list of sacred democratic aims—at the first sign of indocility. The vast fuss of improvements in Indian communities is not aimed at integration. Few are afflicting us any longer with such a tiresome lie. All these measures are primarily aimed at the prevention of civic commotions, secondarily at assuaging the conscience of Whitetown and finally helping the Indians. Priorities tell the story.

The country of Canada is a White man's country conducted according to White customs, and White laws for White purposes. I would not even argue that Whites should not run the country for their own interests, but they can't see that racial integration is one of these interests, except in perilous self-deceit. Whites like Indians so long as they themselves are not disturbed by Indians. Whites have no objection to bettering the Indians' lives so long as it does not cost much, and as long as it leads to the continuance of Indian Reserve and so does not present the threat of genuine integration at any level. The White condition for Indian betterment is, to put it simply, separation.

In giving up on integration I am not giving up on the Indians but on the Whites. Whites attitudes are the problems. Sadly enough, there is only one place where we have registered even a mild success: we have more or less integrated poverty. The liberal view is that patience and persisance will in the end perform the miracle. The enemy is ignorance. Whitetown's resistance, accordingly, is temporary, stubborn perhaps, but penetrable by knowledge and association.

Let me put forward the more general testimony in support of my proposition, the race situation is marked by growing expression of distrust, hate, and fear on the part of both Indians and Whites; growing disillusionment throughout all the reserves; increasing belligerency of young Indians and their leader; increasing impatience of our Dad, Whitey; growing isolation of the Indian middle class who have made it; growing uselessness of treaties between Indians and Whites as Indian demands become more basic and White resistence more determined.

The outside agitation is Whitetown itself. It is important to recognize that separation-not-integration is the way it has always been. The fostering of the illusion that integration is an achievable goal is bad enough in its effects on Indians, some of whom may still entertain a vision of their children foregathering in total equality under the White yum-yum tree. But the illusion is sinister in its likely consequence for Whites. By engaging in it they are leaving themselves unprepared for the grand finale.

What is necessary is the development of a Canadian democratic system which, in itself allows men to be equal and be in peaceful coexistence, but maintains the existence of two or three viable separate societies.

What is meant by?

"We Shall Not Overcome"
"liberal dream"
"White yum-yum tree"
"viable separate societies"

What do you think?

1. *"Racial integration in Canada is impossible". How does Mr. Caibaiosai arrive at this conclusion? Do you agree with him? Why or why not?*
2. *What does Mr. Caibaiosai propose? Why? Argue the case for and against his proposal.*
3. *A "separatist" Indian condition already exists in Canada. Discuss.*
4. *Howard Adams and Lloyd Caibaiosai both call themselves separatists. Compare their views. What do you notice? Explain.*

The White Paper and Responses

In the summer of 1969 the federal government brought out a policy statement on Indian affairs which was to revolutionize the position of the Indian in Canadian society. Was the new policy one of assimilation, integration or separation?

1. OTTAWA'S PROPOSALS

What follows is the case for the new policy given in a White Paper. The official title of the White Paper was "The Statement of the Government of Canada on Indian Policy."

In the past ten years or so, there have been important improvements in education, health, housing, welfare, and community development. Developments in leadership among the Indian communities have become increasingly evident. Indian people have begun to forge a new unity. The Government believes progress can come from these developments but only if they are met by new responses. The proposed policy is a new response.

The policy rests upon the fundamental right of Indian people to full and equal participation in the cultural, social, economic and political life of Canada.

To argue against this right is to argue for discrimination, isolation and separation. No Canadian should be excluded from participation in community life, and none should expect to withdraw and still enjoy the benefits that flow to those who participate.

THE LEGAL STRUCTURE

Legislative and constitutional bases of discrimination must be removed.

Canada cannot seek the just society and keep discriminatory legislation on its statute books. The Government believes this to be self-evident. The ultimate aim of removing the specific references to Indians from the constitution may take some time, but it is a goal to be kept constantly in view. In the meantime, barriers created by special legislation can generally be struck down.

Under the authority of Head 24, Section 91 of the British North America Act, the Parliament of Canada has enacted the Indian Act. Various federal-provincial agreements and some other statutes also affect Indian policies.

In the long term, removal of the reference in the constitution would be necessary to end the legal distinction between Indians and other Canadians. In the short term, repeal of the Indian Act and enactment of transitional legislation to ensure the orderly management of Indian land would do much to mitigate the problem.

The ultimate goal could not be achieved quickly, for it requires a change in the economic circumstances of the Indian people and much preliminary adjustment with provincial authorities. Until the Indian people are satisfied that their land holdings are solely within their control, there may have to be some special legislation for Indian lands.

THE INDIAN CULTURAL HERITAGE

There must be positive recognition by everyone of the unique contribution of Indian culture to Canadian society.

It is important that Canadians recognize and give credit to the Indian contribution. It manifests itself in many ways; yet it goes largely unrecognized and unacknowledged. Without recognition by others it is not easy to be proud.

All of us seek a basis for pride in our own lives, in those of our families and of our ancestors. Man needs such pride to sustain him in the inevitable hour of discouragement, in the moment when he faces obstacles, whenever life seems turned against him. Everyone has such moments. We manifest our pride in many ways, but always it supports and sustains us. The legitimate pride of the Indian people has been crushed too many times by too many of their fellow Canadians.

The principle of equality and all that goes with it demands that all of us recognize each other's cultural heritage as a source of personal strength.

Canada has changed greatly since the first Indian Act was passed. Today it is made up of many people with many cultures. Each has its own manner of relating to the other; each makes its own adjustments to the larger society.

Successful adjustment requires that the larger groups accept every group with its distinctive traits without prejudice, and that all groups share equitably in the material and non-material wealth of the country.

For many years Canadians believed the Indian people had but two choices: they could live in a reserve community, or they could be assimilated and lose their Indian identity. Today Canada has more to offer. There is a third choice—a full role in Canadian society and in the economy while retaining, strengthening and developing an Indian identity which preserves the good things of the past and helps Indian people to prosper and thrive.

This choice offers great hope for the Indian people. It offers great opportunity for Canadians to demonstrate that in our open society there is room for the development of people who preserve their different cultures and take pride in their diversity.

This new opportunity to enrich Canadian life is central to the Government's new policy. If the policy is to be successful, the Indian people must be in a position to play a full role in Canada's diversified society, a role which stresses the value of their experience and the possibilities of the future.

* * * * *

The government recognizes that people of Indian ancestry must be helped in new ways in this task. It proposes, through the Secretary of State, to support associations and groups in developing a greater appreciation of their cultural heritage. It wants to foster adequate communication among all people of Indian descent and between them and the Canadian community as a whole.

Steps will be taken to enlist the support of Canadians generally. The provincial governments will be approached to support this goal through their many agencies operating in the field. Provincial educational authorities will be urged to intensify their review of school curriculae and course content with a view to ensuring that they adequately reflect Indian culture and Indian contributions to Canadian development.

PROGRAMS AND SERVICES

Services must come through the same channels and from the same government agencies for all Canadians.

This is an undeniable part of equality. It has been shown many times that separation of people follows from separate services. There can be no argument about the principle of common services. It is right.

It cannot be accepted now that Indians should be constitutionally excluded from the right to be treated within their province as full and equal citizens, with all the responsibilities and all the privileges that this might entail. It is in the provincial sphere where social remedies are structured and applied, and the Indian people, by and large, have been non-participating members of provincial society.

Canadians receive a wide range of services through provincial and local governments, but the Indian people and their communities are mostly outside that framework. It is no longer acceptable that the Indian people should be outside and apart. The government believes that services should be available on an equitable basis, except for temporary differentiation based on need. Services ought not to flow from separate agencies established to serve particular groups, especially not to groups that are identified ethnically.

Separate but equal services do not provide truly equal treatment. Treatment has not been equal in the case of Indians and their communities. Many services require a wide range of facilities which cannot be duplicated by separate agencies. Others must be integral to the complex systems of community and regional life and cannot be matched on a small scale.

The Government is therefore convinced that the traditional method of providing separate services to Indians must be ended. All Indians should have access to all programs and services of all levels of government equally with other Canadians.

The Government proposes to negotiate with the provinces and conclude agreements under which Indian people would participate in and be served by the full programs of the provincial and local systems. Equitable financial arrangements would be sought to ensure that services could be provided in full measure commensurate with the needs. The negotiations must seek arguments to end discrimination while ensuring that no harm is inadvertently done to Indian interests. The Government further proposes that federal disbursements for Indian programs in each province be transferred to that province. Subject to negotiations with the provinces, such provisions would as a matter of principle eventually decline, the provinces ultimately assuming the same responsibility for services to Indian residents as they do for services to others.

At the same time, the Government proposes to transfer all remaining federal responsibilities for Indians from the Department of Indian Affairs and Northern Development to other departments, including the Departments of Regional Economic Expansion, Secretary of State, and Manpower and Immigration.

It is important that such transfers take place without disrupting services and that special arrangements not be compromised while they are subject to consultation and negotiation. The Government will pay particular attention to this.

ENRICHED SERVICES

Those who are furthest behind must be helped most.

There can be little argument that conditions for many Indian people are not satisfactory to them and are not acceptable to others. There can be little question that special services, and especially enriched services, will be needed for some time.

Equality before the law and in programs and services does not necessarily result in equality in social and economic conditions. For that reason, existing programs will be reviewed. The Department of Regional Economic Expansion, the Department of Manpower and Immigration, and other federal departments involved would be prepared to evolve programs that would help break past patterns of deprivation.

Additional funds would be available from a number of different sources. In an atmosphere of greater freedom, those who are able to do so would be expected to help themselves, so more funds would be available to help those who really need it. The transfer of Indian lands to Indian control should enable many individuals and groups to move ahead on their own initiative. This in turn would free funds for further enrichment of programs to help those who are furthest behind. By ending some programs and replacing them with others evolved within the community, a more effective use of funds would be achieved. Administrative savings would result from the elimination of separate agencies as various levels of government bring general programs and resources to bear. By broadening the base of service agencies, this enrichment could be extended to all who need it. By involving more agencies working at different levels, and by providing those agencies with the means to make them more effective, the Government believes that root problems could be attacked, that solutions could be found that hitherto evaded the best efforts and best-directed of programs.

The economic base for many Indians is their reserve land, but the development of reserves has lagged.

Among the many factors that determine economic growth of reserves, their location and size are particularly important. There are a number of reserves located within or near growing industrial areas which could provide substantial employment and income to their owners if they were properly developed. There are other reserves in agricultural areas which could provide a livelihood for a larger number of family units than is presently the case. The majority of the reserves, however, are located in the boreal or wooded regions of Canada, most of them geographically isolated and many having little economic potential. In these areas, low income, unemployment and under-employment are characteristic of Indians and non-Indians alike.

Even where reserves have economic potential, the Indians have been handicapped. Private investors have been reluctant to supply capital for projects on land which cannot be pledged as security. Adequate social and risk capital has not been available from public sources. Most Indians have not had the opportunity to acquire managerial experience, nor have they been offered sufficient technical assistance.

The Government believes that the Indian people should have the opportunity to develop the resources of their reserves so they may contribute to their own well-being and the economy of the nation. To develop Indians reserves to the level of the regions in which they are located will require considerable capital over a period of some years, as well as the provision of managerial and technical advice. Thus the Government believes that all programs and advisory services of the federal and provincial governments should be made readily available to Indians.

In addition, and as an interim measure, the Government proposes to make substantial additional funds available for investment in the economic progress of the Indian people. This would overcome the barriers to early development of Indian lands and resources, help bring Indians into a closer working relationship with the business community, help finance their adjustment to new employment opportunities, and facilitate access to normal financial sources.

Even if the resources of Indian reserves are fully utilized, however, they cannot all properly support their present Indian populations, much less the population of the future. Many Indians will, as they are now doing, seek employment elsewhere as a means of solving their economic problems. Jobs are vital and the Government intends that the full counselling, occupational training and placement resources of the Department of Manpower and Immigration are used to further employment opportunities for Indians. The government will encourage private employers to provide opportunities for the Indian people.

In many situations, the problems of Indians are similar to those faced by their non-Indian neighbors. Solutions to their problems cannot be found in isolation but must be sought within the context of regional development plans involving all the people. The consequence of an integrated regional approach is that all levels of government—federal, provincial and local—and the people themselves are involved. Helping overcome regional disparities in the economic well-being of Canadians is the main task assigned to the Department of Regional Economic Expansion. The Government believes that the needs of Indian communities should be met within this framework.

CLAIMS AND TREATIES

Lawful obligations must be recognized.

Many of the Indian people feel that successive governments have not dealt with them as fairly as they should. They believe that lands have been taken from them in an improper manner, or without adequate compensation, that their funds have been improperly administered, that their treaty rights have been breached. Their sense of grievance influences their relations with governments and the community and limits their participation in Canadian life.

Many Indians look upon their treaties as the source of their rights to land, to hunting and fishing privileges, and to other benefits. Some believe the treaties should be interpreted to encompass wider services and privileges, and many believe the treaties have not been honoured. Whether or not this is correct in some or many cases, the fact is the treaties affect only half the Indians of Canada. Most of the Indians of Quebec, British Columbia, and the Yukon are not parties to a treaty.

The terms and effects of the treaties between the Indian people and the Government are widely misunderstood. A plain reading of the words used in the treaties reveals the limited and minimal promises which were included in them. As a result of the treaties, some Indians were given an initial cash payment and were promised land reserved for their exclusive use, annuities, protection of hunting, fishing and trapping privileges subject (in most cases) to regulation, a school or teachers in most instances, and, in one treaty only, a medicine chest. There were some other minor considerations such as the annual provision of twine and ammunition.

The annuities have been paid regularly. The basic promise to set aside reserve land has been kept except in respect of the Indians of the Northwest Territories and a few bands in the northern parts of the Prairie provinces. These Indians did not choose land when treaties were signed. The government wishes to see these obligations dealt with as soon as possible.

The right to hunt and fish for food is extended unevenly across the country and not always in relation to need. Although game and fish will become less and less important for survival as the pattern of Indian life continues to change, there are those who, at this time, still live in the traditional manner that their forefathers lived in when they entered into treaty with the government. The Government is prepared to allow such persons transitional freer hunting of migratory birds under the Migratory Birds Convention Act and Regulations.

The significance of the treaties in meeting the economic, educational, health and welfare needs of the Indian people has always been limited and will continue to decline. The services that have been provided go far beyond what could have been foreseen by those who signed the treaties.

The Government and the Indian people must reach a common understanding of the future role of the treaties. Some provisions will be found to have been discharged; others will have continuing importance. Many of the provisions and practices of another century may be considered irrelevant in the light of a rapidly changing society, and still others may be ended by mutual agreement. Finally, once Indian lands are securely within Indian control, the anomaly of treaties between groups within society and the government of that society will require that these treaties be reviewed to see how they can be equitably ended.

Other grievances have been asserted in more general terms. It is possible that some of these can be verified by appropriate research and may be susceptible of specific remedies. Others relate to aboriginal claims to land. These are so general and undefined that it is not realistic to think of them as specific claims capable of remedy except through a policy and program that will end injustice to Indians as members of the Canadian community. This is the policy that the Government is proposing for discussion.

At the recent consultation meeting in Ottawa representatives of the Indians, chosen at each of the earlier regional meetings, expressed concern about the extent of their knowledge of Indian rights and treaties. They indicated a desire to undertake further research to establish their rights with greater precision, elected a National Committee on Indian Rights and Treaties for this purpose and sought government financial support for research.

The Government had intended to introduce legislation to establish an Indian Claims Commission to hear and determine Indian claims. Consideration of the questions raised at the consultations and the review of Indian policy have raised serious doubts as to whether a Claims Commission as proposed to Parliament in 1965 is the right way to deal with the grievances of Indians put forward as claims.

The Government has concluded that further study and research are required by both the Indians and the Government. It will appoint a Commissioner who, in consultation with representatives of the Indians, will inquire into and report upon how claims arising in respect of the performance of the terms of treaties and agreements formally entered into by representatives of the Indians and the Crown, and the administration of moneys and lands pursuant to schemes established by legislation for the benefit of Indians may be adjudicated.

The Commissioner will also classify the claims that in his judgment ought to be referred to the courts or any special quasi-judicial body that may be recommended.

It is expected that the Commissioner's inquiry will go on concurrently with that of the National Indian Committee on Indian Rights and Treaties and the Commissioner will be authorized to recommend appropriate support to the Committee so that it may conduct research on the Indians' behalf and assist the Commissioner in his inquiry.

INDIAN LANDS

Control of Indian lands should be transferred to the Indian people.

Frustration is as great a handicap as a sense of grievance. True cooperation and participation can come only when the Indian people are controlling the land which makes up the reserves.

The reserve system has provided the Indian people with lands that generally have been protected against alienation without their consent. Widely scattered across Canada, the reserves total nearly 6,000,000 acres and are divided into about 2,200 parcels of varying sizes. Under the existing system, title to reserve lands is held either by the Crown in right of Canada or the Crown in right of one of the provinces. Administrative control and legislative authority are, however, vested exclusively in the Government and the Parliament of Canada. It is a trust. As long as this trust exists, the Government, as a trustee, must supervise the business connected with the land.

The result of Crown ownership and the Indian Act has been to tie the Indian people to a land system that lacks flexibility and inhibits development. If an Indian band wishes to gain income by leasing its land, it has to do so through a cumbersome system involving the Government as trustee. It cannot mortgage reserve land to finance development on its own initiative. Indian people do not have control of their lands except as the Government allows, and this is no longer acceptable to them. The Indians have made this clear at the consultation meetings. They now want real control, and this Government believes that they should have it. The Government recognizes that full and true equality calls for Indian control and ownership of reserve land.

Between the present system and the full holding of title in fee simple lie a number of intermediate states. The first step is to change the system under which ministerial decision is required for all that is done with Indian land. This is where the delays, the frustrations and the obstructions lie. The Indians must control their land.

This can be done in many ways. The Government believes that each band must make its own decision as to the way it wants to take control of its land and the manner in which it intends to manage it. It will take some years to complete the process of devolution.

The Government believes that full ownership implies many things. It carries with it the free choice of use, of retention, or of disposition. In our society it also carries with it an obligation to pay for certain services. The Government recognizes that it may not be acceptable to put all lands into the provincial systems immediately and make them subject to taxes. When the Indian people see that the only way they can own and fully control land is to accept taxation the way other Canadians do, they will make that decision.

Alternative methods for the control of their lands will be made available to Indian individuals and bands. Whatever methods of land control are chosen by the Indian people, the present system under which the Government must execute all leases, supervise and control procedures and surrenders, and generally act as trustee, must be brought to an end. But the Indian land heritage should be protected. Land should be alienated from them only by the consent of the Indian people themselves. Under a proposed Indian Lands Act full management would be in the hands of the bands and, if the bands wish, they or individuals would be able to take title to their land without restrictions.

As long as the Crown controls the land for the benefit of bands who use and occupy it, it is responsible for determining who may, as a member of a band, share in the assets of band land. The qualifications for band membership which it has imposed are part of the legislation—the Indian Act—governing the administration of reserve lands. Under the present Act, the Government applies and interprets these qualifications. When bands take title to their lands, they will be able to define and apply these qualifications themselves.

The Government is prepared to transfer to the Indian people the reserve lands, full control over them and, subject to the proposed Indian Lands Act, the right to determine who shares in ownership. The Government proposes to seek agreements with the bands and, where necessary, with the Governments of the provinces. Discussions will be initiated with the Indian people and the provinces to this end.

What do you think?

1. *Outline the proposals of the White Paper briefly. To what extent does it deal with Indian grievances? What are its chief concerns and why? Do you feel it omits anything? Explain.*
2. *"Legislative and constitutional bases of discrimination must be removed." Would Kahn Tineta Horn agree? Why or why not? What is your feeling and why?*
3. *"There must be positive recognition by everyone of the unique contribution of Indian culture to Canadian society." How does the White Paper say this could be done? Are its proposals sufficient? Why or why not?*
4. *"There can be no arguments about the principle of common services. It is right." Why was the White Paper so dogmatic on this point? Do you agree with its assertion?*
5. *It is in "the provincial sphere where social remedies are structured and applied. . . ." Do you agree? Explain.*
6. *"Those who are furthest behind must be helped the most." What does the Government mean by this? How does it propose to implement this policy? What do you think the Indian reaction to this policy might be?*
7. *Explain the White Paper's policy on treaties. How do you feel about it? How do you think Indians might feel about it?*
8. *"Control of Indian lands should be transferred to the Indian people." What does the White Paper mean by this, and how does it intend to put it into effect? What problem does it intend to correct? Should Indian lands be taxable? Why or why not?*
9. *What safeguards for the Indian people does the White Paper intend to use while the policy is being enacted? Why does it feel they are necessary? Do you think they are sufficient?*

2. WHITE BY ACT OF PARLIAMENT

The next few selections are a representative sampling of reactions to the White Paper. The first article, "The Last Years of the Indian Nation," is by Indian activist Lloyd Caibaiosai.

I heard a loud voice proclaiming from Parliament Hill:

> Now at last the just society has come to men. They shall dwell decently and with dignity. The just society will wipe away poverty; there shall be an end to strikes and to discrimination and lack of medical care and employment, for the old order has passed away.
>
> The Book of Trudeau
> The New Liberal Testament
> Revelation 25:7

I heard refrains from the Centennial Tower: "Aye, hosanna to the highest!"

The consultations were publicly launched in wrappings of nobility of purpose and yet with a certain dedication which smacked of sanctimoniousness.

The disguises of the consultations program were thin and clumsy. . . . It was a repulsive lie. The demands, the recommendations, the changes for the Indian Act fell on unhearing ears, unseeing eyes. It was a shameful waste of money.

The revolutionary new program that Jean Chrétien, minister of Indian Affairs, fashioned does not even smack of anything I have heard Indian people, the Indian nation, say, request or demand. The stated long-range objective of this new Indian policy is the integration and assimilation of Indian people into the mainstream of Canadian society. Last year, at Glendon College, I stated the proposition that integration is an impossibility within Canadian society. At the Federation of Labor Conference here in Toronto, I further elaborated on that proposition stating that integration is impossible because of the inherent racism existing within the cultural life of the Western "civilization." The rationale of the new Indian policy is integration. When integration is on the White man's terms; it is assimilation. To be deliberately separated or segregated means to be controlled. To be assimilated means to be controlled. It means to be not in control of your own destiny. How can our "land heritage" be protected if our cultural heritage is White-washed? Look at the French Canadians, fanatically fighting to keep their identity.

The Minister of Indian Affairs, or rather Prime Minister Trudeau who pushed Chrétien to publicize the New Indian Policy, fails to contend with the fact that the Indian will remain a series of separate and identifiable people, even if individuals are absorbed into the dominant society with the result that Indian people will continue to be discriminated against, regardless of the equality of services or taxation burden; Indians are discriminated against because they are of a different color, a different race. Another important consideration neglected, but known to the Indian people, is that the interests of the dominant society will take precedence over the interests of Indians in any policy decision; Indian interests will be considered only when they coincide or at least do not contradict "White interests" (taxation, rich reserves).

So the Government is prepared to transfer to the Indian people the reserve lands, full control over them and, subject to the proposed Indian Lands Act. But the new deal only gives the Indians a bigger say in the fields of housing, education, welfare services, and citizenship rights. There is no guarantee for the protection of the Indian lands; free education up to and including university tuition and residence fees will be terminated; free medical care will be terminated; exemption from land and income tax on income earned on the reserve will be terminated. All this is rationalized under the pretext that "Canada cannot seek the 'just society' and keep discriminatory legislation on its statute books."

According to the enlightened authors of Indian Policy 1969, Indians will be given equal rights and responsibilities as other Canadians; that the doors of opportunity will be opened to Indians. This belief is supposed to enable the Indian people to realize their needs and aspirations. The mainstream mentality does not even know what an Indian is. That is why it keeps asking. "What does the Indian want?" What does any man want? To be left alone with his life and have some hope of making that life what he wants it to be. As we all know from the past, the stated goals of a policy may be and usually are quite different from the consequences of a policy—with the goals usually being more favorable to the Indians than the consequences. One that comes to my mind is "that services come through the same channels and from the same government agencies for all Canadians." This may be an undeniable part of equality. But who can say there is an argument about the principle or separate services for separate peoples. Equal but separate services cannot be argued, really if the second people decide to establish those services. The consequences may be said to be the extinction of the Indian nation as a visible people, as recognized first-citizens; they are denied their existence.

The Indians will receive social services from the province, which if given the federal funds, will assume responsibility for serving Indians the same health, welfare, and educational facilities as other residents of the provinces.

To my mind, the turning over of Indian affairs to the provinces was inevitable. At a time when "a forceful and articulate Indian leadership has developed to express the aspirations and needs of the Indian community," now was the time to "pass the buck." But a deeper penetration cuts to the bone of the matter. "Divide and rule" time is here. Anyone who is not too blind will realize the provincial administrations are more hostile to Indians than is the federal government. Not only are the provincial governments less able to render health and welfare services comparable to those of the federal government, the provincial governments are run by persons in competition with the Indians and less likely to take Indian interests into account. (Here in Ontario Robarts would like to get a hold of that approximately $42 million—he would have the opportunity to get rid of the proposed Crown Corporation as submitted by the Union of Ontario Indians.)

So there we have it, the revolutionary new Indian policy isn't as radical as it would appear to be. It is just another presumptuous, arrogant declaration of government ineptitude, shortsightedness, and "buck-passing".

What do you think?

1. *What are Caibaiosai's complaints against the White Paper? Do you agree with him? Why or why not?*
2. *"When integration is on the White man's terms, it is assimilation. To be deliberately separated or segregated is to be controlled. To be assimilated means to be controlled." What do you think Caibaiosai sees as a possible solution? Explain his position.*

3. AN AMERICAN PARALLEL

The following is a full text of a Letter to the Editor written by Professor James Duran of Canisius College in Wyoming. Professor Duran's letter appeared in the Toronto Globe and Mail, *July 15, 1969.*

The "new" Indian policy of the Government of Canada announced in June 25 by Minister Jean Chrétien is in reality not "new." The same policy was actively pursued by the United States from 1953 through 1960, though its harshest aspects were mitigated after September 1958. During those years, the U.S. Congress passed many laws and amendments recommended by the executive branch designed to "get the United States out of the Indian business" and to shift responsibility for Indian affairs from the federal government to the states.

The Congress, restless about the necessity to consider the continuing heavy volume of legislation on Indian affairs and to appropriate sums of money in seeming perpetuity, approved mandatory termination, i.e., the withdrawal of the federal government from its historic obligations to the Indian people even without their consent. Forty-one reserves were "liberated" as Secretary of the Interior Douglas McKay once described the process. Careful study of three of the most important groups terminated, i.e.

four bands of Paiutes, the Klamath, and the Menominee, has shown that the consequences have been—to say the least—disastrous for the vast majority of the Indians involved.

It must be noted that "municipalization" (I understand this is supported by the New Democratic Party) was implemented in the case of the Menominee and has proved that these ably-led Indians were not ready to meet the precipitous revolution forced upon them. In most cases, the Indians were consulted, but it is now clear that they simply did not understand what was happening. So obviously terrible were the consequences that Secretary of the Interior Fred A. Seaton on September 18, 1958, announced the end of the involuntary termination.

It must also be noted that the various states for the most part refused to allow the federal government to surrender its responsibilities even though federal financial assistance had been promised. When faced with the issue, California, Nevada and Wisconsin legislatures memorialized Congress to continue federal control. The legislatures of New Mexico, Arizona, North Dakota and Montana, instead of preparing to include Indians within their administrative framework, actually requested the federal government to increase its appropriations for Indians on federal reservations within their states.

The complexity of transferring such responsibilities was grossly underestimated. With rapidly rising budgets in the post Second World War years, the states simply were unwilling to add what admittedly must be an additional heavy burden if the life of America's most deprived minority is to be their human rights, including the right of cultural freedom.

In *The Report of the Commission on the Rights, Liberties and Responsibilities of the American Indian*, published in 1966, it was concluded that the termination policy if executed would only lead to each state assuming such responsibilities having a department of Indian affairs and the federal government ending up "with a multifunctional Department of Indian Termination, costing more to operate than the Bureau of Indian Affairs."

In view of the U.S. experience, Mr. Chrétien's hope to wipe out his department within five years seems to be an ill-founded dream which, if executed, will be done over the objections of the Indians themselves. Considering the actions of John Yaremko in the province of Ontario and the failure of the government of British Columbia to honor the property rights of the Indians there, what indeed can the Indians of Canada expect from provincial governments?

The statement of the Indian National Brotherhood released in Ottawa records the bitter opposition of the Indian community to the termination of federal responsibility in Canada. This was also the case in the United States, but the federal government proceeded to execute a policy of termination with tragic results. Is the Canadian government going to disregard the record of human tragedy that occurred in the United States and pursue what in so many phases is a policy identical to that of the Eisenhower years?

Both the United States and Canada have a common national minority and could benefit by studying the experience of each other. The central governments of both countries can intelligently reach but one conclusion, that this is a responsibility which the governments of both countries are obligated to continue until such time as the Indian nations themselves choose to request termination.

In the United States, the Kennedy-Johnson administrations represented a reversal of prior policy. There has even been "resumption" of federal services to tribes from which they had been withdrawn and *The Report of the Interagency Task Force on American Indians*, released in the fall of 1967, illustrates the important change in attitude during the past twelve years. I hope the government will not again return to the cruel policy of termination which amounts to an attempt at forced assimilation by legislation.

What do you think?

1. *Why does Professor Duran oppose the new policy?*
2. *What policy does he advocate?*
3. *What is the importance of the American experience for Indian-White relations in Canada?*

4. MINISTER DEFENDS POLICY

An article written by Jean Chrétien, the minister of Indian Affairs and Northern Development responsible for the 1969 White Paper, appeared in the Globe and Mail *of July 8, 1969.*

For a long time now Indian people have been asking for the right to manage their own affairs in the same way as other Canadians, for equal treatment and opportunity with other Canadians. They have asked for an end to bureaucratic control of their lives, for an end to paternalism. Other Canadians have said the same things on the Indians' behalf.

This is why the Government has proposed to end the federal trusteeship of Indian land, to return the land to the Indian people, to phase out the Department of Indian Affairs, to repeal the Indian Act and to work with the provincial governments to insure that Indian people are treated as full Canadian citizens by being treated as citizens of the provinces in which they reside.

We as a Government were faced with a basic choice; we could keep on with the existing framework, knowing full well that this set Indian people apart and hindered their development, or we could change the existing framework to enable Indian people to be free—free to develop Indian cultures in an environment of legal, social and economic equality with other Canadians.

The Government chose to try to break the pattern of two hundred years and change the existing framework. It did so knowing that the proposals would be controversial. It did so knowing that the proposals were not the solution to the so-called "Indian problem," knowing that the only real solutions would be those which came from within the Indian community itself. It did so knowing that if it did not make these proposals and did not try to break the existing pattern it would be avoiding the basic issues.

After a year of intensive consultations and review of past policies, it became clear that the existing framework under which Indian people were governed was wrong. It was wrong because it discriminated against people on the basis of race and set them apart. It was wrong because it denied one group of citizens in this country the same freedom to manage their own affairs as other Canadians have.

There are those who say the policy is too revolutionary, that it requires too much too soon. There are those who say the Government is trying to evade its responsibilities and abandon Indian people. Others may say that Indian people need specialized help, that a policy of legal equality and independence is not enough. Some have gone so far as to say that integration is equivalent to cultural genocide. All these doubts must be set at rest through discussion and consultation, for they are the antithesis of what is being proposed.

Many will criticize but few will defend the present system. The persistent control of other people's lives is ruinous to them and futile for government. How in all conscience can the Government pursue a policy of gradualism when it comes to giving people human dignity? What right does government have to decide for a group of people the nature and extent of their dignity? This is not something to be weighed and measured, apportioned out to those whom the Government in its wisdom has decided are deserving of it.

It seems to me that gradualism is the ultimate indignity and I am convinced that those who call our proposals precipitous now would be the first to complain if the Government continued on its past course.

The fear has been expressed that if moves are made too quickly the Indian will be separated from his land by the first sharp trader who comes along and will then become a homeless vagrant (that was how Sir John A. Macdonald put it in the House of Commons in 1872).

The policy statement is clear about the transfer of control of reserve lands to the Indian people. It will take longer than five years. I made it clear that Indian people should have the opportunity to control what is theirs: the reserve lands. This is their right, but they can choose, if they want, to assume this control gradually.

The federal Government is not evading its responsibilities by calling on the provincial governments to extend their services to Indian people who live within their boundaries. This is a basic right of Canadian citizenship. The provinces are being asked, in effect, to treat Indian people as citizens, as people, not as a race apart. Where there are additional needs, they are largely regional rather than ethnic. Regional problems must be met on a regional basis and cannot be dealt with in isolation.

The present system of governing a group of people on the basis of race involves a system of "head-counting." One of the hardest problems to solve is defining who is and who is not an Indian. Many heads have been left out in the process. The fault, of course, lies not in the heads but in the process.

This is the real problem of the Métis people. Their problems cannot be solved separately from those of their Indian neighbors. The Indian people's problems in many instances cannot be solved separately from those of their Métis neighbors. The consequence of the divided responsibility has been that neither group has had its problems solved and neither has been able to progress.

The strongest argument for provincial services was advanced in a recent issue of the *Globe and Mail* in a column by Scott Young. Although he drew quite different conclusions, the plain fact is that sooner or later Indian people do come into contact with the larger society around them. Whether this happens in a primary schoolroom, a high school, on the job or on a village street, the encounter comes.

The question of whether the schoolroom in which both the Indian student and the non-Indian student are classmates will be hostile or friendly ground for the Indian must lie with provincial school authorities. The federal Government can operate schools with only Indian pupils and thus defer the ultimate meeting of the two cultures. It is within the power of the provincial authorities to decide what sort of environment there will be in the schoolroom that contains both Indian and non-Indian pupils. Indian people involved in school boards will be able to make their voices heard, to insure the two cultures will come together in the best possible way.

The Canadian public and some Indian people themselves have not acknowledged the great contribution of Indian people to the richness of the Canadian mosaic. Indian people are a proud people with a great heritage. The policy statement emphasizes this important point. Government can create awareness of this strong Indian identity.

We do not feel this is incompatible with increased opportunities in a political, social and economic sense. Assimilation is a word which should be abolished from Canadian usage. Canada is a country with many different peoples; this is our strength. Canadians, however, do not have to have a separate status to have a different identity and to have a pride in their own particular cultures and traditions.

Success does not develop in a vacuum. The existence of a special department does much to create such a vacuum, to make of the Indian people a race apart, isolated from the mainstream of Canadian society.

Some people, both Indians and non-Indians, have criticized the new policy. Some have supported it. What the final outcome will be is up to the Indian people, up to the provinces and up to the Canadian public—all those who will directly or indirectly be involved in helping a new future take shape. The overriding responsibility facing the federal Government now is to try to break the patterns of the past, to explain to people why the system should be changed and to suggest how it can be changed.

The statement is not legislation, it is not an order from above drafted in a vacuum. It was written in response to many different things which many different Canadians—both Indian and non-Indian alike and members of Parliament from both sides of the House—have said over the years. We will not push anything down anyone's throat. We will not abandon anyone or any problem. We will be flexible. We do want to discuss.

The Government believes the proposals are the right ones. It is committed to discussion, negotiating, consulting, to make them the right ones. It wants the chance to do this and it seeks the full and continuing involvement and understanding of those whose decisions will affect its chances.

What is meant by?

"gradualism"

What do you think?

1. *According to Chrétien how does the new policy help the Métis and non-treaty Indians?*
2. *"Government can create awareness of this strong Indian identity." How does Chrétien think this could be done? Do you agree? Why or why not?*
3. *Does Chrétien adequately defend the policy against its critics? Defend your answer.*
4. *Is Mr. Chrétien arguing for assimilation, integration or separation? What evidence is there for your choice?*

5. CITIZENS PLUS: THE RED PAPER

In June of 1970 the Indian Chiefs of Alberta presented a brief to the federal government which represented their reaction to the White Paper. Taking their cue from the Hawthorn Report, *a government-*

commissioned inquiry into Indian affairs released in 1967, the Indian chiefs called their brief Citizens Plus *after the* Hawthorn Report *stated that "Indians should be regarded as citizens plus; in addition to the normal rights and duties of citizenship, Indians posses certain additional rights as charter members of the Canadian community." However, the brief quickly became known as the Red Paper.*

Citizens Plus *is a lengthy document and so has been divided for the purposes of this book. The selection here, is the Indian Chiefs' reaction to the White Paper. Later, in "Indian Proposals" their suggestions for future programs will be seen.*

INDIAN STATUS

The White Paper policy said "that the legislative and constitutional bases of discrimination should be removed."

We reject this policy. We say that the recognition of Indian status is essential for justice.

Retaining the legal status of Indians is necessary if Indians are to be treated justly. Justice requires that the special history, rights and circumstances of Indian people be recognized. The Chrétien policy says, "Canada cannot seek the just society and keep discriminatory legislation on its statute books." That statement covers a faulty understanding of fairness. [A study done by a] Professor L. C. Green found that in other countries minorities were given special status. Professor Green has concluded:

> The 1969 *Statement of the Government of Canada on Indian Policy* is based on the assumption that any legislation which sets a particular segment of the population apart from the main stream of the citizenry is conducive to a denial of equality and therefore discriminatory and to be deplored. . . .
>
> Equality in law precludes discrimination of any kind, whereas equality in fact may involve the necessity of different treatment in order to obtain a result which establishes an equilibrium between different situations. . . .

The legal definition of registered Indians must remain. If one of our registered brothers chooses, he may renounce his Indian status, become "enfranchised," receive his share of the fund of the tribe, and seek admission to ordinary Canadian society. But most Indians prefer to remain Indians. We believe that to be a good useful Canadian he must first be a good, happy and productive Indian.

THE UNIQUE INDIAN CULTURE AND CONTRIBUTION

The White Paper Policy said "that there should be positive recognition by everyone of the unique contribution of Indian culture to Canadian life."

We say that these are nice-sounding words which are intended to mislead everybody. The only way to maintain our culture is for us to remain as Indians. To preserve our culture it is necessary to preserve our status, rights, lands and traditions. Our treaties are the bases of our rights.

There is room in Canada for diversity. Our leaders say that Canada should preserve her "pluralism," and encourage the culture of all her peoples. The culture of the Indian peoples are old and colorful strands in that Canadian fabric of diversity. We want our children to learn our ways, our history, our customs, and our traditions.

Everyone should recognize that Indians have contributed much to the Canadian community. When we signed the treaties we promised to be good and loyal subjects of the Queen. The record is clear—we kept our promises. We were assured we would not be required to serve in foreign wars: nevertheless many Indians volunteered in greater proportion than non-Indian Canadians for service in two world wars. We live and are agreeable to live within the framework of Canadian civil and criminal law. We pay the same indirect and sales taxes that other Canadians pay. Our treaty rights cost Canada very little in relation to the Gross National Product or to the value of the lands ceded, but they are essential to us.

CHANNELS FOR SERVICES

The White Paper Policy says "that services should come through the same channels and from the same government agencies for all Canadians."

We say that the federal government is bound by the British North America Act, Section 9k, Head 24, to accept legislative responsibility for "Indians and Indian lands." Moreover in exchange for the lands which the Indian people surrendered to the Crown the treaties ensure the following benefits:

(a) To have and to hold certain lands called "reserves" for the sole use and benefit of the Indian people forever and assistance in the social, economic, and cultural development of the reserves.

(b) The provision of health services to the Indian people on the reserve or off the reserve at the expense of the federal government anywhere in Canada.

(c) The provision of education of all types and levels to all Indian people at the expense of the federal government.

(d) The right of the Indian people to hunt, trap, and fish for their livelihood free of governmental interference and regulation and subject only to the proviso that the exercise of this right must not interfere with the use and enjoyment of private property.

These benefits are not "handouts" because the Indian people paid for them by surrendering their lands. The federal government is bound to provide the actual services relating to education, welfare, health, and economic development.

ENRICHED SERVICES

The White Paper policy says "that those who are furthest behind should be helped most." The policy also promises "enriched services."

We do not want different treatment for different tribes. These promises of enriched services are bribes to get us to accept the rest of the policy. The federal government is trying to divide us Indian people so it can conquer us by saying that poorer reserves will be helped most.

All reserves and tribes need help in the economic, social, recreational, and cultural development.

LAWFUL OBLIGATIONS

The White Paper policy says "that lawful obligations should be recognized." If the Government meant what it said we would be happy. But it is obvious that the Government has never bothered to learn what the treaties are and has a distorted picture of them.

The Government shows that it is willfully ignorant of the bargains that were made between the Indians and the Queen's commissioners.

The Government must admit its mistakes, and recognize that the treaties are historic, moral and legal obligations. The Red men signed them in good faith, and lived up to the treaties. The treaties were solemn agreements. Indian lands were exchanged for the promises of the Indian commissioners who represented the Queen. Many missionaries of many faiths brought the authority and prestige of the White man's religion in encouraging Indians to sign.

In our treaties of 1876, 1877, and 1899, certain promises were made to our people: some of these are contained in the text of the treaties, some in the negotiations, and some in the memories of our people. Our basic view is that all these promises are part of the treaties and must be honored.

The intent and spirit of the treaties must be our guide, and not the precise letter of a foreign language. Treaties that run forever must have room for the changes in the conditions of life. The undertaking of the government to provide teachers was a commitment to provide Indian children the educational opportunity equal to their White neighbors. The machinery and livestock symbolized economic development.

The White Paper policy says "a plain reading of the words used in the treaties reveals the limited and minimal promises which were included in them . . . and in one treaty only a medicine chest." But we know from the commissioners' report that they told the Indians that medicine chests were included in all three.

Indians have the right to receive, without payment, all health-care services without exception and paid by the Government of Canada.

The "medicine chests" that we know were mentioned in the negotiations for Treaties Six, Seven and Eight, mean that Indians should now receive free medical, hospital and dental care. . . .

We agree with the judgment of Policha, J. in *Regina* vs. *Walter Johnston*:

> Referring to the "medicine chest" clause of Treaty Number Six, it is common knowledge that the provision for caring for the sick and injured in the areas inhabited by the Indians in 1876 were somewhat primitive compared to present-day standards. It can be safely assumed that the Indians had limited knowledge of what provisions were available and it is obvious that they were concerned that their people be adequately cared for. With that in view and possibly carrying the opinion of Angers J. a step further, I can only conclude that the "medicine chest" clause and the "pestilence" clause in Treaty Number Six should be properly interpreted to mean that the Indians are entitled to receive all medical services, including medicines, drugs, medical supplies and hospital care free of charge. Lacking proper statutory provisions to the contrary, this entitlement would embrace all Indians within the meaning of the Indian Act, without exception.

The principle thus laid down by Policha J. is that all the provisions of the treaties are to be interpreted in favor of the Indians with full regard given to changing social and economic conditions.

The Indian people see the treaties as the basis of all their rights and status. If the Government expects the cooperation of Indians in any new policy, it must accept the Indian viewpoint on treaties. This would require the Government to start all over on its new policy.

INDIAN CONTROL OF INDIAN LANDS

The White Paper policy says "that control of Indian lands should be transferred to Indian people."

We agree with this intent but we find that the Government is ignorant of two basic points. The Government wrongly thinks that Indian reserve lands are owned by the Crown. The Government is of course, in error. These lands are held in trust by the Crown but they are Indian lands.

The Indians are the beneficial (actual) owners of the lands. The legal title has been held for us by the Crown to prevent the sale or breaking up of our land. We are opposed to any system of allotment that would give individuals ownership of rights to sell.

According to the Indian Act, R.S.C. 1952, the land is safe and secure, held in trust for the common use and benefit of the tribe. The land must never be sold, mortgaged or taxed.

The second error the Government commits is making the assumption that Indians can have control of the land only if they take ownership in the way that ordinary property is owned. The Government should either get some legal advice or get some brighter legal advisers. The advice we have received is that the Indian Act could be changed to give Indians control of lands without changing the fact that the title is now held in trust.

Indian lands must continue to be regarded in a different manner than other lands in Canada. It must be held forever in trust of the Crown because as we say, "The true owners of the land are not yet born."

What do you think?

1. *What are the areas of disagreement between the White and Red papers? In each case why do you think they disagree?*
2. *In the Red Paper the Indian Chiefs of Alberta rejected the ending of legislative and constitutional discrimination.*
   (a) Explain their position.
   (b) What would be their position towards the Indian Act?
3. *Why are the treaties seen as safeguards for the Indian culture?*
4. *"The true owners of the land are not yet born." Explain the significance of this statement. Why do the authors of the Red Paper support this assertion?*

6. THE GOVERNMENT RETREATS

During his visit to the Australian National University on May 18, 1970, Prime Minister Trudeau fielded a question about the Canadian Indian after his address.

We published our policy paper on this subject. As some of you may know, the essence of it was to do away with the special status of the Indians, who've had a special Indian Act, who were treated as different, who came under federal jurisdiction rather than provincial jurisdiction in the area of education, state health, and so on. We said we were going to make the Indian an equal citizen. We would abolish all laws discriminating against him. We were not going to permit him to be assimilated into our society because we hoped he would preserve his values. But we were going to help him integrate into our society, preserving those of his values that he can, while still not being a second-class citizen.

The first thing we knew, many Indians in the country were saying: "We don't want this." Many White people were saying: "The Indians are right, this is not good; you're taking away from the Indians their special rights. You're trying to assimilate them. This is a corrupt society. It's based on material values, and you're trying to make the Indian just a slave of progress as the rest of us are. The Indian lives, as you know, in the forest. He's a trapper, he's happy and you're going to bring him into our polluted cities," and so on. I may be over-simplifying the case, but it has become a very, very real issue. And, of course, very soon the Opposition party was giving us hell for having brought in this very awful policy paper on Indians, which was going to destroy their values, and so on.

So the discussion is raging and this is participation as we never expected it would come. Now, whatever the ultimate reaction is, and I don't know what the result will be, if the White people and the Indian people in Canada don't want the proposed policy, we're not going to force it down their throats.

What do you think?

1. *According to Mr. Trudeau why do Indians and Whites object to the new Indian policy? From your reading to this point what evidence seems to support or deny his interpretations?*
2. *What is the significance of the government "retreat"?*

Indian Proposals

What proposals are being made by various Indian spokesmen for resolving some of the problems faced by Indians? What ideas have been put into action in this area, and how successful have they been?

The following section deals with these questions and raises others: What difficulties do Indians face in defining their goals and in achieving them? Do the suggestions made by Indians and their leaders seem to favor the integration of the Indian people with White society, the assimilation of Indians into White society, or the separation altogether of Indians and Whites?

1. WHO SHOULD CHANGE?

George Mortimore, a professor of anthropology at Guelph University made some recommendations for the betterment of reserve life in an article of October 27, 1968.

There have been many examples of industrial corporations moving into Indian or Eskimo country—country for which the Indians and Eskimos have never been paid—extracting millions of dollars worth of profits from the ground or the forests, and refusing to hire any Indians or Eskimos, or hiring only token numbers with the excuse that the work patterns and life patterns of the local people are not suited to the needs of modern industry. But let's look at the question from the other direction: Why can't modern industry alter itself somewhat to suit the native life pattern? For example, why not have Indian work groups serving as labor contractors, undertaking to get a specified work done within an agreed time, but having a licence to do the job in their own rhythm, on their own hourly, daily or weekly schedule. This has been tried and my understanding is that it has been successful. In other words why should the Indians and Eskimos be required to do all the changing? The companies are using resources which really belong to the public. Why doesn't the government show enough courage to impose conditions on the use of those resources? Why doesn't it impose, as one condition, the requirement that the country does something effective to make a place for Indian and Eskimo labor, not just in token numbers, but in large numbers? Why doesn't it demand that the companies show some imagination in fitting native workers into jobs and into communities? I am convinced that such measures would be in the companies' self-interest in the long run, in terms of a steady labor supply and a good public image.

What do you think?

1. *Would Mr. Mortimore's suggestions diminish Indian poverty? If so, how? What other benefits or problems might result if his suggestion were implemented?*
2. *What is Mortimore saying about the present relationship between Indians and Whites? What do you think he would like to see in the future?*

2. POLITICAL AMBITIONS

This news item is taken from the Toronto Telegram, *April 28, 1969.*

Chippewa Indian Chief Fred Plain is en route to Ottawa today to demand up to twelve House of Commons seats for Indians. The 43-year-old Chief's plan would mean creation of a new constitution giving Indians and Eskimos equal legislative rights. Indians are tired of being "spectators, not players" Chief Plain protested. Unless Indians have a complete voice, "Canada is doomed." Chief Plain says he expects his plan will be ridiculed with the same type of argument which has "kept the aboriginal in his place" the past three hundred years. There is already one MP who is an Indian. "But he is an MP who happens to be an Indian, not an Indian who is an MP," he said.

The Chief and his followers are not completely set on the twelve MP plan. If the same ratio of MPs to population for the rest of the country is kept, he said then seven would be enough. He pointed out that New Zealand already has such a plan in effect for its Maori population. "Four are elected to parliament with all rights by their own people. There is no reason this couldn't be done in Canada."

Chief Plain describes himself as a militant opposed to violence. While renouncing violence, he warned it could come if some progress is not made.

What do you think?

1. *"Chief Plain's proposal entails the unequal treatment of Indians." Discuss.*
2. *How would Chief Plain's proposal, if enacted, change the relationship between Indians and Whites, if at all? Would you call his plan one of assimilation, integration, or separation? Why?*
3. *What justification, if any, is there for guaranteeing Indians, as opposed to other groups, seats in the House of Commons?*

3. CROWN CORPORATIONS

The remarks of Wilmer Nadjiwon, one-time president of the Union of Ontario Indians, were reported in the Toronto Globe and Mail, *June 5, 1969.*

To Chief Wilmer Nadjiwon, Red Power means partnership between Indian and White. The new president of the Union of Ontario Indians, chief of the Cape Croker band, accepts the fact the Indian must co-operate with the White man since the White man possesses the economic resources the Indian needs to progress.

In an interview last week, the 48-year-old Ojibway sculptor and former steelworker spelled out in considerable detail his ideas and proposals for Indian development. They are all keyed to the concept of partnership, but they nevertheless aim toward a greater degree of Indian autonomy. The chief roadblock to successful Indian dealings with the federal and provincial governments has been the red tape resulting from the involvement of a multiplicity of departments in Indian affairs, the chief said. Last week, the UOI came up with a proposal submitted to Premier John Robarts, which they believe will cut through the red tape, and combine a fair degree of Indian autonomy with the need to maintain government control over public money.

The proposal is a Crown corporation to administer Indian affairs in Ontario. Chief Nadjiwon sees no constitutional reason for the province not being able to establish it. Under the 1966 federal-provincial agreement, Ontario took over complete responsibility for Indian community development, he said, and it is to this area that the corporation would be directed. The corporation, as proposed by the UOI, would have at least a majority of Indian directors. Yet, like other Crown corporations, it would report to to the legislature through a particular minister and thereby be accountable for its expenditures of public money. Its finances would come from all government departments currently providing sums for some aspect of Indian affairs. Instead of these departments spending their money separately, the money would be channeled to the corporation.

Chief Nadjiwon is willing for the government to see how such a concept would work through a pilot project. If the project is successful, it would become province-wide. And then, if that works, other provinces and the federal government might become interested, Chief Nadjiwon said.

The Crown Corporation concept reflects the growing determination among Indian leaders that the Indian must be involved in, if not entirely responsible for, his own welfare and development. "Unless the Indian approach is taken, there is bound to be failure," Chief Nadjiwon said. "There is no person better qualified to advance the Indian people than the Indian himself. Present government machinery is far too cumbersome."

Chief Nadjiwon said an important part of the Crown corporation concept would be insuring that the Indian maintained his ancient treaty rights and title to his lands. The Indian is very suspicious, and would want a watchdog over his treaty rights," he said. "The reserves, at least if they are economically viable, should be maintained at this point in history. The Indian must have some base from which to find his past and develop his pride."

The chief agreed that many of his proposals could be criticized for affording the Indian a special status above other citizens. "We always have had special status. No other people live in outdoor zoos. Before, it was a negative special status, and what we want now is to make it positive."

What is meant by?

"Crown corporation"
"negative special status"

What do you think?

1. *Would a Crown corporation increase or decrease government involvement in Indian affairs?*
2. *Which policy would Wilmer Nadjiwon seem to favor: assimilation, integration, or separation? Explain.*

4. THE RED PAPER'S PROPOSALS

The Indian Chiefs of Alberta in their 1970 brief to the federal government, Citizens Plus (or the Red Paper), presented specific proposals for improving the situation of Canadian Indians. The Chiefs' reaction to the White Paper was seen on page 218. How do their proposals reflect their response to the government policy?

IMMEDIATE REQUIREMENTS

MINISTER OF INDIAN AFFAIRS

We demand a full-time Minister of Indian Affairs immediately. The prime minister should redefine the responsibilities of the minister responsible for Indians. At the moment, the problems of Arctic sovereignty and National Parks policy are heavy. The Government is quite unrealistic in expecting one minister to handle other responsibilities at the same time that new policies are being suggested for Indians and Indian lands. We are insulted because it is clear that the Government does not intend to regard its Indian people as deserving proper cabinet representation. As soon as we get a full time minister, there will be some hope for useful consultations.

RECOGNIZE THE TREATIES

The Government must declare that it accepts the treaties as binding and must pledge that it will incorporate the treaties in updated terms in an amendment to the Canadian constitution. The preamble or introduction to this amendment should contain a reaffirmation of the treaties and an undertaking by the Government to abide by the treaties.

When this declaration is given, Indians will be prepared to consider some specific details of policy changes.

The treaties could be clarified in several ways:

(a) The Government should appoint a permanent standing committee of the House of Commons and Senate with members from all parties to deal only with registered Indians and their affairs.

(b) The treaties could be referred to the Supreme Court of Canada with the understanding that the Court will examine all supporting evidence and not merely the bare treaty.

(c) We would agree to referring the interpretation of the treaties to an impartial body such as the International Court of Justice at the Hague.

When the Government applies the same intent to the treaties as our forefathers took them to mean, the Government must enact the provisions of the treaties as an act of the Canadian Parliament. We would regard this act as an interim and temporary measure indicating good faith. Then with the consent of the provinces, the Government of Canada should entrench the treaties in the written consitution.

Only by this entrenching will Indian rights be assured as long as the sun rises and the river runs.

THE STEPS

THE INDIAN ACT

The White Paper policy says that the Government would "propose to Parliament that the Indian Act be repealed and take such legislative steps as may be necessary to enable Indians to control Indian lands and to acquire title to them."

We reject the White Paper proposal that the Indian Act be repealed.

It is neither possible nor desirable to eliminate the Indian Act.

It is essential to review it, but not before the question of the treaties is settled. Some sections can be altered, amended, or deleted readily. Other sections need more careful study, because the Indian Act provided for Indian people the legal framework that is provided in many federal and provincial statutes for other Canadians. Thus the Indian Act is very complicated and cannot simply be burned.

The Indian Act provides the basis for the Indian Affairs Branch. It confers on the minister very sweeping powers. It often frustrates Indians in their individual efforts to earn a living and the entire tribe in its attempts toward greater self-government and better stewardship of the assets of the tribe.

The whole spirit of the Indian Act is paternalism.

These paternalistic prescriptions thus confine the Indian and the tribe as if they were incompetent, not able to conduct their personal business affairs, or be responsible for local self-government.

As one example, under Section 32, an Indian rancher might spend four days and one hundred miles of driving to obtain authority to sell a calf, obtain permission to receive the proceeds and cash the cheque!

Many tribes have now had valuable experience in managing their local government affairs. Other tribes are now ready to accept greater responsibility. We believe that there should be a commitment from the Government that, as time passes and Indians choose, we should be given those responsibilities we feel we are capable of taking on.

The tribe should choose its own arrangements for this local government. Sections 73–85 of the Indian Act now provide for the election of officers and prescribe the powers of the council. The Indian Act can therefore be rewritten to establish the legal basis for tribal government in all matters usually delegated to local government. The provincial governments are not competent to pass legislation which includes reserve lands or persons as part of nearby counties.

TRANSFER TO THE PROVINCES

The White Paper policy said that the federal government would "propose to the governments of the provinces that they take over the same responsibility for Indians that they have for other citizens in their provinces.

The take-over would be accompanied by the transfer to the provinces of federal funds normally provided for Indian programs, augmented as may be necessary."

The current arrangement for education is unacceptable because the provincial and federal governments can make agreements without consulting Indian tribal councils.

Our education is not a welfare system. We have free education as a treaty right because we have paid in advance for our education by surrendering our lands.

The funds for education should be offered to the tribal councils. Then the tribe can decide whether it will operate schools itself or make contracts with nearby public schools for places for some or all of its students. These contracts would provide for Indian voice and vote in the operation of those schools. Opportunity could be provided for children of other Canadians to attend schools on the reserves.

ECONOMIC DEVELOPMENT

The Government White Paper policy promises to "make substantial funds available for Indian economic development as an interim measure."

We say that it is not realistic to suppose that short-term assistance with economic development as an interim measure will be adequate. The promise of substantial funds must be followed by actually making these monies available. This help in economic development is in keeping with the intent of the treaties which provided machines and livestock, the ingredients of economic development one hundred years ago. It is important that everyone recognize that giving up our Indian identity is not necessary for economic development.

It should also be recognized that other groups in society enjoy special legislation to ensure their economic, social or cultural well-being. Doctors and teachers are licensed as members of their professions. Labor negotiates for wages. Industry has tariff protection. Tax savings are given by the federal government to attract industry to underdeveloped regions. Special circumstances require special programs or benefits. Why not Indian reserves too?

Every group gets special treatment, concessions—even special status. We need and are entitled to special consideration—at the very least we expect that the promises made when we signed the treaties ceding our lands will be honored. The promise to help us help ourslves was an important promise and one still largely unfulfilled.

GUIDING PRINCIPLES

One guiding principle in our strategy must be that no program can succeed if it rests solely on continuing government appropriations, which depend in turn on annual legislative action. Government at all levels—

federal, provincial, and local—will have to play key roles in any such program. But total reliance on government would be a mistake. It would be astronomically costly to the taxpayer; and would continue to make our people totally dependent on politics, on year-to-year appropriations, and the favor of others.

It is therefore imperative that we enlist the energies, resources and talents of private enterprise in this most urgent effort. All of our programs have been designed in Ottawa. Their funds have been voted and run by government agencies. They are not enough and only a part of it even gets to the Indian people, the rest being gobbled up in administration at all levels.

To rely exclusively, even primarily, on governmental efforts is unwise. We must no longer ignore the potential contribution of private enterprise. It is probable that the lack of private enterprise participation is one of the main causes of failure to solve the problems of the poor and underdeveloped.

LOCAL EFFORT

The primary effort must be the labor and sacrifice of the local tribes. The elimination of poverty and want is a responsibility we all share—but if it is to be met, tribal councils themselves must take the initiative. Leadership within Indian communities is important for its own sake. The objectives are group achievement, stability of family, and growth of community pride. But it is also important to end the psychological isolation of these areas—to bring not just individual persons but the entire community, into the mainstream of Canadian life. And it is vital that children and young people see change and development take place through the work of their own fathers and brothers.

Freedom depends on having financial and social security first. The immediate problem before us, therefore, is to enable the bands to achieve basic, financial and social security where they live now, and it is crucial that they do so as a community.

There are two major categories of employment to be developed: the performance of tasks and works that the community needs (self-government) and the development of jobs in private industry.

There is an enormous potential for work on the needs of the community and within the tribal administrations as self-government develops. We also need large numbers of workers to staff our schools, clinics, and community centers. Even now we face serious shortages of nurses, teachers, policemen, health and welfare workers, recreation and sanitation workmen that could be alleviated by employing people from the communities they serve to aid them and by giving these aides the opportunity to move up the career ladder as they are trained.

The school curricula should be revised to prepare Indians to play their rightful part in the fields of public service employment, tribal administration, and in the new industries to be established.

GOVERNMENT SUPPORT TO PRIVATE INDUSTRY

There will be enormous potential in the private sector as well. We can and must make our communities into centers of profitable and productive private industry, creating dignified jobs, not welfare handouts, for the men and youth who now languish in idleness.

Large-scale investment in Indian communities will certainly be more costly and more difficult than investment elsewhere. Land transportation, insurance against fire, training of workers, extra supervision, all these are so costly in most reserve areas as to make investment there uneconomical under present conditions. If private enterprise is to play its full part in Indian communities, it must have the support of government to help make up the increased costs.

The most effective way to encourage new enterprise in reserve communities is through tax incentives, training incentives, and labor guarantees. This concept of government incentives to induce desired investments by private industry is not new. Tax credits, charitable contribution deductions, oil and mineral development incentives, accelerated depreciation, extra payroll deductions, low-interest loans, and numerous other ways have always been used by government as incentives to develop special areas or to handle special situations.

The entry of private enterprise must be in tune with the life and spirit of the community. Its role must complement the other efforts being made in the community.

COMMUNITY DEVELOPMENT CORPORATION

Private enterprise and local government will be assisted by all the resources of a provincial community development corporation set up by the Indian Association of Alberta.

The community corporation would ensure that what is done to create jobs and build homes builds the community as well, and builds new and continuing opportunities for its residents. They would ensure that what is done involves not just the physical development of the community, but the development of its educational system, its health services—in short, all the services its residents need. They would be the source of technical assistance to local business men. And they would be the main channel through which outside aid—government or private—enters the community. They would have the opportunity to make every government program and many private efforts more effective than before.

The programs cannot come from the top down. The leadership for these self-help initiatives must come from the people who live where the problems are. The people must know that the programs belong to them, and that the successes as well as the failures will be theirs too.

This Community Development Corporation must enter into partnership with industry to enlist resources thus far not available to Indian communities—sufficient to mount a real attack on the intertwined problems of housing and jobs, education, and income. This will require loans and technical cooperation from industry and commerce, trained manpower and organization from labor unions, academic and educational partnership with the universities, funds for education and training such as those provided under many present government programs.

The corporation would make special efforts in the field of on-the-job training. Not only will job training be needed to make initial employment possible; just as important, the availability of jobs will make the training programs more meaningful than they have been before.

THE INDIAN AFFAIRS BRANCH

The White Paper policy proposes that the Government will "wind up that part of the Department of Indian Affairs and Northern Development which deals with Indian Affairs. The residual responsibilities of the federal government for programs in the fields of Indian affairs would be transferred to other appropriate federal departments."

We reject this proposal to abolish the Indian Affairs Branch.

There will always be a continuing need for an Indian Affairs Branch. The Indian Affairs Branch should change to a smaller structure closely attuned to the well-being of Indian people.

The Branch needs to change its outlook. It should stop being authoritarian and it should start to serve the people. The Branch should be given a new name to signify that it has turned over a new leaf. This smaller successor body should serve mainly as the keeper of the Queen's promises, the treaties and the lands. It should channel federal funds to the tribes or to the provincial association depending on circumstances.

Tribes should also have direct access to Ottawa. The Branch should report to a minister of the Crown who has no other responsibility than the well-being of the Canadian Indian people.

Over the years the Indian Affairs Branch has been out of touch, a long ways away, unresponsive, and even unthinking. This has made the Indians feel that the Indian Affairs Branch has been bureaucratic and paternalistic. We know too that many good-hearted individuals have worked there, including some of our Indian people. But the good people seem to leave. They become discouraged or they are squeezed out. Thus we conclude that the recruitment and promotion policies of the Branch need a thorough review soon.

The Government's proposal to eliminate the Indian Affairs Branch ignores the advice given by the Hawthorn Committee which the Government itself set up to look into Indian Affairs. The Indian Affairs Branch could make a valuable contribution. For example, the Hawthorn *Report* recommended than the Branch play a valuable role in the Canadian community:

> The Indian Affairs Branch should act as a national conscience to see that social and economic equality is achieved between Indians

and Whites. This role includes the persistent advocacy of Indian needs, the persistent exposure of shortcomings in the governmental treatment that Indians receive and the persistent removal of ethnic tensions between Indians and Whites.

Indians should be regarded as "citizens plus"; in addition to the normal rights and duties of citizenship, Indians possess certain additional rights as charter members of the Canadian community. The Indian Affairs Branch has a special responsibility to see that the "plus" aspects of Canadian citizenship are respected, and that governments and the Canadian people are educated in the acceptance of their existence.

INDIAN CLAIMS COMMISSION

The White Paper policy said: "In addition, the Government will appoint a Commissioner to consult with the Indians and to study and recommend acceptable procedures for the adjudication of claims."

We reject the appointment of a sole Commissioner because he has been appointed without consultation and by the Government itself. He is not impartial and he has no power to do anything but a whitewash job.

WHAT A CLAIMS COMMISSION WOULD BE

A Claims Commission would be established by consultation with the Indians. The Comissioners would be impartial. The Commission would have the power to call any witness the Indians or the Commission wanted or any documents that either wanted. The Commission would make binding judgments.

WHAT WOULD A CLAIMS COMMISSION DO

The Claims Commission could:

(a) Help modernize the treaties

(b) Award compensation to aboriginal peoples who are registered Indians who have no treaties. The Royal Proclamation of 1763 issued following the acquisition of Canada by the British provided that no Indian could be dispossessed of his land unless with his consent and the consent of the Crown. This common consent was given in the treaties under which Indians were to be compensated for giving up their title to the lands.

(c) Examine the boundaries of reservations and recognize the need to include as part of reserves the lakes that are on the edge of the reserves.

(d) Prepare draft legislation to overcome the bad effects of the Migratory Birds Convention Act and other improper restrictions on Indians fishing in lakes and rivers.

(e) Hear all other claims that Indian persons or tribes want to have heard.

What do you think?

1. *Outline the proposals of the Red Paper briefly. To what extent does it deal with the array of Indian grievances. What are its chief concerns and why? What do you think it has left out? Can you give reasons for this?*
2. *Why does the Red Paper want the treaties entrenched in the constitution? Why do some Canadians favor an entrenched Bill of Rights?*
3. *Explain how you think the authors of the Red Paper would like to see the Indian Act changed. Compare their views to Walter Currie and Kahn Tineta Horn (pages 90 and 95).*
4. *What do the authors have to say about education? How do you think they feel this would improve Indian education?*
5. *In the field of economic development explain what the Red Paper means by:*
   (a) special status,
   (b) the role of private enterprise,
   (c) local effort,
   (d) government support,
   (e) Community Development Corporation
   What are the similarities and differences between this program and present-day arrangements? Compare it with other Indian proposals. Discuss and evaluate.
6. *How effective do you think a Claims Commission would be? Explain.*
7. *Is the Red Paper a "radical" document? Explain.*
8. *Outline the relationship you feel the Red Paper envisages for the Indian people with regard to White society. Is it one of assimilation, integration or separation?*
9. *Evaluate the proposals of the Red Paper with respect to the protection of the Indian culture.*

Innovations

What are some of the practical programs now being conducted across Canada to improve the Indian situation? What are these innovations designed to accomplish and how do they mean to accomplish it?

Perhaps in themselves the programs are not sweeping in scope, yet their implications are broad enough, for if successful, they will influence the thinking of many different people: Indians, Whites, radicals and moderates alike. Do these measures on the whole seem to favor the assimilation of the Indian people into White society, the integration of Indians and Whites, or the virtual separation of the two peoples?

1. THE BLOOD RESERVE IS VIABLE

An Indian success story was reported in Time Magazine *April 19, 1971.*

The 351,575-acre Blood Indian reserve in Southern Alberta is the largest in Canada. A band of the Blackfoot nation, the Bloods once roamed the area as splendid horsemen and canny fur traders. Eventually, as the North West Mounted Police noted in 1874, the White man's influence—especially his booze—reduced the Bloods from "the most opulent Indians in the West to abject poverty, in rags, without horses or guns." The fur traders' whiskey forts ultimately disappeared, but over the years the living conditions of the Bloods have only marginally improved. Until recent years, life on the reserve largely meant subsisting on the band's $1 million-a-year in gas royalties and land leases as well as federal welfare checks, and drinking up a storm in nearby Lethbridge on Saturday nights.

Now the Blood reserve (pop. 4,397) is in the midst of a remarkable economic and social rebirth that may serve as a model for other native communities. Even at their lowest ebb, the Bloods were not entirely down and out—or at least not all of them were. Five years ago, the band's leadership—Indians who were themselves successful as farmers and cattle ranchers—recognized that the band could never throw off its lethargy without providing decent jobs for its people. They formed an industrial development committee, hired Oblate Father Denis Chatain as an adviser, and went shopping.

The objective was to find a manufacturer who would set up shop on the reserve and be prepared to train Indian workmen—and management. Said a member of the industrial development committee, Stephen Fox, "We wanted to be able to operate completely on our own, from janitor to president, within fifteen years." After a broad search, the Bloods found their company in their own backyard: Lethbridge's HaiCo Manufacturing Ltd., a large builder of mobile homes.

An 80,000 sq. ft. plant on a sere bluff overlooking the reserve's main community of Standoff is now turning out one prefab house a day, and expects to increase its production to four a day by the end of the year. The Bloods borrowed $876,000 from Jean Marchand's Department of Regional Economic Expansion to build the plant; HaiCo is providing operating capital, on-the-job training and management for the first five years—when the Bloods have an option to take over the operation entirely. The prefabs will sell for $15,000–$20,000 each. Already a Lethbridge real estate firm has signed a contract estimated at $20 million to buy the plant's production run for the next three years.

But first the operation will turn out several hundred houses for a modern townsite at Standoff. The project has so far brought water, sewage, telephones and natural gas services to the town; soon it will employ 240 Indians and provide a payroll of $1 million a year. Says Father Chatain:

"This is just the beginning. Imagine the rippling effect—the service industries needed, the possibilities for auxiliary manufacturing and so on." Among the ripples already being felt, the Safeway supermarket chain has opened a small market in Standoff, and the Bank of Nova Scotia has established a branch in the town—the first on an Alberta reserve. Plans are being formulated for nothing less than a subdivision with several hundred homes, a shopping center, schools, churches, and all of the other amenities of suburban life.

The quest for economic independence is mirrored in changing social attitudes among the Bloods. Fred Gladstone, a cattle rancher, a former North American calf-roping champion and the son of Canada's first Indian senator, is president of Red Crow Developments, the band-owned company that is HaiCo's partner in the plan. He says: "Our motto is "Get off the welfare line and on the production line'." According to Father Chatain, the sentiment is more than a slogan. "People who never have worked have come in for a job," he reports. "Suddenly it is the in thing on the reserve to quit drinking." Father Chatain predicts that within two years there will be no unemployment on the reservation, and, "If everything goes as we project, we will be hiring Indians from other reserves."

Federal Indian Affairs officials are both impressed and somewhat startled by the Bloods' initiative in throwing off the government's tutelage. Says Tom Turner, the department's district supervisor: "The exciting thing is that it is their baby. They call us when they need us. Otherwise, what they want is for us to stay the hell out of the way, and they make it just that plain."

What do you think?

1. *Why do you think this project is a success?*
2. *Compare this project to the proposals seen in the Red Paper.*
3. *Discuss what you think the benefits or problems that the Blood Reserve project could create for the protection of the Indian culture.*
4. *Why would you say that the Blood Reserve project increases the likelihood of assimilation, integration or separation?*

2. THE RIVERS HALFWAY HOUSE

In the September 28, 1971 issue of the Toronto Globe and Mail, *there was an article describing a new measure to facilitate the move of Indians from the reserve to urban life.*

Almost 90 per cent of those among Manitoba's 35,000 Indians who move to an industrial center from a reserve fail to adjust to urban life. But with the help of the federal government and Manitoba businessmen, the transition soon may become much easier.

This could happen because a new approach to Indian job training and self-development is to be introduced this fall at a recently closed Canadian Forces air base at Rivers, Manitoba. The base, one hundred and fifty miles northwest of Winnipeg, is to be converted into a multi-million-dollar industrial park that will house half a dozen manufacturing plants staffed mainly by Indian workers.

The Rivers experiment will differ from previous training programs. Entire Indian families will live at the base industrial park for a two-year period. During their stay, they will learn as a unit to cope with the pressures of earning a living in the modern industrial world. The bread-winner of each family will have an opportunity to acquire an industrial skill at one of the plants in the base complex. At the same time, his wife and children will receive instruction in such matters as shopping and banking when they visit the service facilities at the base. In short, the Rivers training and environmental center will be sort of a halfway house where Indian families will have time to adjust from rural isolation to an industrial wage economy.

It is being founded on the premise that Indians are failing to make the grade in the city because they lack the experience to function in a new and completely different environment. Even if he is skilled, an Indian worker often becomes disenchanted with urban living when he and his family have difficulty with things like shopping. "Many Indians have trouble plugging into our society," says Frank Price, president of a Winnipeg consulting firm that developed the plan for the Rivers training center. "Because of unfamiliarity, they have problems with commonplace items that White people take for granted. . . . So the objective of the Rivers center is to train Indian families to live and make their way in urban society. It is definitely not a vocational school teaching specific trades—but rather a place where Indians can broaden their options if they desire a change in their way of life."

About fifty Indian workers and their families will be installed at the Rivers base when it opens this fall. Annual intake will rise to two hundred and fifty families within three years, with the federal government spending $1.3 million every twelve months to sustain the experiment.

While government involvement is predictable in this field, a unique aspect of the Rivers venture will be the large-scale participation by private business. Mr. Price expects that at least six manufacturers will occupy a series of former air force hangers that are going to be transformed into manufacturing plants. Already signed up are two Winnipeg companies, Unistican Trail Motel Ltd., a manufacturer of mobile motel units, and Soto Industries Ltd., a builder of portable homes. In addition, Mr. Price's company is negotiating with several other manufacturers who might lease the remainder of the 350,000 square feet of space allotted for industrial purposes. "Part of the deal is that industries coming here must agree to accept Indian workers as trainees in their plants," Mr. Price said in an interview. "Commercial facilities, such as stores and a bank, will be leased to concessionaires on the same basis. . . . Personally, we think the base is suitable for a variety of light industrial activities, ranging from metal working to electronics to garment production."

In some cases, business interest in the Rivers industrial park may be less than altruistic. Manufacturers, in fact, can qualify for sizeable federal grants if they decide to settle at the base. For example, they are eligible to apply for the maximum Department of Regional Economic Expansion grant of $4,500 for each job created. Ottawa also will bear fifty per cent of each trainee's wages for twelve months until the worker is ready to join the regular labor force during the final year of his Rivers training. As a further "carrot" to prospects, there will be transportation subsidies so that manufacturers can ship their products to market from the base's rather remote location.

Management of the Rivers center will be in the hands of nine directors, who have been jointly nominated by the federal government and the Manitoba Indian Brotherhood. Representing a cross-section of government-business-Indian interests, the directors include Robert Connelly, Manitoba director for the Department of Indian Affairs, and Howard Fontaine, a key Indian Brotherhood official.

"This is the first time that Indians and industry have come together to prepare the head of an Indian household to live and work in a wage economy," Mr. Connelly said. "I don't know of any other scheme of this type in North America. . . . And it is needed because Indian families are having a hard time in urban society."

Basically, Rivers was chosen as the center site because urban conditions can be closely simulated under controlled conditions. In addition to the proposed manufacturing buildings, the base has 405 housing units, a 22-room school, a community core, a swimming pool, curling rink and indoor hockey arena. While at the base, Indian families will be expected to manage their affairs—earning wages, tackling shopping and paying rent on their dwellings. However, there will be one counsellor to each fifteen families, helping the base residents to progress in their new environment.

"We have only scratched the surface of potential projects that could take place at Rivers," says Mr. Price. "For example, there will probably be extension courses, plus training programs for band councils. And some base residents may enter the mature student program at Brandon University, which is only 27 miles away. . . . [But] Mr. Price thinks the Rivers experiment may be "the most exciting social change project in North America." He also says that if the family training approach is successful in Manitoba, it probably will be tried in other Canadian provinces.

A note of caution, however, is voiced by Howard Fontaine, the Indian Brotherhood official who is also a Rivers director. He says there must be some followup to ensure that Indian workers will find jobs after they leave Rivers. "We must not make the same mistake that has hampered previous training programs for Indians. . . . When training is completed, the graduates must not be abandoned without anything for them to do."

What do you think?

1. *". . . the objective of the Rivers center is to train Indian families to live and make their way in urban society."*
   (a) What difficulties do Indian families have in making a transition to the city from the reserve?
   (b) How is the Rivers center designed to help overcome these difficulties?
   (c) Does this innovation seem to favor the assimilation, integration or separation of Indian and White societies? Explain.
2. *Discuss the significance of the involvement of the private business. Would the authors of the Red Paper support this? Why?*
3. *Explain why the whole Indian family is involved in the Rivers center program. Where can this policy be applied in other parts of Canadian society?*

3. CHANGES ON THE CURVE LAKE RESERVE

An intensive campaign has made the Curve Lake Reserve, near Peterborough, Ontario, flourish. Staff reporter Douglas Sheppard described the situation there in the Toronto Telegram, *April 10, 1971.*

Probably no native community in Ontario has undergone such dramatic social changes in the past decade as this tiny Ojibwa reserve thirty miles north of Peterborough. Today, with unemployment rates soaring across Canada, just the opposite is happening in this village where only nine are on welfare compared to the more than one hundred who qualified in 1965.

But although most of the 667 people here believe the changes are for the better, there are some, as in any community, who have different views and question the effect of such rapid change.

Interest-free federal government loans have been provided for construction of 38 new three- and four-bedroom brick homes which would stand out in any suburban development. Other loans under the same scheme were made available for repairs on reserve homes which met area building standards but had fallen into disrepair. "The loans (most about $8,000 a family, payable at $40 monthly) have allowed us to really transform the face of our reserve and restore a dignified standard of living for our people," said Chief Elsie Knott. And Mrs. Knott points with some pride to the way residents have maintained their new homes, thus effectively destroying the myth—at least in the Peterborough area—that native peoples cannot maintain general housing standards.

Leading to the new homes, which have replaced one-room shacks so common to native communities, is a paved highway—among the few, if not the only one, leading into a reserve community in Ontario. Running water is available for all homes as well as hydro and telephone service, often unheard-of amenities in native communities.

And the need for higher education has become almost an obsession with leaders, many of whom believe early assimilation into non-native schools several years ago is responsible for the extremely low drop-out rate here.

Councillor Douglas Williams, however, questions if the "White washing" of this village might be destroying the Ojibway value system and culture. "Many people here and in surrounding non-native communities are putting too much stress on the changes. The quickness of the change and the stress on it has subconsciously coerced many into believing that materialism, the American way, is the best and only way," said Mr. Williams. The 27-year-old former community development officer with Indian Affairs who is now a student of Indian studies at Trent University wonders whether if the change had been a little slower, would his people not have ended up with the best of both worlds. "I know I am one of those with a new house. I appreciate it but it isn't everything. It doesn't mean as much as knowing that my children will retain their culture and be proud and aware of their ancestry. It is wrong that we sell our identity for a few bricks and pipes. But the people here, unlike their brothers in other areas throughout the province where I have worked, fail to see that this is appending," said Mr. Williams.

Mr. Williams and his wife Alice, a teacher, strongly criticize the assimilation of children here into non-native schools after grade three in Lakefield, about fifteen miles away. Chief Knott agrees that the assimilation of Curve Lake students into non-native schools at such an early age might be wrong. But she adds: "It is too late now to return to the old system."

Sparking many changes here has been the development of a private resident-owned retail and wholesale craft center now doing in excess of $100,000 business annually. The Whetung Craft Center has brought at-home employment for sixty households with more than two hundred people manufacturing in excess of one hundred lines of native crafts ranging from beadwork headbands to carved paddles.

Manager Mike Whetung, 25, a recent Waterloo economics student whose father, Cliff, started the center in the early '60s, believes the sucess of the business is largely responsible for the "general level of prosperity here today. Some people can make a lot of money if they want to work hard and they can do it all on their own time at home. And you must remember that all of the money they make is tax-free because this is a reserve," said Mr. Whetung.

Mr. Williams, however, asks if the gap between what the craft center pays for goods and sells them for is not in some cases too wide. And he wonders why the project could not have involved all the community as shareholders because it was financed for expansion by Indian Affairs (current interest rate) loans, along with Royal Bank demand loans.

What do you think?

1. *Are the changes taking place on the Curve Lake Reserve examples of government "paternalism"? Explain.*
2. *(a) Why are some Indians dissatisfied with what is occurring? Is their dissatisfaction a criticism of the focus of government policy? Explain. Compare their views to Canon Scott's (page 55).*
   (b) Is this dissatisfaction well-founded? Why or why not?
3. *Compare the Curve Lake Reserve project, the Blood Reserve project and the Rivers center project. Does the Curve Lake experience suggest any future problems for the other two projects? Give reasons.*
4. *What are Williams's objections to the way the craft center is operated? Do you agree with him? Why or why not?*

4. NEW CONCEPT IN INDIAN EDUCATION

This report of the innovative community college on the Blackfoot reserve near Gleichen, Alberta, appeared in the Toronto Globe and Mail, *April 8, 1972.*

On the Blackfoot reserve near here [Gleichen, Alberta] there is a campus with a difference. Old Sun is a community college, a satellite of Mount Royal College in Calgary, and it is bilingual—English and Blackfoot. There is no curriculum as such and the enrolment fluctuates from day to day; there are no grades, no admission standards. Officially there are one hundred students, but most days somewhere between fifty and seventy put in an appearance.

A curriculum of sorts will probably be chosen in time, by the students, and the only suggestion that has come from Mount Royal College is that it include a course on Indian lore and culture. Mount Royal itself is a traditional college, offering courses in such fields as journalism, electronics, machine shop and the liberal arts.

Old Sun got under way in an abandoned missionary school on the reserve, sixty miles east of Calgary, with help from Ernest Tyson, a teacher at Mount Royal, who came up with Ken Bradford, a University of Toronto graduate and the founding president of Loyalist College at Belleville, as director. The unconventional college received approval from the Department of Indian Affairs last summer.

At the moment the college is concentrating on basic adult education: English and mathematics, skills, and something called the support program which is designed to give students the time, equipment and facilities to explore whatever interests them. Mr. Bradford calls this "browsing in education," and it will lead eventually to a curriculum, once students determine where they're going. After all, it's hard to want to be a typist if you've never seen a typewriter.

Eventually, Mount Royal sees Old Sun as a complete campus, with standards of admission and diplomas. But that's for the future. At the moment, Indians are still finding out what they need, rather than being told what they should have. This hasn't been true in the past. Mr. Tyson and Mr. Bradford distrust more conventional approaches to Indian education. Indians have been uprooted from reserves and dropped into alien cities to be retrained. They've been expected to adhere to White man's time: nine-to-five, Monday-to-Friday. And they've been expected to adapt to White man's educational system—classroom discipline, rows of seats, each man an island in front of a lecturer, starting at level one and proceeding according to timetable. Retraining courses have had rigid admission standards.

And there are great differences between Indian and White cultures. Mr. Bradford describes the Indian as "a round person." He's a member of a family, a clan, and a society. He works in a group. And students themselves joke about Indian time—you eat when you're hungry, sleep when you're tired, do something as long as it interests you. At Old Sun, the Blackfoot bus co-operative delivers students to the door at 9 a.m., approximately. But there's cushion time before classes start—a daily Oomoowap, which translates as "people get together." If someone dies on the reserve, classes aren't held because almost everyone will be going to the funeral. Students work in groups, under the tutorship of four instructors. When they master what one group is working on, they find another where something new is happening. If there's farming to be done, families to be cared for, they drop out for a week or a month, come back when they want. "A student might not turn up at 9, but he's just as likely to stay all night if he likes what he's doing. It's not like White society, which operates by the clock," Mr. Bradford says.

By being flexible, Old Sun thinks it reaches more people than it would otherwise. For example, Canada Manpower sent a man out to the reserve to register farmers for a retraining course. Somehow, the word of the course didn't get around until the day before the deadline. The only way to register then was to go to Calgary, so the school hired a bus and sent thirty-four Indians into town. Twenty were later accepted for the course, which will be held on campus. And two weeks before the course started, ten men voluntarily turned up to brush up on mathematics. At Old Sun, a math class has no trouble coping with ten unexpected students.

Another story Bradford likes to tell is about a man whose wife enrolled in mathematics. The husband scorned the idea of school, but when a general farm-maintenance course started, he enrolled. He could see the sense in learning how to fix his tractor. But he soon discovered he didn't know enough English to understand the operator's manual. So he joined the English class. As work on his tractor progressed, he discovered he needed some math. He joined that class, too.

"If we had standards of admission," Mr. Bradford says, "that man would have been tested before starting mechanics and refused entrance until he'd taken English and math. And he would have said to hell with the whole idea. But if you get a man interested, he learns what he needs to know to fulfill his interest." Mr. Tyson suggests that approach might not only apply to Indians. "It could go far beyond the confines of reserve. Anyway, it's working at Old Sun."

Old Sun sees its staff expanding to a dozen from the current four major instructors. There will be a Blackfoot language class and, the staff hopes, a fine arts department that will translate Blackfoot color and form into modern art. In three or four years, basic adult education may be phased out if Indian children no longer drop out of public schools so early. The library, which has tossed out the usual missionary school mishmash of discarded donations it inherited, is to be a full-fledged one, emphasizing Indian literature. At least that's the hope.

And one day the Indians will decide they don't need Mount Royal's help at all to run their campus. "That day," Mr. Bradford says, "will be the day we are a complete success."

What do you think?

1. *What criticisms of the education so far offered to Indians are met in the Old Sun idea?*
2. *Does Old Sun promote the assimilation, integration or separation of White and Indian societies? Explain. How do you feel about the experiment?*
3. *What would be the opinions of Howard Adams (page 101) on this project?*
4. *Describe new modes of education now being experimented with in White society which are similar to that of Old Sun. Why are these alternative systems of education being attempted? With what foreseeable results?*

Suggested Readings

Contemporary

BURNFORD, SHEILA: *Without Reserve*. Toronto: McClelland and Stewart, 1969.

CANADA. DEPARTMENT OF INDIAN AFFAIRS AND NORTHERN DEVELOPMENT. *The Bankslanders: Economy and Ecology of a Frontier Trapping Community*. Ottawa: Information Canada, 1971.

————. *The Canadian Indian*. Ottawa: Information Canada, 1966.

————. *Canadian Indian Treaties and Surrenders*. Ottawa: Information Canada, 1965.

————. *Discussion Notes on the Indian Act*. Ottawa: Information Canada, 1968.

————. *Fur-Trade Posts of the Northwest Territories, 1870-1970*. Ottawa: Information Canada, 1969.

————. *The Indian Economic Development Fund*. Ottawa: Information Canada, 1968.

————. *Indian Facts and Figures*. Ottawa: Information Canada, 1970.

————. *Indians of British Columbia*. Ottawa: Information Canada, 1967.

————. *Indians of Ontario*. Ottawa: Information Canada, 1967.

————. *Indians of the Prairie Provinces*. Ottawa: Information Canada, 1967.

————. *Indians of Quebec and the Maritime Provinces*. Ottawa: Information Canada, 1967.

————. *Indians of the Yukon and Northern Territories*. Ottawa: Information Canada, 1967.

————. *Indians on Skid Row*. Ottawa: Information Canada, 1970.

————. *Linguistic and Cultural Affiliations of Canadian Indian Bands*. Ottawa: Information Canada, 1970.

————. *A Survey of the Contemporary Indians of Canada*. Two volumes. Ottawa: Information Canada, 1966 and 1967.

CANADIAN CORRECTIONS ASSOCIATION: *Indian and the Law*. Ottawa: Information Canada, 1967.

CARDINAL, HAROLD: *The Unjust Society*. Edmonton: M. J. Hurtig, 1969.

DEPREZ, PAUL: *The Economic Status of the Canadian Indian*. Winnipeg: Center for Settlement Studies, University of Manitoba, 1969.

The Education of Indian Children in Canada. Indian Affairs Education Division. Toronto: Ryerson Press, 1965.

FODLER, DICK: *Red Power in Canada*. Toronto: Vanguard Publications, 1970.

HAYCOCK, R. G.: *The Image of the Indian*. Waterloo Lutheran University Monograph Series. Waterloo, 1971.

HENDRY, CHARLES: *Beyond Traplines*. Toronto: Anglican Church of Canada, 1969.

INDIAN-ESKIMO ASSOCIATION: *Education for What?* Toronto: Indian-Eskimo Association, 1965.

————. *Final Report: Indians and the City*. Toronto: Indian-Eskimo Association, 1971.

————. *Native Rights in Canada*. Toronto: Indian-Eskimo Association, 1970.

JENNESS, DIAMOND: *The Indians of Canada*. Ottawa: Information Canada, 1963.

GOODERHAM, KENT: *I Am an Indian*. Toronto: J. M. Dent and Sons, 1969.

MELLING, JOHN: *Right to a Future*. Toronto: United Church of Canada and the Anglican Church of Canada, 1967.

NAGLER, MARK: *Perspectives on the North American Indian*. Carleton Library, No. 60. Toronto: McClelland and Stewart, 1972.

National Conference on the Indian in the City. Toronto: Indian-Eskimo Association, 1966.

ROBERTSON, HEATHER: *Reservations are for Indians*. Toronto: James Lewis and Samuel, 1970.

ROSENTHAL, JOE: *Indians: A Sketching Odyssey*. Toronto: Clarke, Irwin, 1971.

SCHUMIATCHER, MORRIS C.: *Welfare: Hidden Backlash.* Toronto: McClelland and Stewart, 1971.

VANDERBERGH, ROSAMOND M.: *The Canadian Indian in Ontario School Texts.* Toronto: Indian-Eskimo Association, 1971.

WAUBAGESHIG, ed. *The Only Good Indian.* Toronto: New Press, 1970.

The Way of the Indian. Toronto: Canadian Broadcasting Corporation, 1963.

WUTTUNEE, WILLIAM I. C.: *Ruffled Feathers.* Calgary: Bell Books, 1971.

Historical

BAILEY, ALFRED G.: *The Conflict of European and Eastern Algonkian Cultures, 1504-1700: A Study in Canadian Civilization.* Toronto: University of Toronto Press, 1969.

BRETON, PAUL EMILE: *The Big Chief of the Prairies: The Life of Father Lacombe.* Dorval, Quebec: Palm Publishers, 1956.

CHAMPLAIN, SAMUEL DE: *Voyages, 1604-1618.* Edited by W. L. Grant. New York: Barnes and Noble, 1959.

DICKENS, FRANCIS: *The Diary of Francis Dickens, N.W.M.P.* Kingston: The Jackson Press, 1930.

ECCLES, W. J.: *The Canadian Frontier, 1534-1760.* New York: Holt, Rinehart and Winston, 1969.

HARMON, DANIEL: *Sixteen years in the Indian Country: The Journal of Daniel Williams Harmon.* Edited and with an introduction by W. Kaye Lamb. Toronto: Macmillan, 1957.

HODGETTS, J. E.: *Pioneer Public Service.* Toronto: University of Toronto Press, 1955.

JESUITS: *Letters from Missions: Black Gown and Redskin.* Selected and edited by Edna Kentor. Introduction by Reuben Gold Thwaites. New York: Longmans, Green, 1958.

KENNEDY, JOHN HOPKINS: *Jesuit and Savage in New France.* New Haven: Yale University press, 1950.

LONGSTRETH, THOMAS M.: *The Silent Force: Scenes from the Mounted Police of Canada.* New York: Century, 1927.

MAC INNIS, T. R. L.: "History of Indian Administration in Canada." *Canadian Journal of Economics and Political Science* 12:387-394.

MACKENZIE, *Sir* ALEXANDER: *Alexander Mackenzie's Voyage to the Pacific Ocean in 1793.* Historical introduction and footnotes by Milton Quaife. New York: Citadel Press, 1967.

MORRIS, ALEXANDER: *The Treaties of Canada with the Indians of Manitoba and N.W.T.* Coles Canadiana Collection. Toronto: Coles Publishing, 1970.

PATTERSON, E. PALMER: *The Canadian Indian: A History since 1500.* Don Mills: Collier-Macmillan, 1972.

PECKHAM, H. H.: *Pontiac and the Indian Uprising.* Chicago: University of Chicago Press, 1947.

SILVER, A. I.: *The North-West Rebellion.* Vancouver: Copp Clark, 1967.

SLUMAN, NORMAN: *Poundmaker.* Toronto: McGraw-Hill Ryerson, 1967.

STANLEY, G. F. G.: *The Birth of Western Canada.* Toronto: University of Toronto Press, 1962.

SURTEES, R. J.: "The Development of an Indian Reserve Policy in Canada." *Ontario History* 61:87-98.

SYMINGTON, FRAZER: *The Canadian Indian: The Illustrated History of the Great Tribes of Canada.* Toronto: McClelland and Stewart, 1969.

USHER, JEAN: "Duncan of Metlakatla: The Victorian Origins of a Model Indian Community" in Morton, W. L. *The Shield of Achilles.* Toronto: McClelland and Stewart, 1969. pp. 286-334.

VAN STEEN, MARCUS: *Pauline Johnson.* Toronto: Mustang, 1965.

Films

The Indian Speaks. (NFB. 16 mm. 35 mm. 40 min.)
A film about Indians in many parts of Canada who are concerned about preserving what is left of their own culture and restoring what is gone. It is the consciousness of the Indian tradition slipping away, with nothing equally satisfying or significant to take its place, that this film discovers wherever it goes.

The Longer Trail. (NFB. 16 mm. 30 min.)
The story of a young Alberta Indian and the problems he finds in the world of the White man. In learning a trade and getting a job he encounters prejudices that make his adjustment all the more difficult.

The Longhouse People. (NFB. 16 mm. 23 min.)
The life and religion of the Longhouse People. We see how the Iroquois of today maintain a link with their proud past. The film shows a rain dance, a healing ceremony and a celebration in honor of a newly chosen chief.

Mission of Fear. (NFB. 16 mm. 35 mm. 79 min.)
The story of the Jesuit martyrs who lived with the Huron people in the region near what is now Midland, Ontario. The film reconstructs a period of Canadian history, especially of Indian life at the beginning of European settlement. The Indian village and the Jesuits buildings are exact models from archeologists' reconstructions. The story is based on the Jesuit Relations, the actual journals of mission life that still make thrilling reading.

No Longer Vanishing. (NFB. 16 mm. 35 mm. 27 min.)
This film outlines the present status of Canada's Indian population and shows how the 20th-century Indian is stepping forward in his own affairs and those of his country. The film spotlights Indians who are making full and lasting contributions to Canadian life.

Pikangikum. (NFB. 16 mm. 35 mm. 9 min.)
John Gould, a young Toronto artist, draws sketches of life as he sees it while living on an Indian reserve in northern Ontario. Winter hunger, sickness, cold, enthusiasm in the faces of children in the classroom and strength in other faces show life of a people rich in spirit.

Pow-Wow at Duck Lake. (NFB. 35 mm. 14 min.)
A discussion at Duck Lake, Saskatchewan, where Indian-Métis problems are presented before a gathering of Indians and non-Indians. Among matters discussed are schooling available to Indians and the limited education that restrict their opportunities to develop in their own way.

The Ballad of Crowfoot. (NFB. 16 mm. 35 mm. 10 min.)
This film recalls some of the tragic incidents where Indian people suffered from the coming of the White man. It was created by a Micmac Indian who is part of a film crew composed of Canadian Indians in the Challenge for Change Program. It makes use of illustrations and photographs from various private and public archive collections. Words and music of the song that forms the film commentary are by Willie Dunn, the film-maker.

Charley Squash Goes to Town. (NFB. 16 mm. 4 min.)
This film is a satirical animation which, in a gentle and restrained way, resists the idea that it is the manifest destiny of Indian boys and girls to follow the advice of well-meaning Indians and Whites, to work hard at school and to be like everybody else in society. The film, from idea to screen, is largely the work of Duke Redbird, an articulate young Cree Indian.

Encounter with Saul Alinsky. (NFB. 16 mm. 32 min.)
A provocative film in which young, articulate Indians talk about their philosophy with pragmatic Saul Alinsky. Alinsky advocates a development of power to bring about the changes.

These Are My People. (NFB. 16 mm. 13 min.)
This is the first film by an Indian film crew under the Challenge for Change program and was filmed at the St. Regis Reserve. Two band members explain

the historical and other aspects of the Longhouse religion, culture and government. They examine the impact of the White man's arrival on the Indian way of life.

Indian Dialogue. (NFB. 16 mm. 27 min.)
Canadian Indians discuss their many problems, particularly those which threaten their own culture. Some forthright views are expressed by the younger generation. They seem very much aware of the economic and spiritual deprivation. It is a candid film that reveals the White man's predicament as well as that of the Indian.

Indian Relocation: Elliot Lake—A Report. (NFB. 16 mm. 29 min.)
An experiment to prepare Indians for city life through a program of vocational and academic education, families are moved to the town of Elliot Lake in northern Ontario from neighboring reserves. The film makes you part of discussions and interviews with some families who stayed and others who went back. It offers insights into the kind of adjustments Indians face in this kind of program.

You Are on Indian Land. (NFB. 16 mm. 36 min.)
A film report of a protest demonstration by Mohawk Indians of the St. Regis Reserve on the international bridge between Canada and the United States near Cornwall, Ontario. The blocking of the bridge which is located on Indian land drew public attention to their grievance that Canadian authorities prohibited duty-free passage of personal purchases across the border.

Audiotapes

Canada's Indians. (1 hr.)
Canadian Broadcasting Corporation Learning Series, No. 385. Toronto: Canadian Broadcasting Corporation, 1970.

A Conversation with Duke Redbird. (1 hr.)
Canadian Broadcasting Corporation Learning Series, No. 144. Toronto: Canadian Broadcasting Corporation, 1971.

On My Way to School. (1 hr.)
Canadian Broadcasting Corporation Learning Series, No. 145. Toronto: Canadian Broadcasting Corporation, 1971.

The Way of the People. (1 hr.)
Canadian Broadcasting Corporation Learning Series, No. 307. Toronto: Canadian Broadcasting Corporation, 1971.